NEW PARENT SMELL

BY
BEN ROSENFELD
AND
MICHELLE SLONIM ROSENFELD

ISBN: 978-0-9908552-2-4

Illustrated by Jonathan Antonio
Book design by Chris Havel

For more visit:

NewParentSmell.com
BigBenComedy.com
MichelleSlonim.net

New York, NY

"I was a wonderful parent before I had children."

- Adele Faber and Elaine Mazlish

How To Talk So Kids Will Listen & Listen So Kids Will Talk

DEDICATIONS

This book is dedicated to the following people who made this project possible:

"A-nan-ee" for being our little, kind-but-strong-willed muse

Howard and Paula Slonim

All of Judy Segal's first cousins and first cousins once removed
For the duckies, the platypuses, the comics and the children
Jordan Jitzchaki

Team Jake
The Begeman Family
Linda Schlesinger
Michael Codispoti
Sal, Sarah & Posy Ortiz
Robert Punchur (Neat Guy)
Barbara Kimmel, devoted (read: patient) wife and mother
Rutgers Football - The 2007 International Bowl Champions

TABLE OF CONTENTS

INTRODUCTION

MEET MICHELLE

I WAS BORN IN NEW YORK CITY AND HAVE A WIDE ACTING RANGE.
I CAN PLAY A...

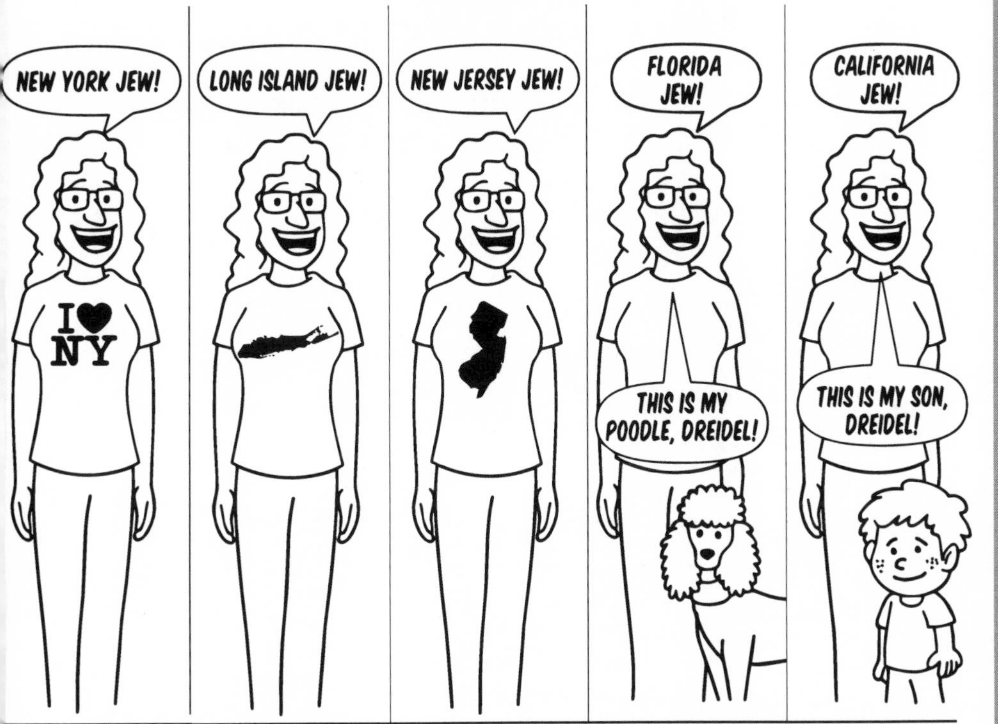
NEW YORK JEW!
I ♥ NY
LONG ISLAND JEW!
NEW JERSEY JEW!
FLORIDA JEW!
THIS IS MY POODLE, DREIDEL!
CALIFORNIA JEW!
THIS IS MY SON, DREIDEL!

AS A NATIVE NEW YORKER, I'VE TRIED MANY DIFFERENT FORMS OF THERAPY.

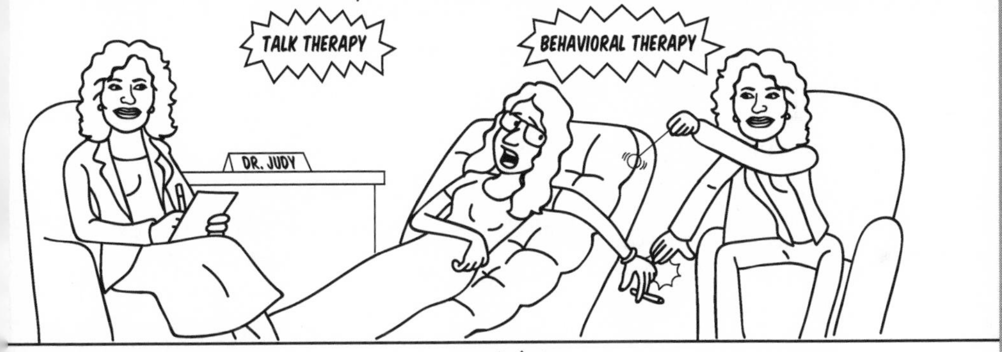
TALK THERAPY
DR. JUDY
BEHAVIORAL THERAPY

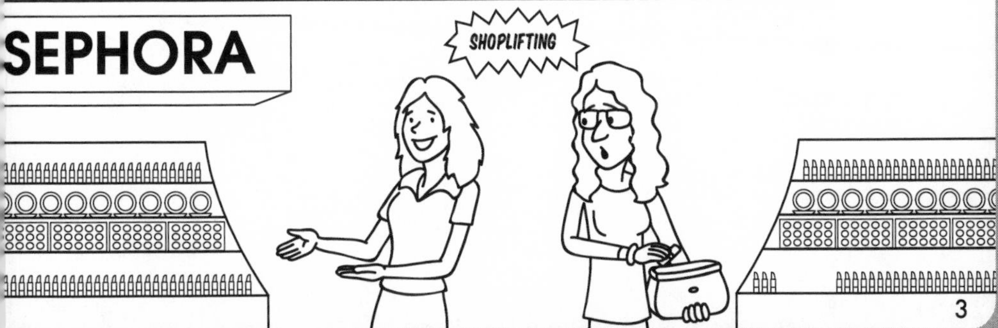
SEPHORA
SHOPLIFTING

I WENT TO PRIVATE SCHOOL IN MANHATTAN.

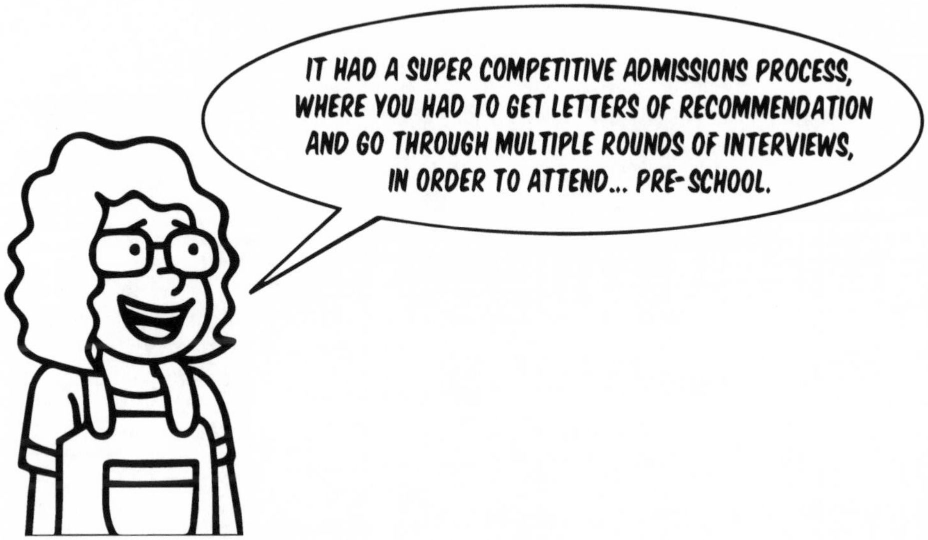
IT HAD A SUPER COMPETITIVE ADMISSIONS PROCESS, WHERE YOU HAD TO GET LETTERS OF RECOMMENDATION AND GO THROUGH MULTIPLE ROUNDS OF INTERVIEWS, IN ORDER TO ATTEND... PRE-SCHOOL.

WHAT DO YOU ASK A FOUR-YEAR-OLD?

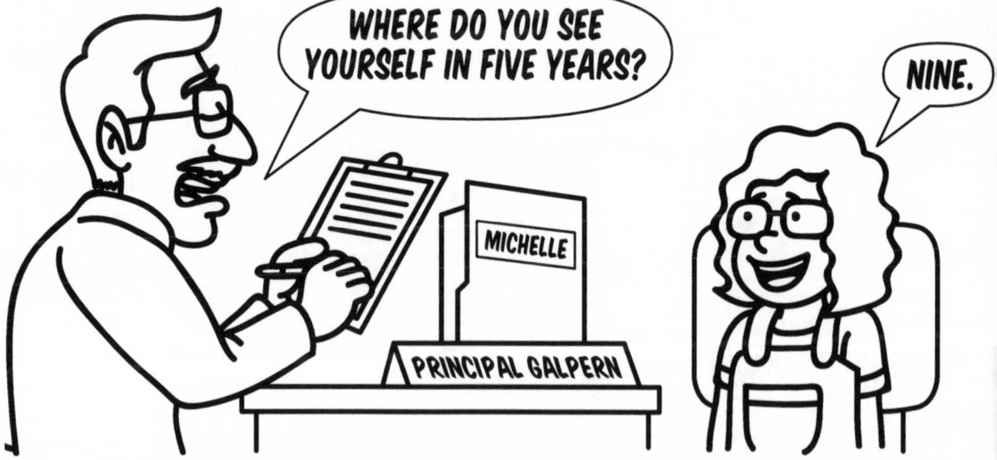
WHERE DO YOU SEE YOURSELF IN FIVE YEARS?
NINE.
MICHELLE
PRINCIPAL GALPERN

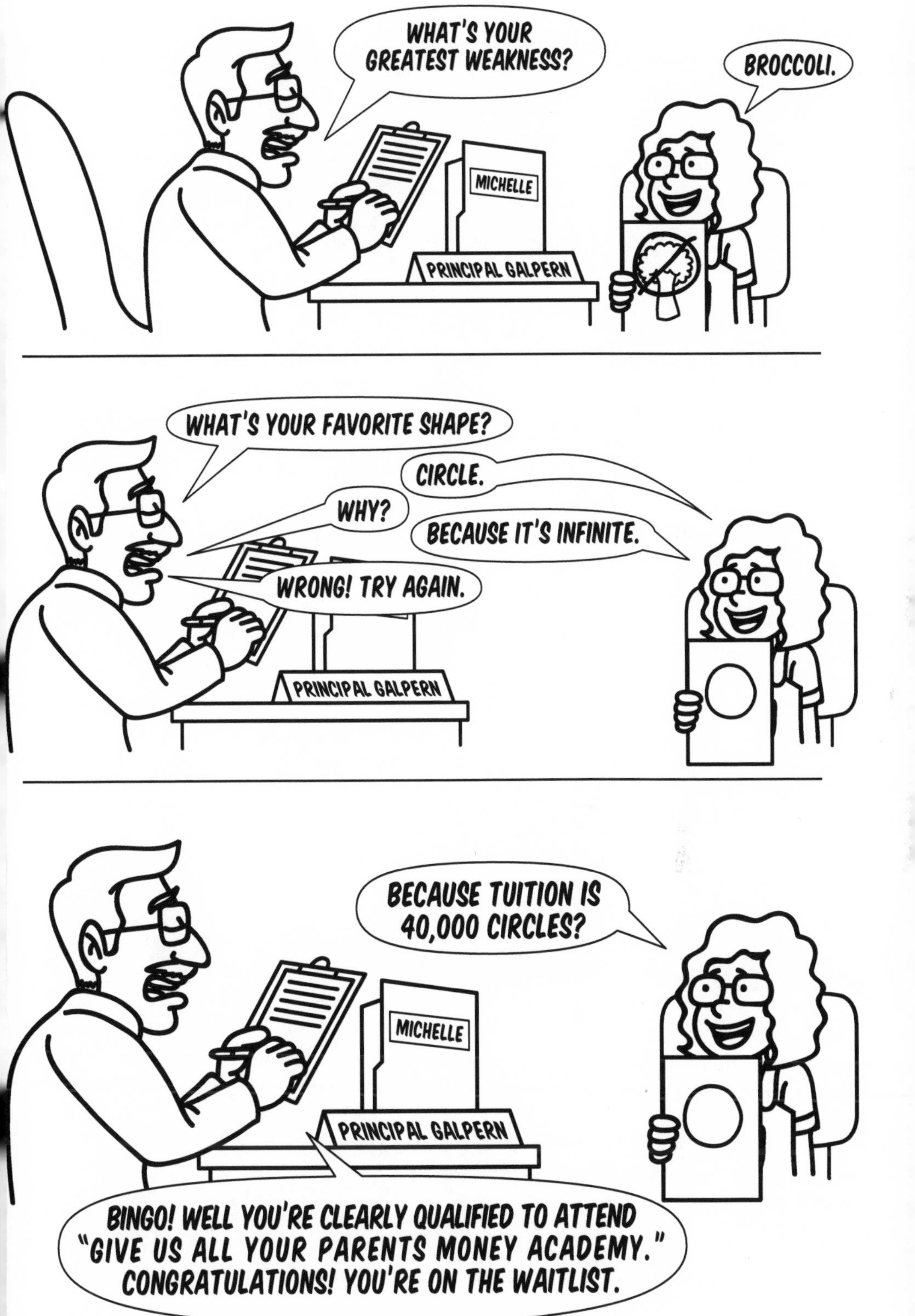
WHAT'S YOUR GREATEST WEAKNESS?
BROCCOLI.
MICHELLE
PRINCIPAL GALPERN
WHAT'S YOUR FAVORITE SHAPE?
CIRCLE.
WHY?
BECAUSE IT'S INFINITE.
WRONG! TRY AGAIN.
PRINCIPAL GALPERN
BECAUSE TUITION IS 40,000 CIRCLES?
MICHELLE
PRINCIPAL GALPERN
BINGO! WELL YOU'RE CLEARLY QUALIFIED TO ATTEND "GIVE US ALL YOUR PARENTS MONEY ACADEMY." CONGRATULATIONS! YOU'RE ON THE WAITLIST.

GROWING UP, MY DAD WOULD SPEAK FAKE YIDDISH.

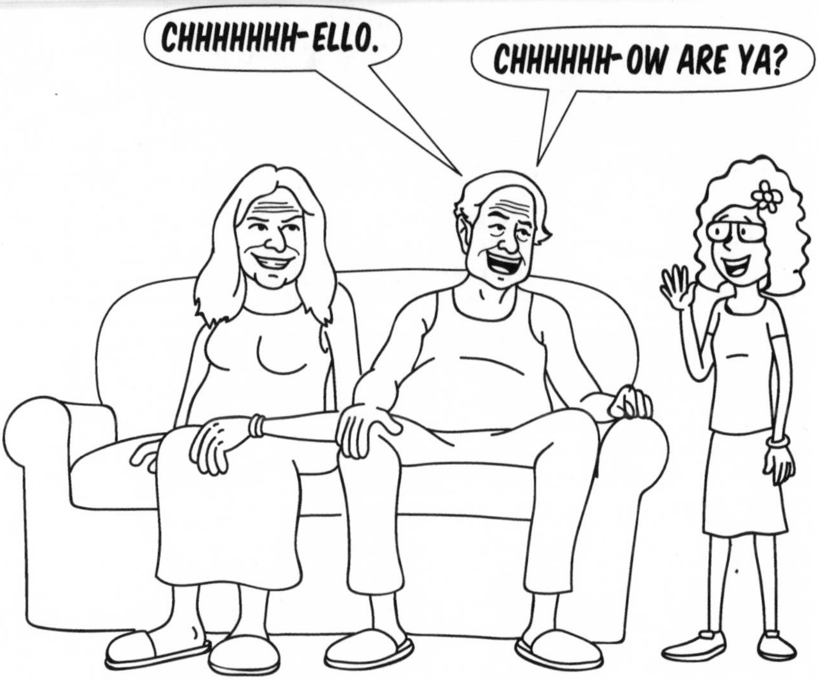
CHHHHHHH-ELLO.
CHHHHHH-OW ARE YA?

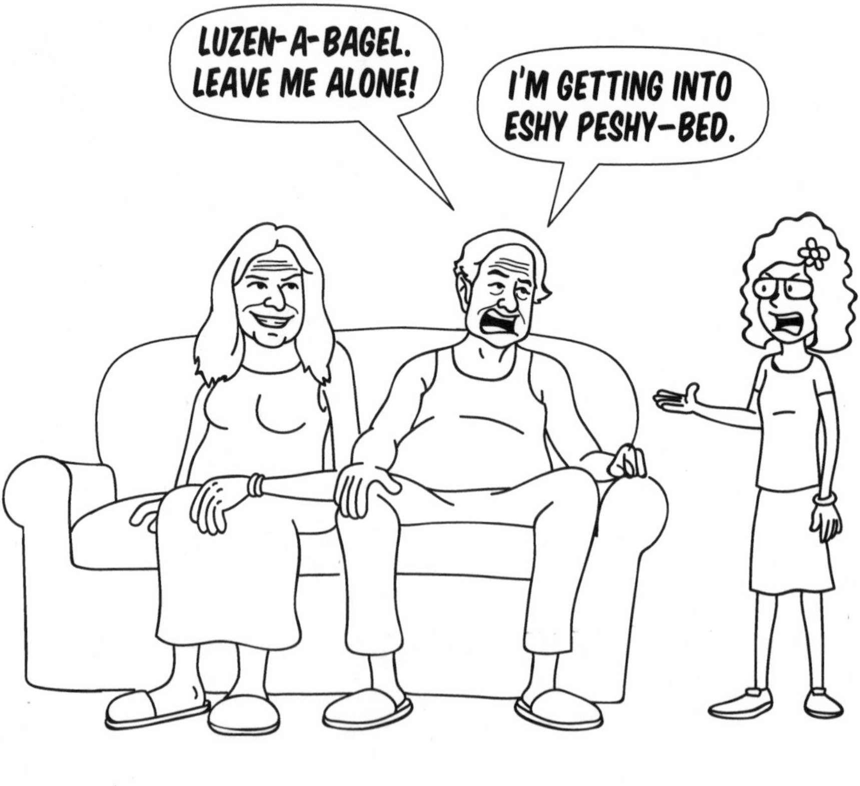
LUZEN-A-BAGEL. LEAVE ME ALONE!
I'M GETTING INTO ESHY PESHY-BED.

A WHILE BACK, I WAS AT A BAR, AND A LAME GUY WAS HITTING ON ME. SO I STARTED MESSING WITH HIM.

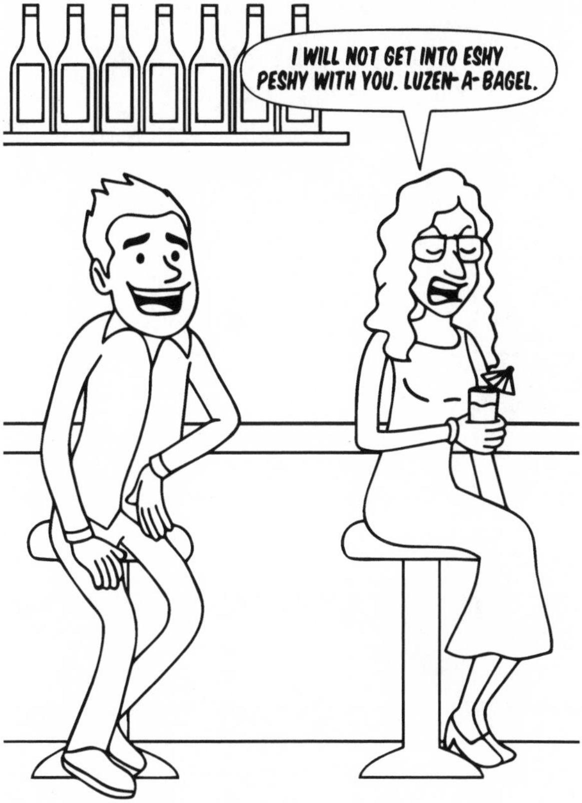
I WILL NOT GET INTO ESHY PESHY WITH YOU. LUZEN-A-BAGEL.

BUT THIS GUY DIDN'T CARE. HE STOOD HIS GROUND, LOOKED ME IN THE EYE AND SAID...

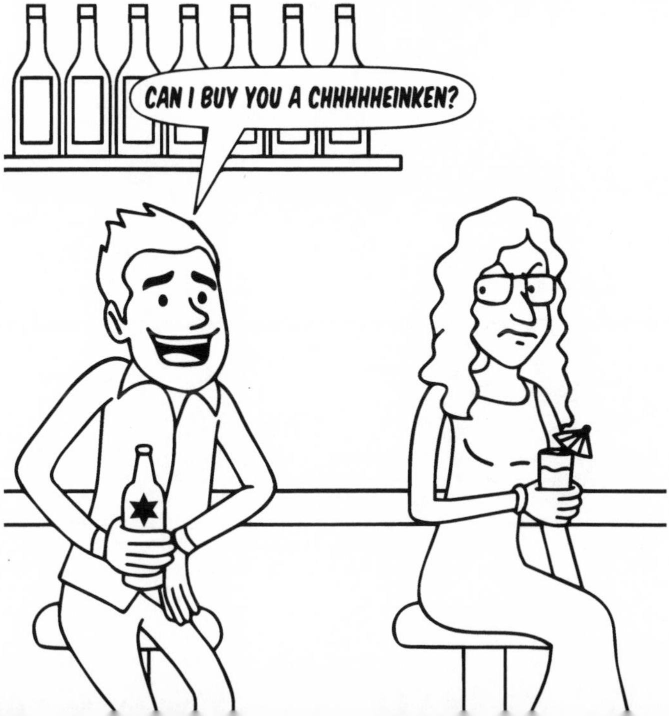
CAN I BUY YOU A CHHHHHEINKEN?

MEET BEN

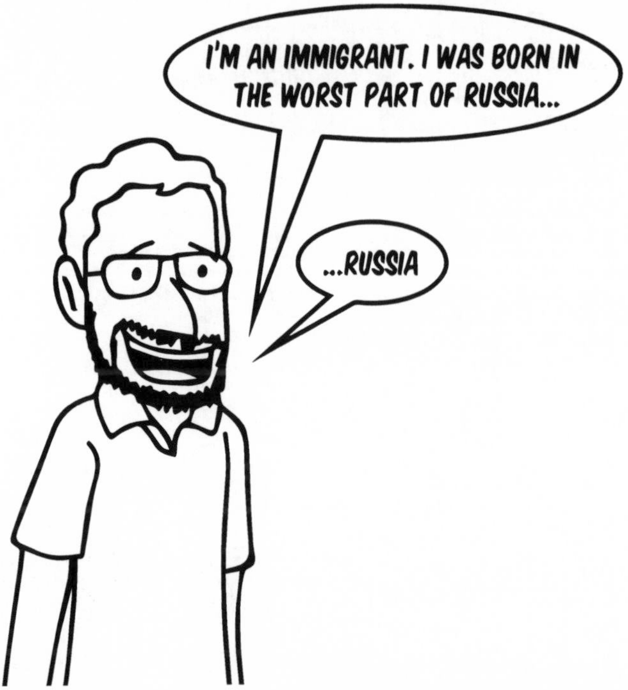
I'M AN IMMIGRANT. I WAS BORN IN THE WORST PART OF RUSSIA...
...RUSSIA

AS A KID, WHEN I CAME TO AMERICA, I WANTED TO FIT IN, SO I BECAME... OVERWEIGHT.

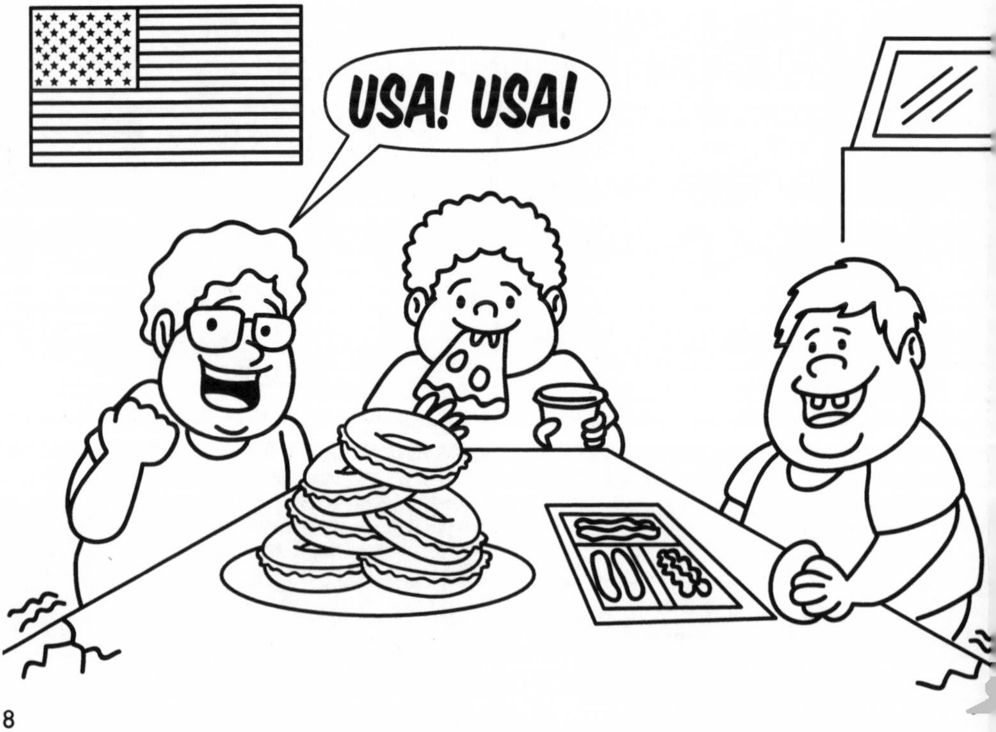
USA! USA!

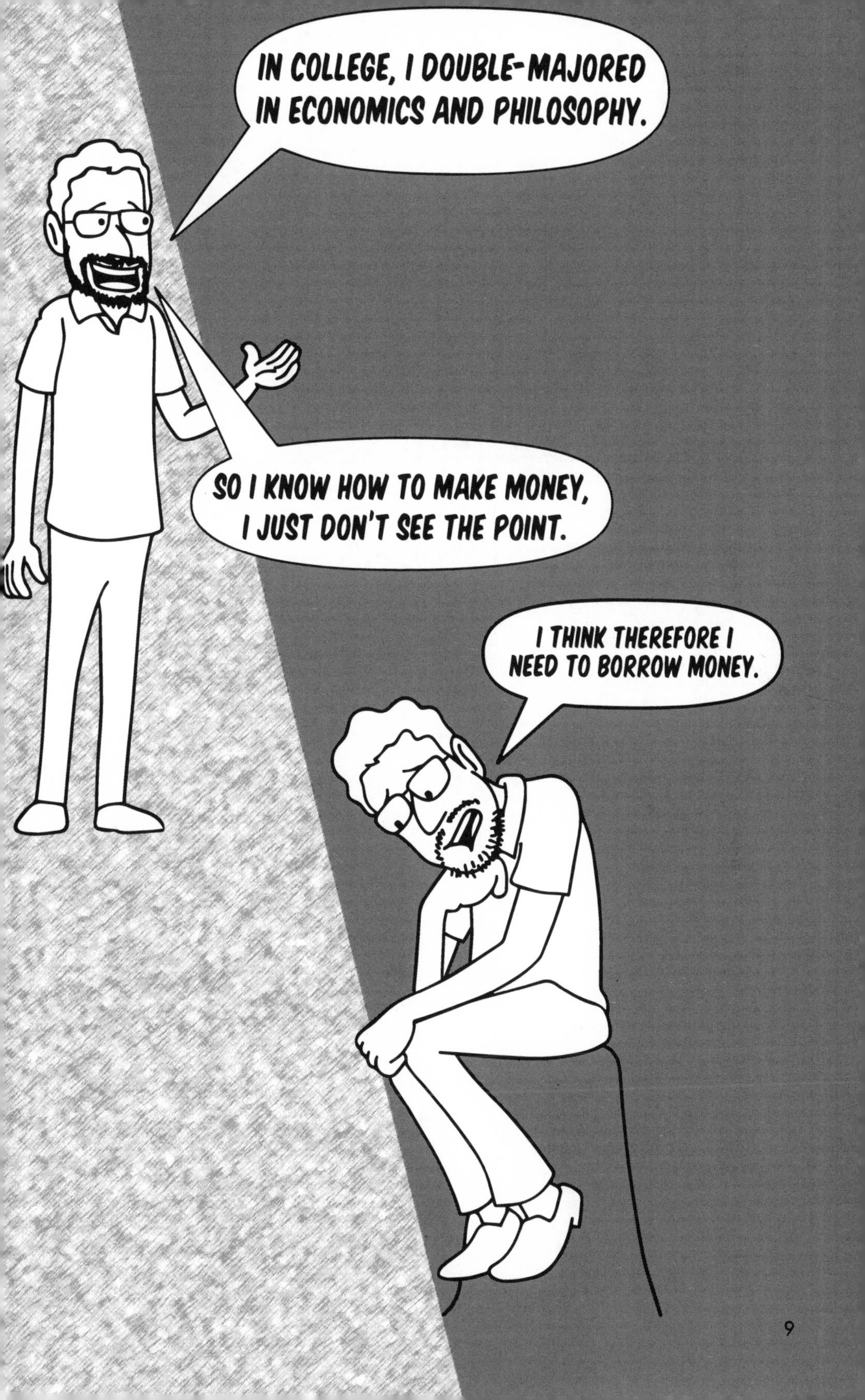
IN COLLEGE, I DOUBLE-MAJORED IN ECONOMICS AND PHILOSOPHY.
SO I KNOW HOW TO MAKE MONEY, I JUST DON'T SEE THE POINT.
I THINK THEREFORE I NEED TO BORROW MONEY.

MR. AND MRS. BEN AND MICHELLE

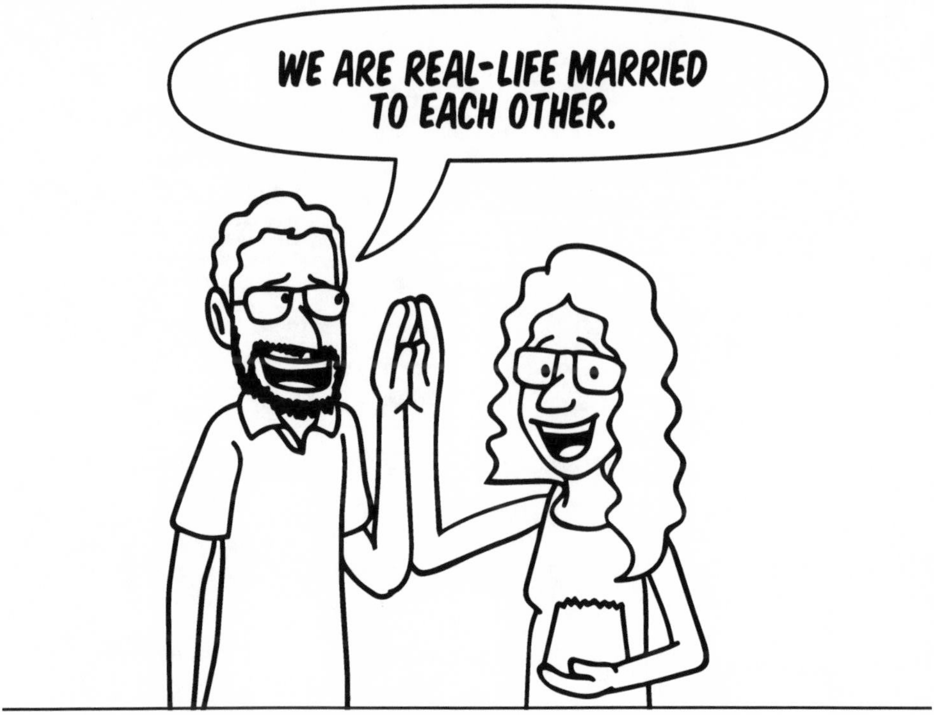
WE ARE REAL-LIFE MARRIED TO EACH OTHER.

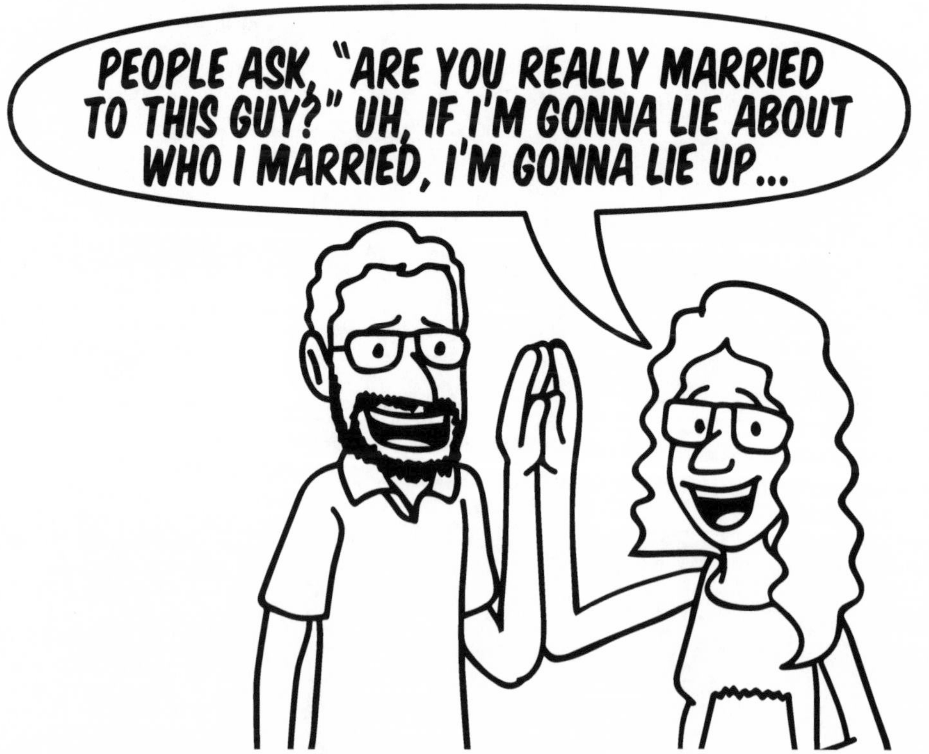
PEOPLE ASK, "ARE YOU REALLY MARRIED TO THIS GUY?" UH, IF I'M GONNA LIE ABOUT WHO I MARRIED, I'M GONNA LIE UP...

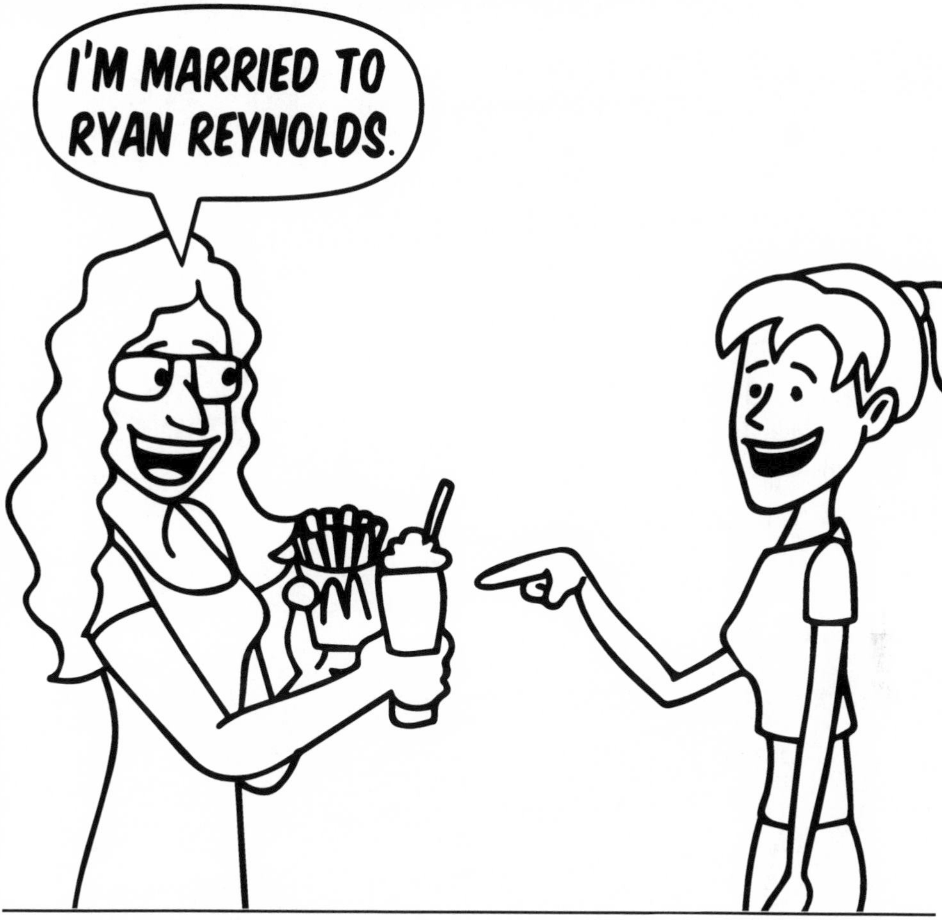
I'M MARRIED TO RYAN REYNOLDS.

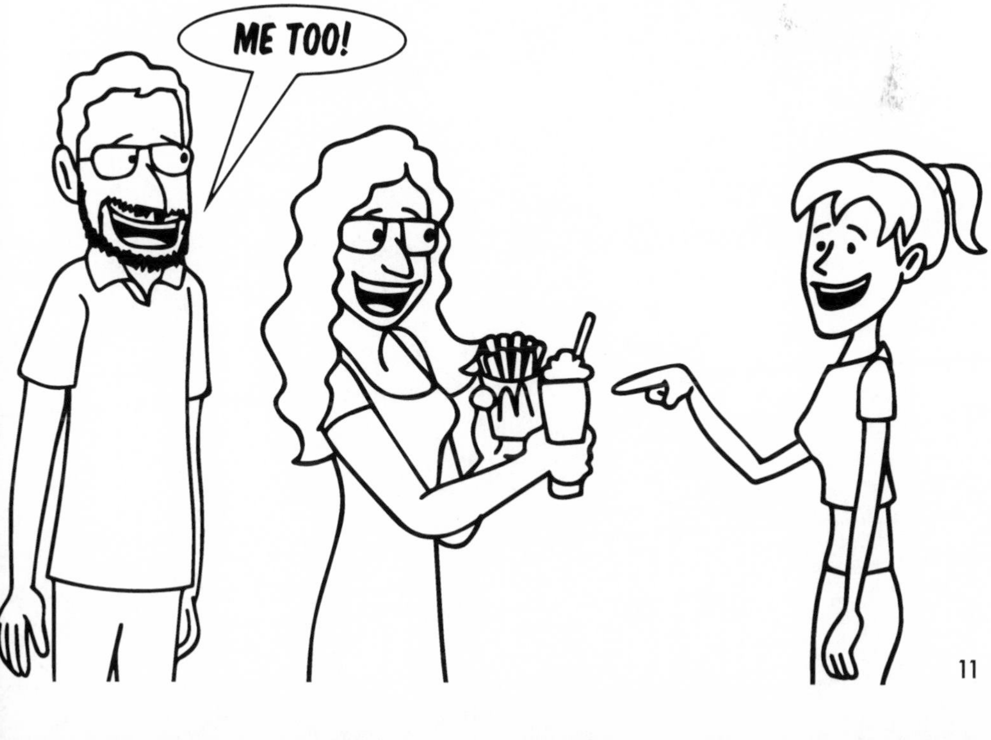
ME TOO!

WHY THIS BOOK EXISTS

A FEW YEARS BACK, WE WERE THINKING OF BECOMING PARENTS BECAUSE...
MICHELLE GAVE BIRTH.

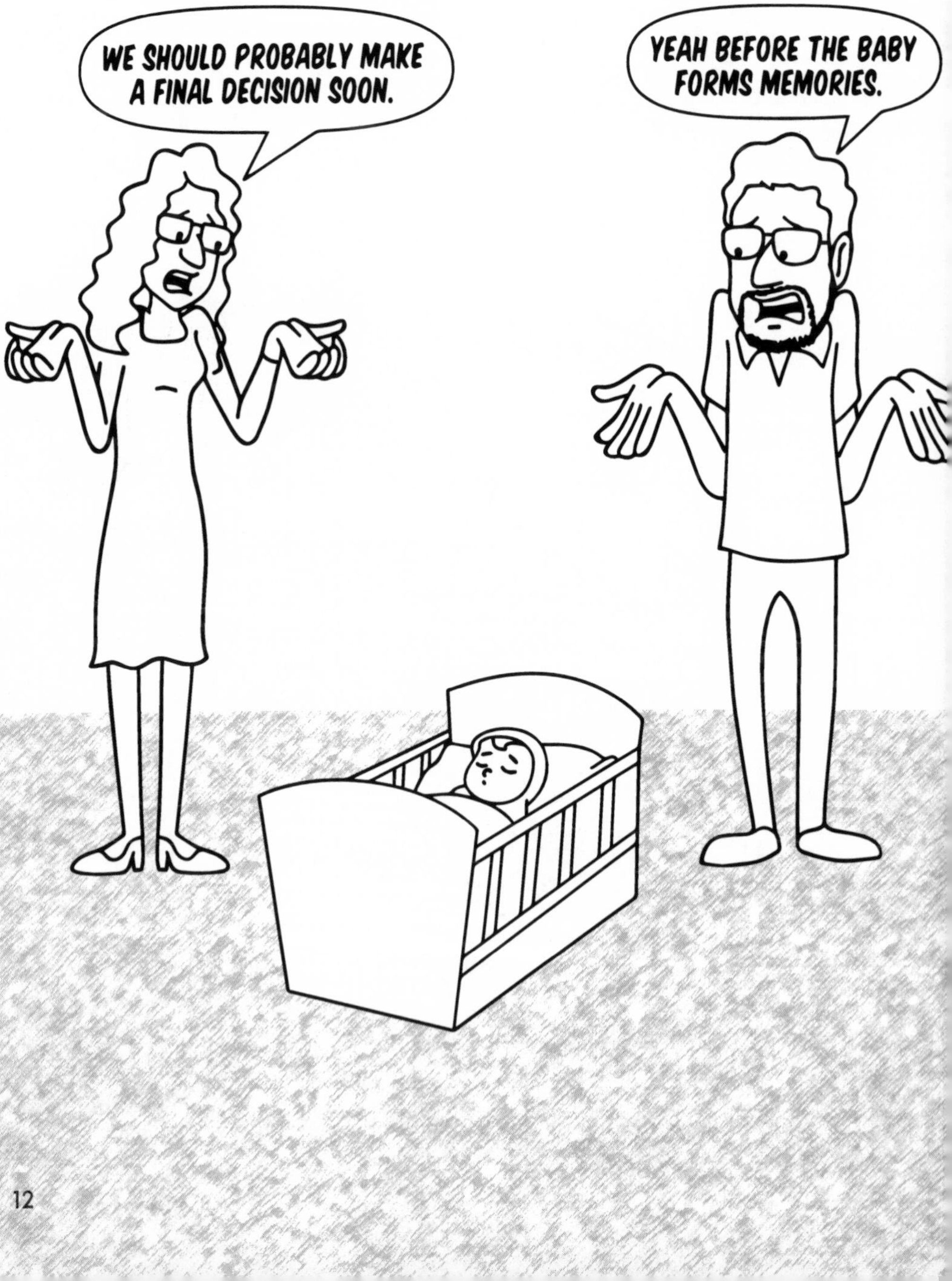
WE SHOULD PROBABLY MAKE A FINAL DECISION SOON.
YEAH BEFORE THE BABY FORMS MEMORIES.

WHAT FOLLOWS IS OUR PARENTHOOD JOURNEY SO FAR – FROM CONCEPTION UNTIL THE BABY TURNED ONE-YEAR-OLD.

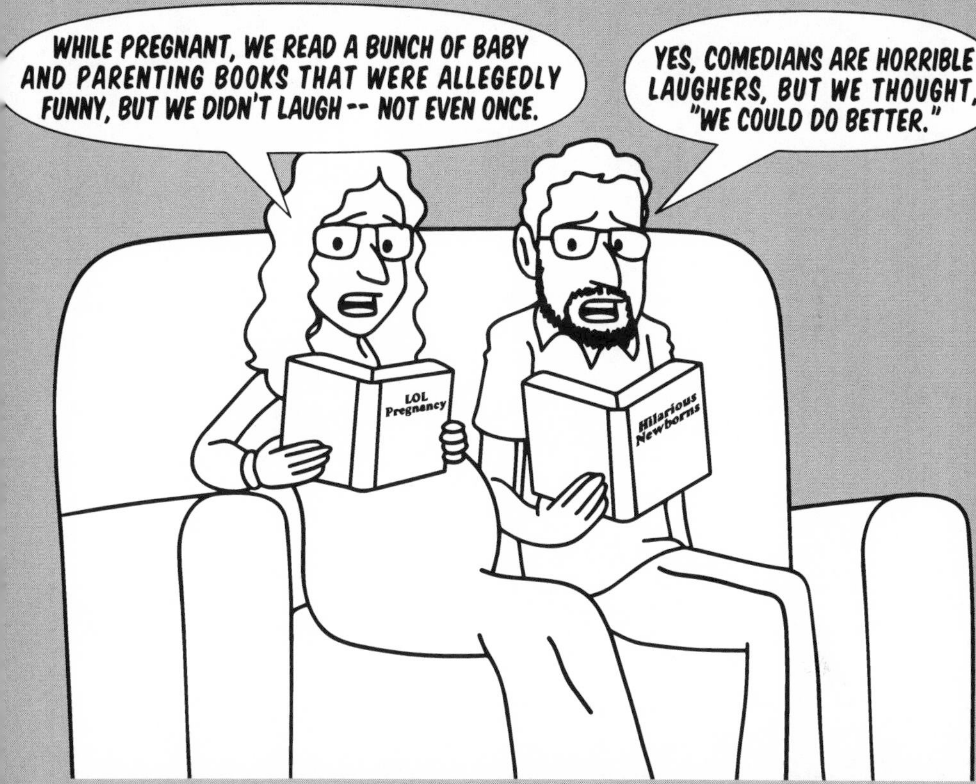
WHILE PREGNANT, WE READ A BUNCH OF BABY AND PARENTING BOOKS THAT WERE ALLEGEDLY FUNNY, BUT WE DIDN'T LAUGH -- NOT EVEN ONCE.
YES, COMEDIANS ARE HORRIBLE LAUGHERS, BUT WE THOUGHT, "WE COULD DO BETTER."
LOL Pregnancy
Hilarious Newborns

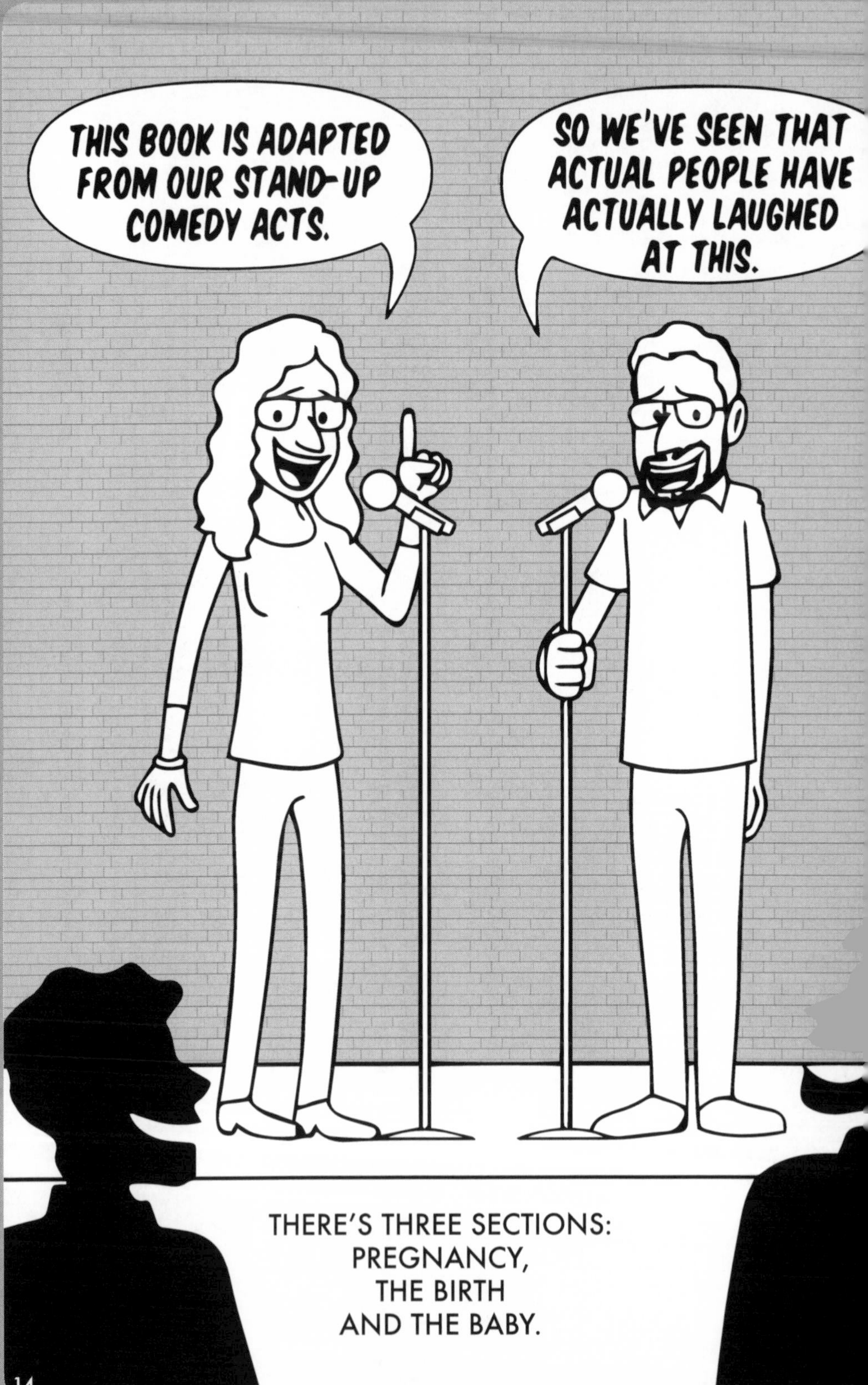
THIS BOOK IS ADAPTED FROM OUR STAND-UP COMEDY ACTS.
SO WE'VE SEEN THAT ACTUAL PEOPLE HAVE ACTUALLY LAUGHED AT THIS.
THERE'S THREE SECTIONS: PREGNANCY, THE BIRTH AND THE BABY.

PREGNANCY

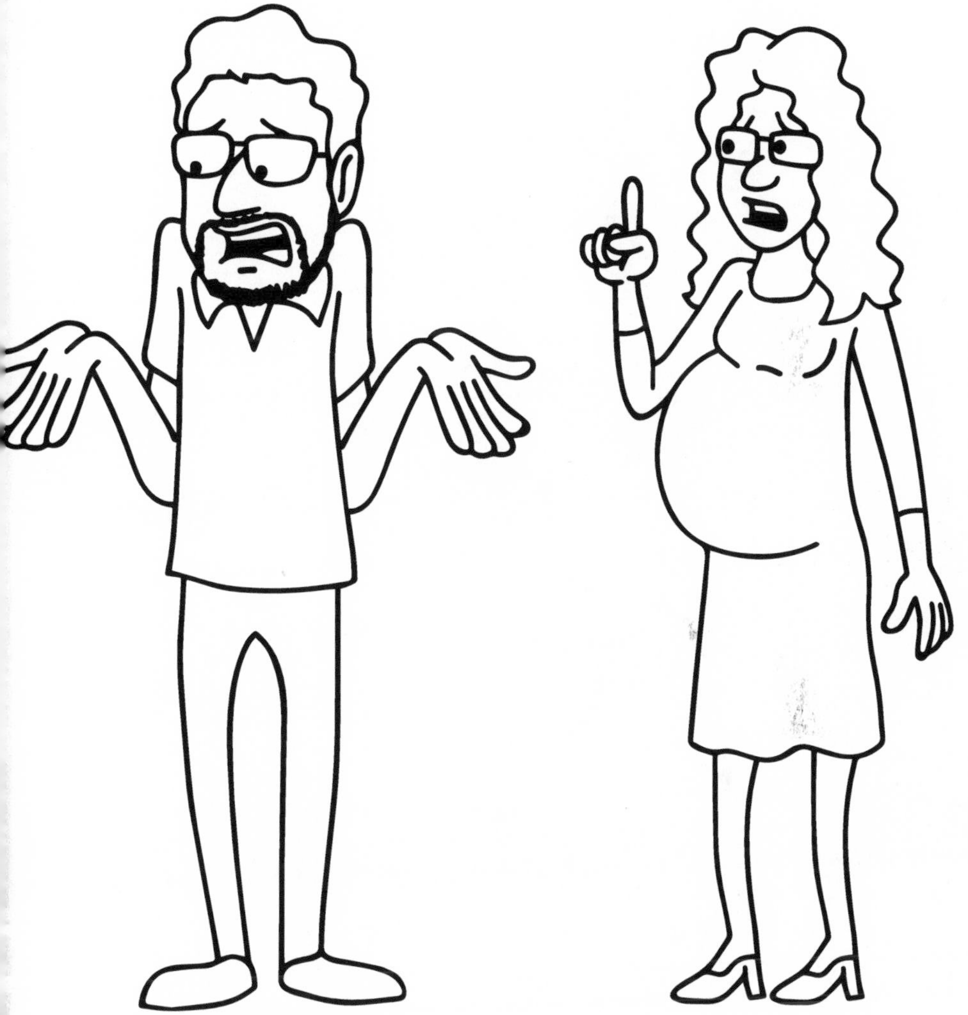

MICHELLE'S PREGNANCY JOKES

COCO LOCO

I DIDN'T KNOW IF I WAS READY TO HAVE KIDS.

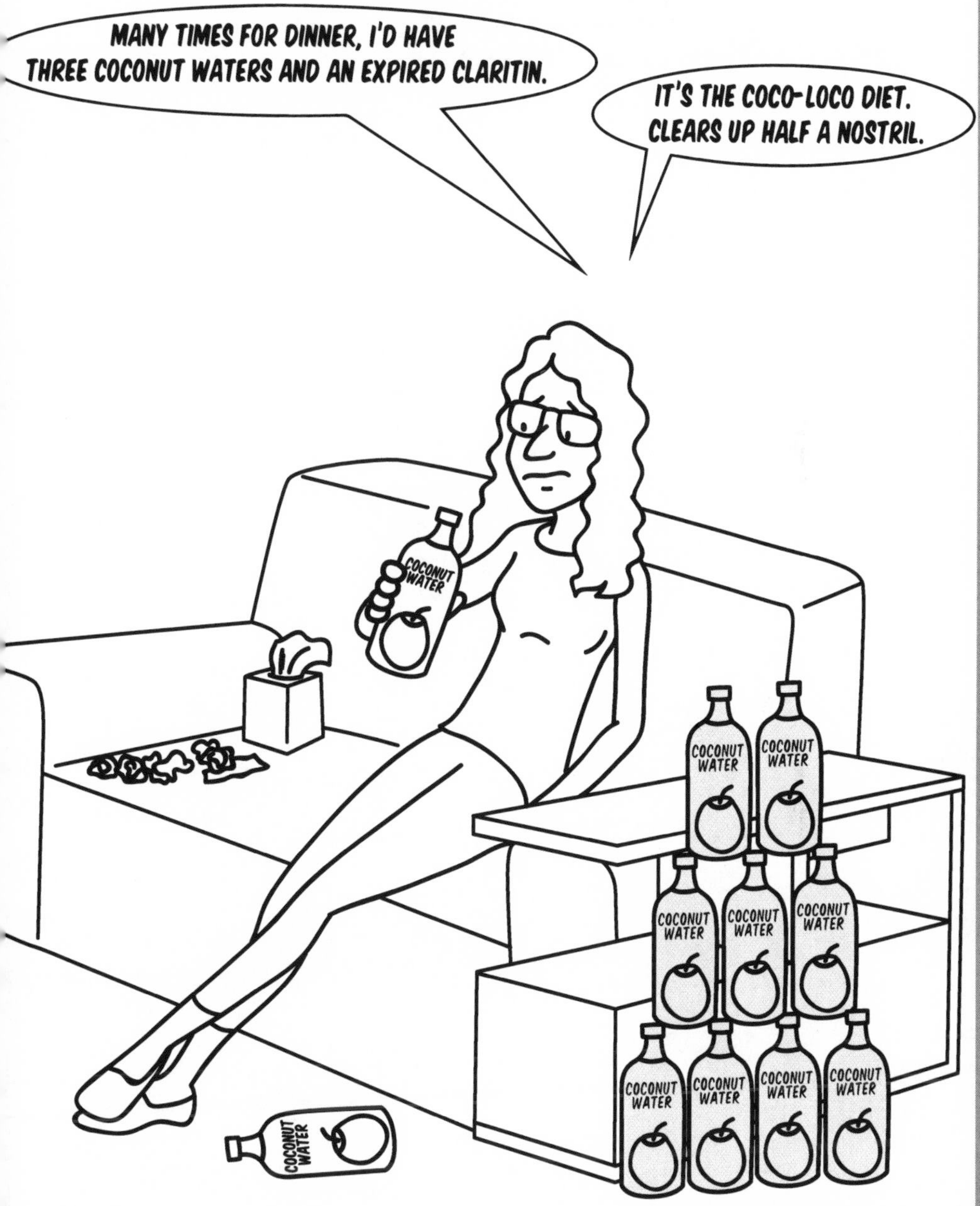

MANY TIMES FOR DINNER, I'D HAVE THREE COCONUT WATERS AND AN EXPIRED CLARITIN.
IT'S THE COCO-LOCO DIET. CLEARS UP HALF A NOSTRIL.
COCONUT WATER

BABY PICS

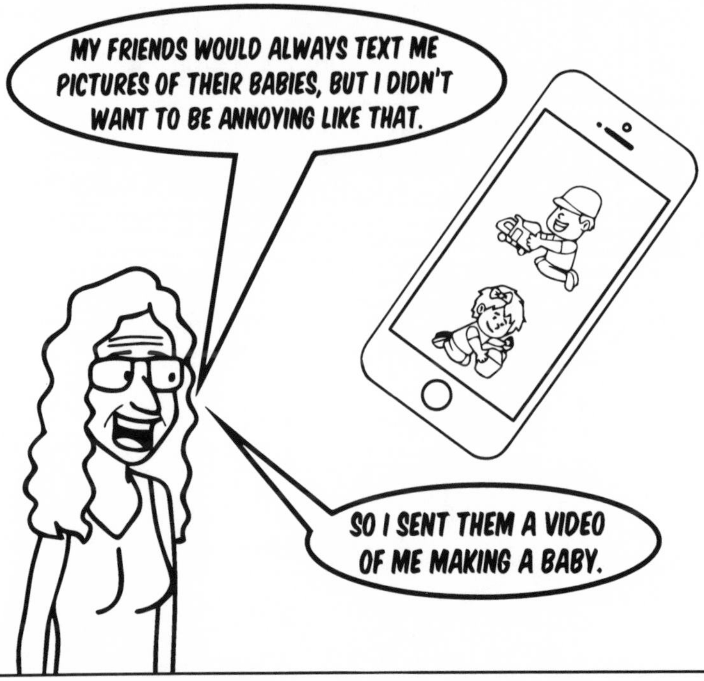
MY FRIENDS WOULD ALWAYS TEXT ME PICTURES OF THEIR BABIES, BUT I DIDN'T WANT TO BE ANNOYING LIKE THAT.
SO I SENT THEM A VIDEO OF ME MAKING A BABY.

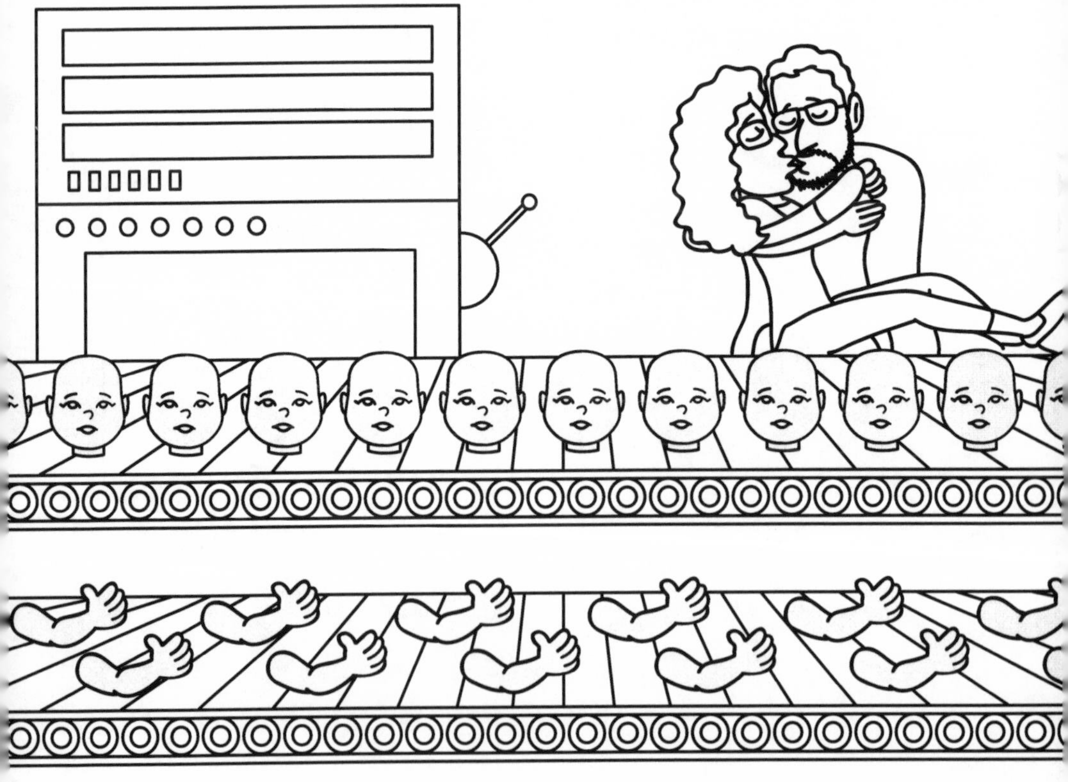

STOP ASKING ME IF I'M PREGNANT

I WAS AT A RESTAURANT, AND THIS WOMAN I'D NEVER MET APPROACHED ME...

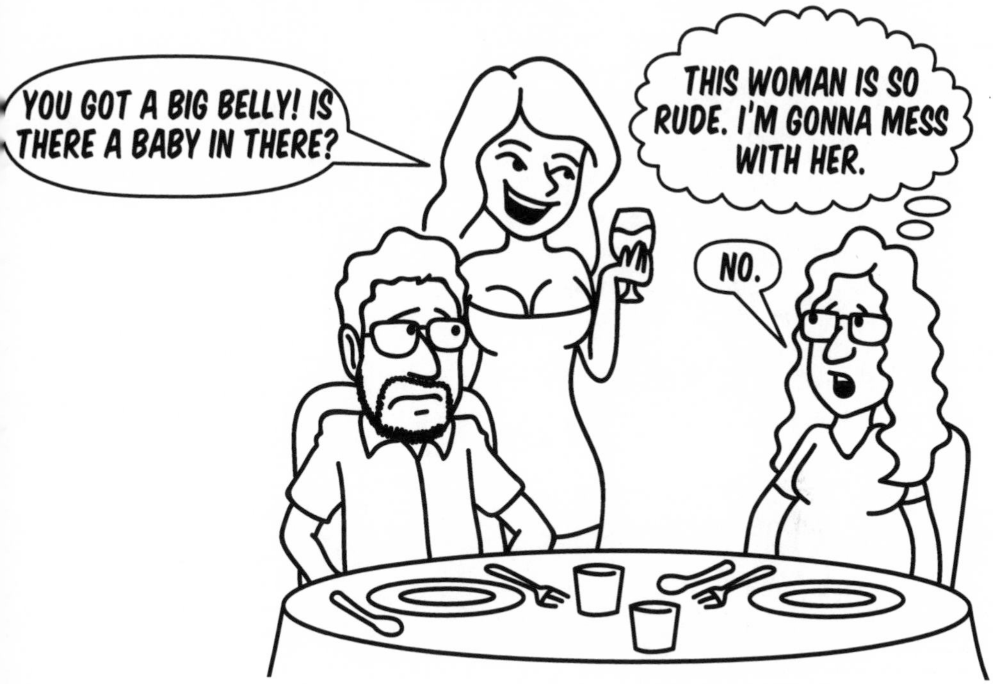
YOU GOT A BIG BELLY! IS THERE A BABY IN THERE?
THIS WOMAN IS SO RUDE. I'M GONNA MESS WITH HER.
NO.

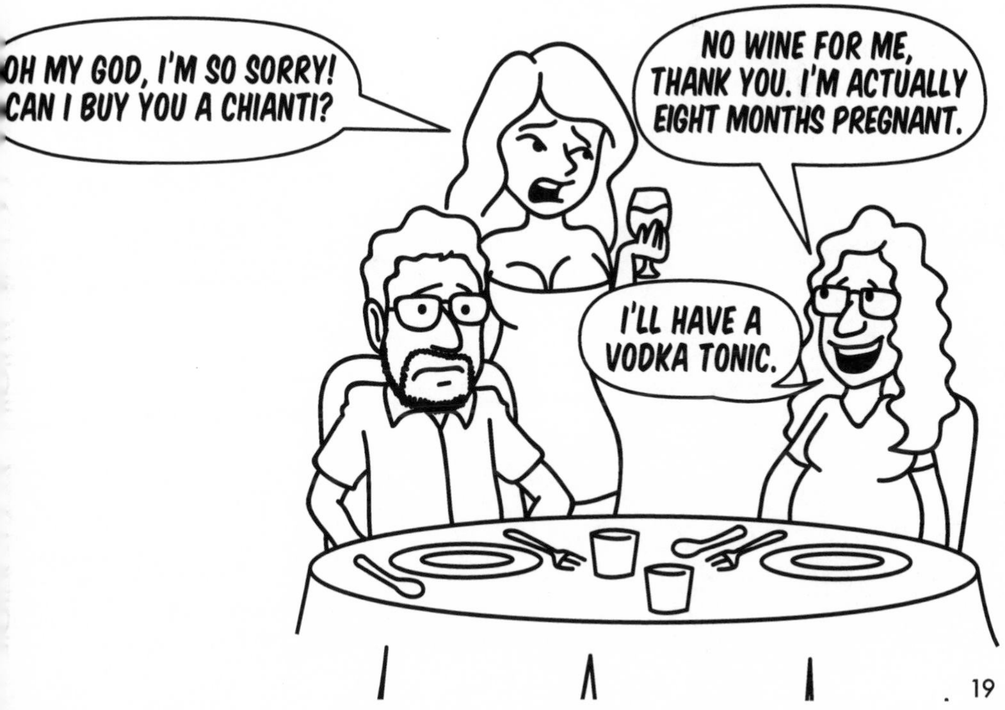
OH MY GOD, I'M SO SORRY! CAN I BUY YOU A CHIANTI?
NO WINE FOR ME, THANK YOU. I'M ACTUALLY EIGHT MONTHS PREGNANT.
I'LL HAVE A VODKA TONIC.

STRANGERS

EVENTUALLY YOU GET SICK OF STRANGERS ASKING ABOUT YOUR BELLY, SO YOU GET SNARKY.

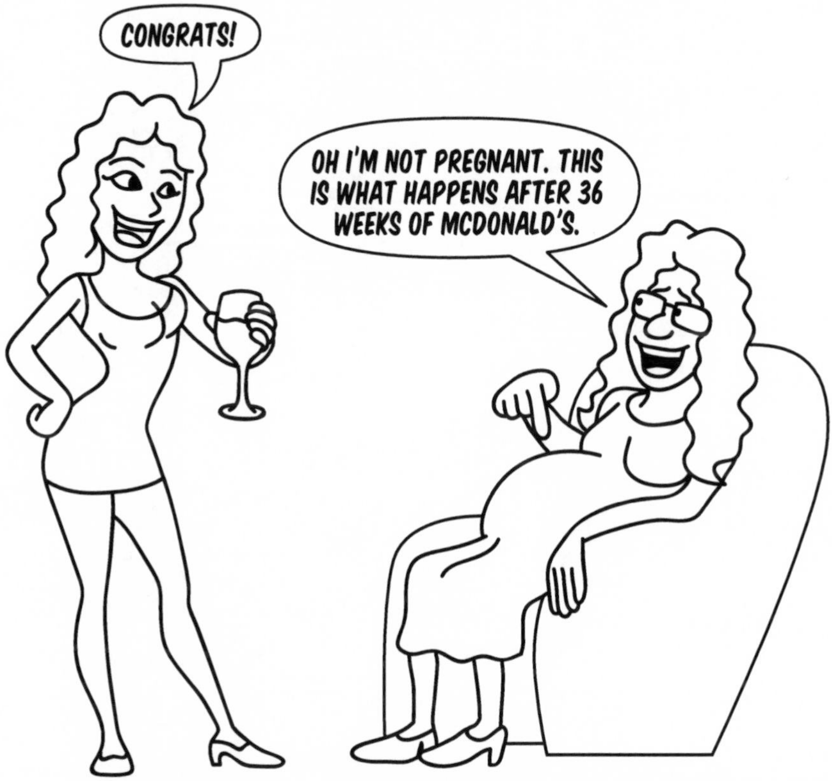
CONGRATS!
OH I'M NOT PREGNANT. THIS IS WHAT HAPPENS AFTER 36 WEEKS OF MCDONALD'S.

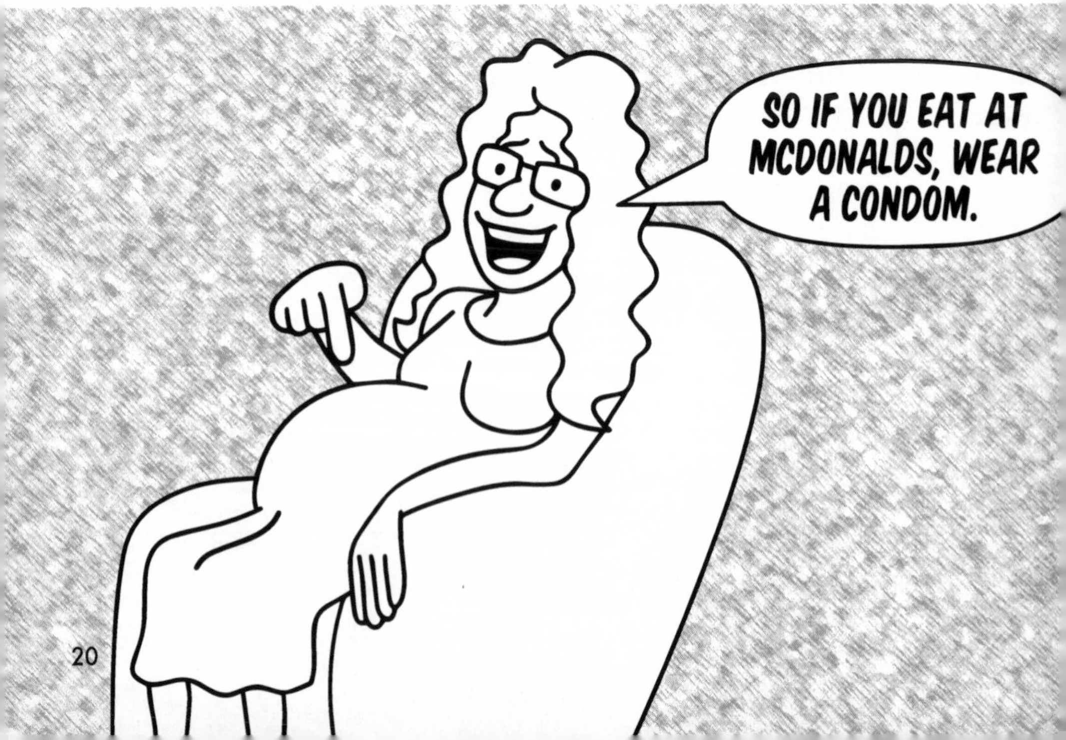
SO IF YOU EAT AT MCDONALDS, WEAR A CONDOM.

CAT CALLING

JUST BECAUSE YOU'RE PREGNANT, DOESN'T MEAN MEN STOP CAT CALLING YOU. WHEN I WAS 8 MONTHS PREGNANT...

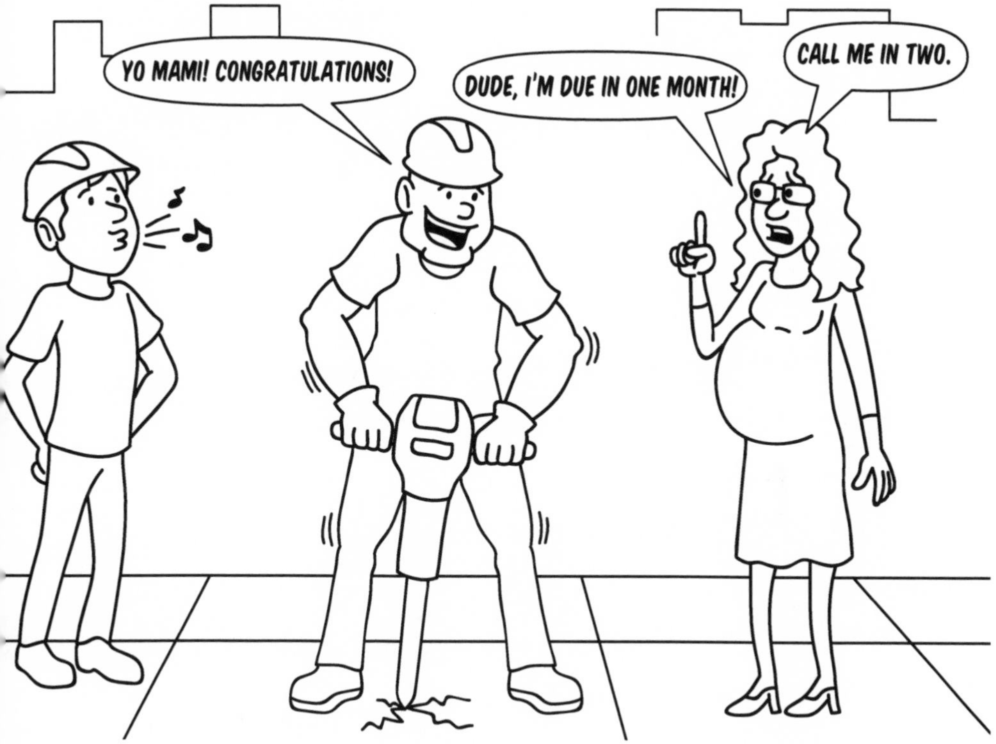
YO MAMI! CONGRATULATIONS!
DUDE, I'M DUE IN ONE MONTH!
CALL ME IN TWO.

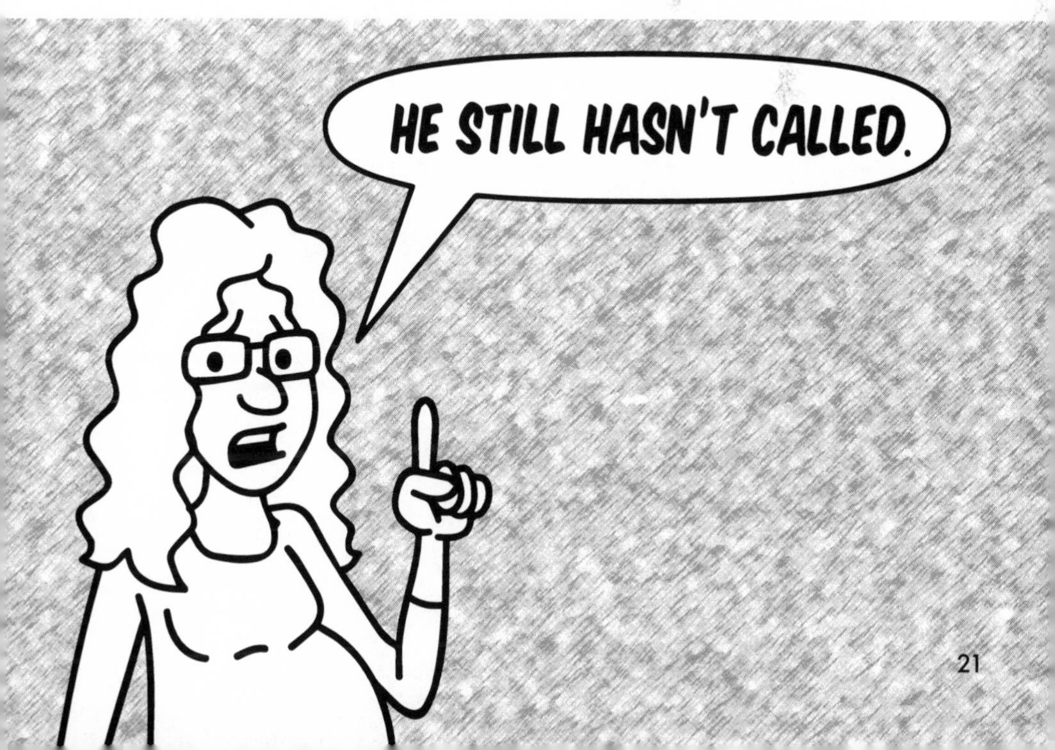
HE STILL HASN'T CALLED.

BIG APPETITE

PREGNANCY MAKES YOU HUUUUUUNGRY.

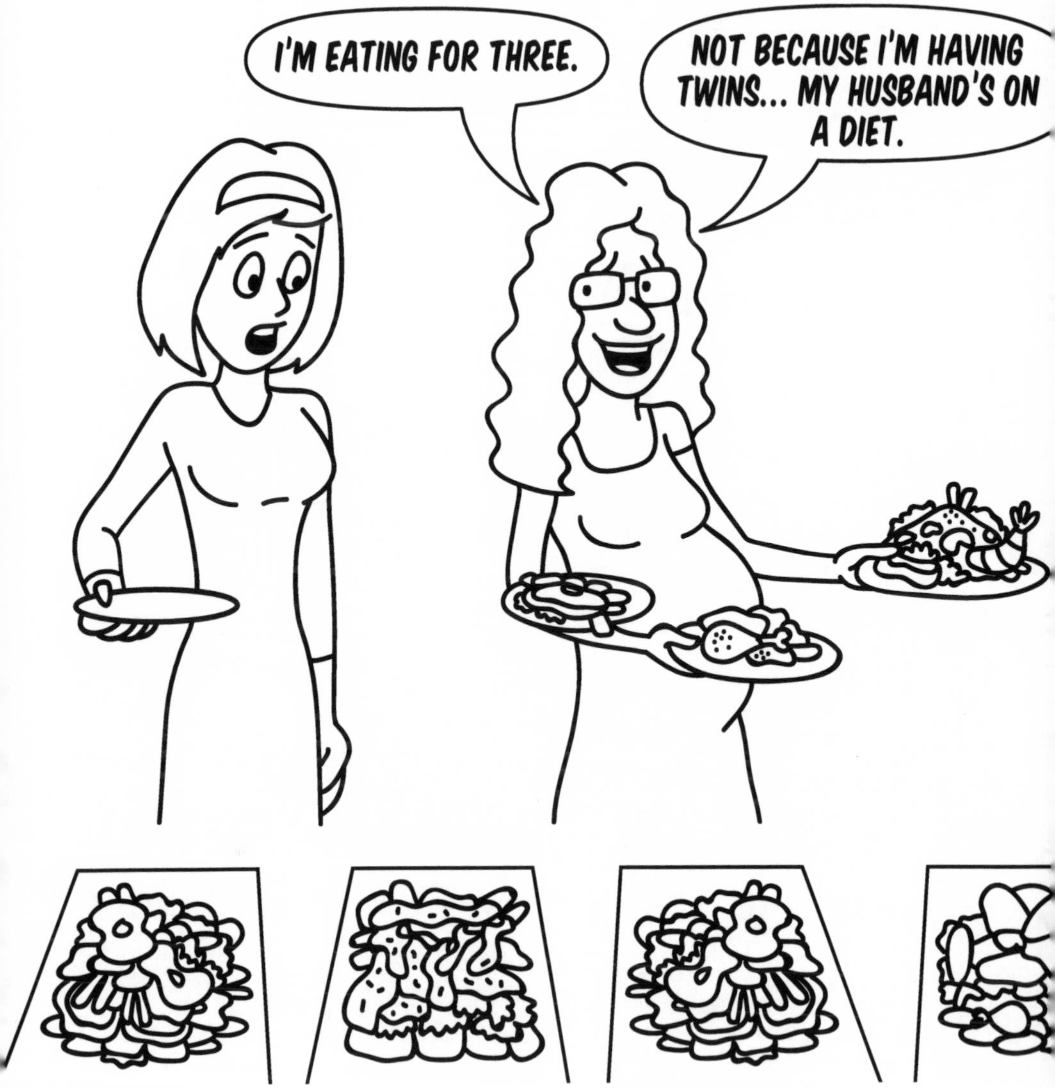

I'M EATING FOR THREE.
NOT BECAUSE I'M HAVING TWINS... MY HUSBAND'S ON A DIET.

RECOGNIZE VOICES

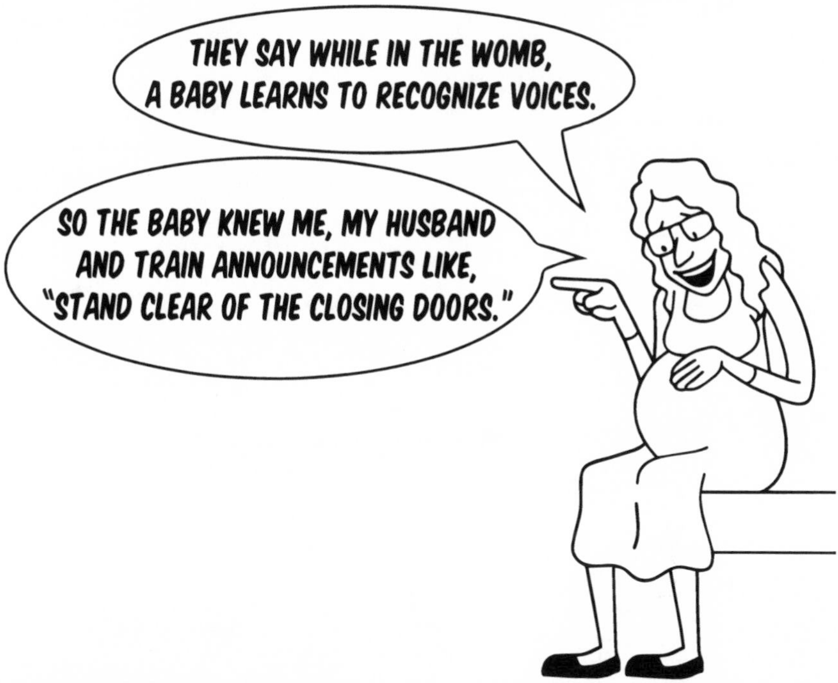
THEY SAY WHILE IN THE WOMB, A BABY LEARNS TO RECOGNIZE VOICES.
SO THE BABY KNEW ME, MY HUSBAND AND TRAIN ANNOUNCEMENTS LIKE, "STAND CLEAR OF THE CLOSING DOORS."

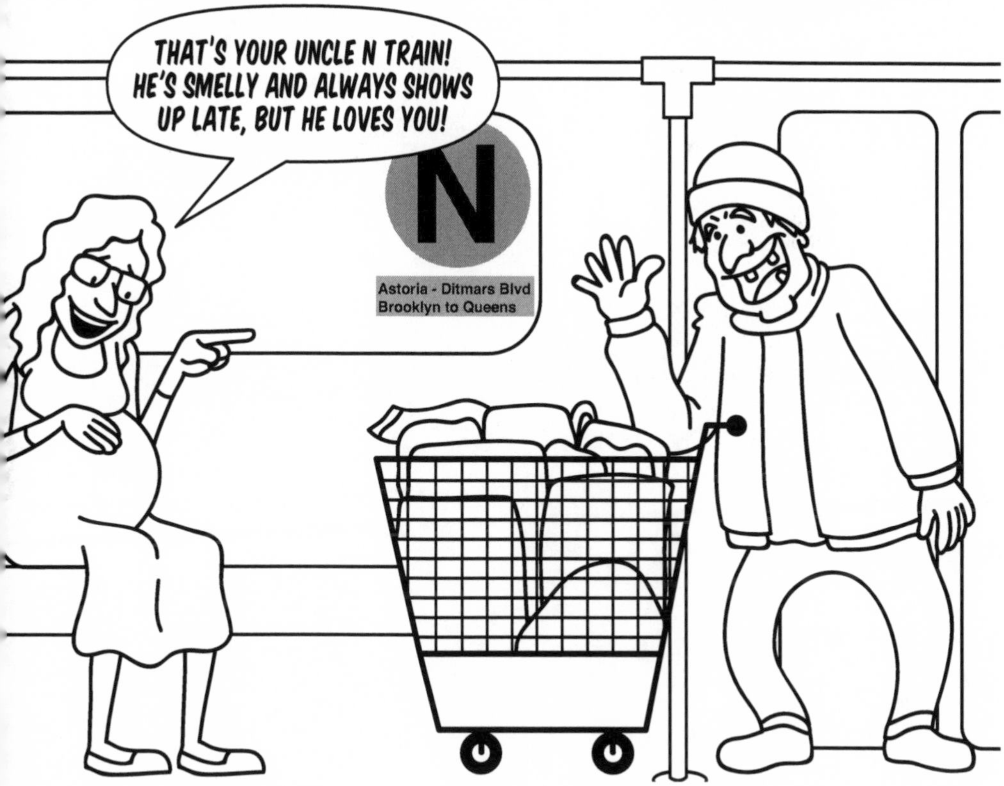
THAT'S YOUR UNCLE N TRAIN! HE'S SMELLY AND ALWAYS SHOWS UP LATE, BUT HE LOVES YOU!
N
Astoria - Ditmars Blvd
Brooklyn to Queens

SONOGRAM

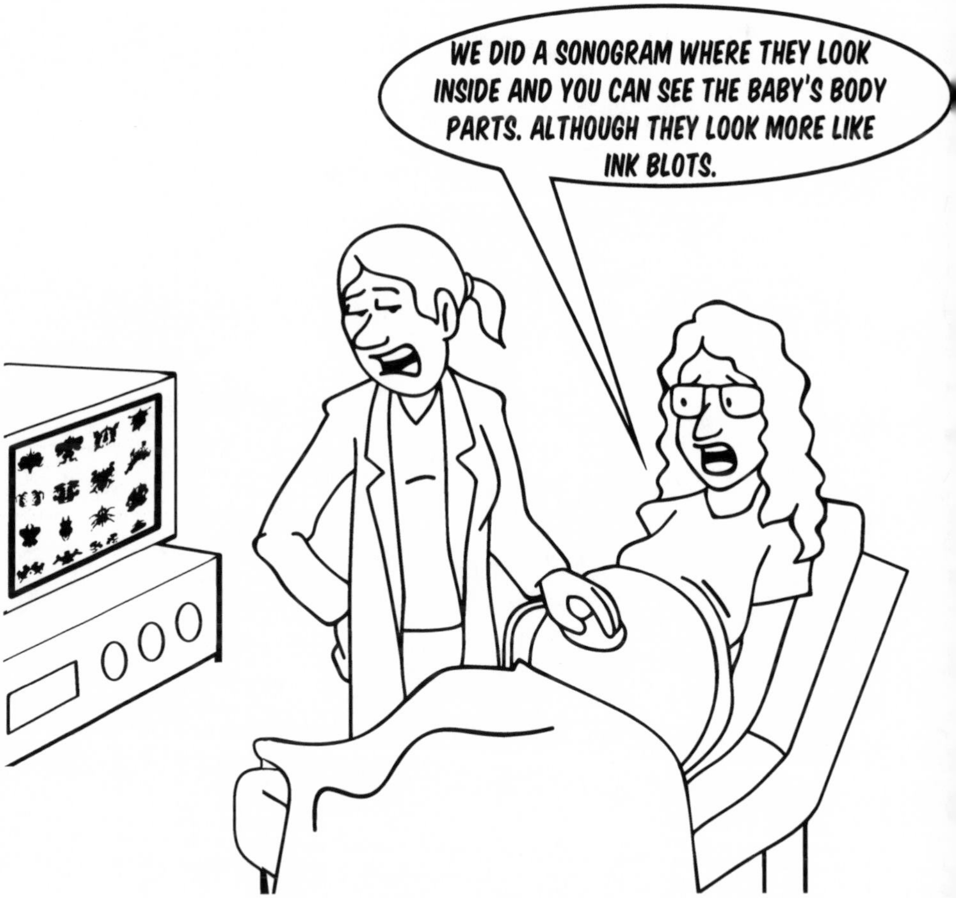
WE DID A SONOGRAM WHERE THEY LOOK INSIDE AND YOU CAN SEE THE BABY'S BODY PARTS. ALTHOUGH THEY LOOK MORE LIKE INK BLOTS.

MY HUSBAND STARTED GUESSING WHAT BODY PARTS WE WERE SEEING ON THE SONOGRAM.

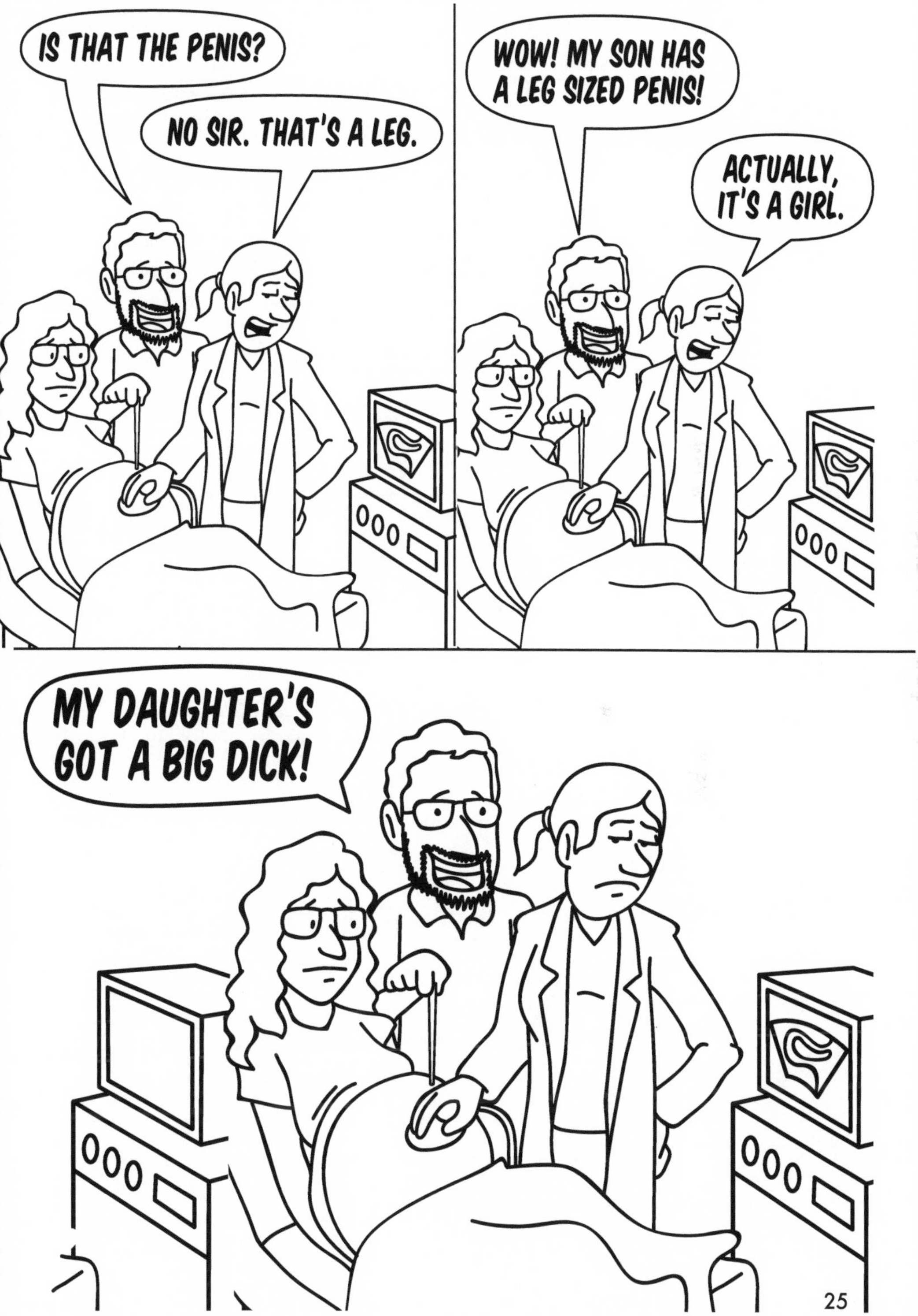
IS THAT THE PENIS?
NO SIR. THAT'S A LEG.
WOW! MY SON HAS A LEG SIZED PENIS!
ACTUALLY, IT'S A GIRL.
MY DAUGHTER'S GOT A BIG DICK!

MOM EMAIL

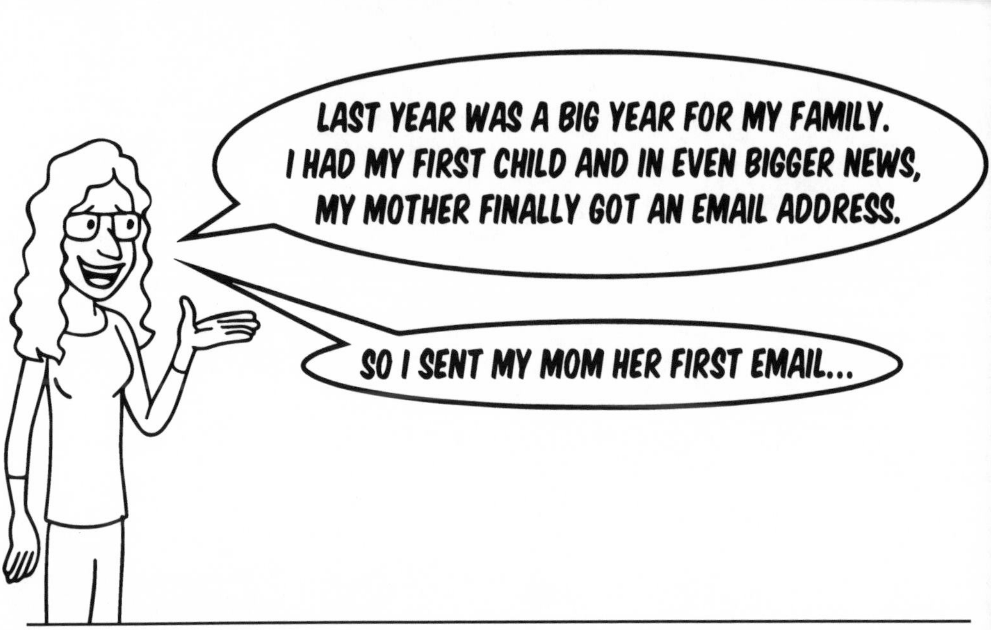
LAST YEAR WAS A BIG YEAR FOR MY FAMILY. I HAD MY FIRST CHILD AND IN EVEN BIGGER NEWS, MY MOTHER FINALLY GOT AN EMAIL ADDRESS.
SO I SENT MY MOM HER FIRST EMAIL...

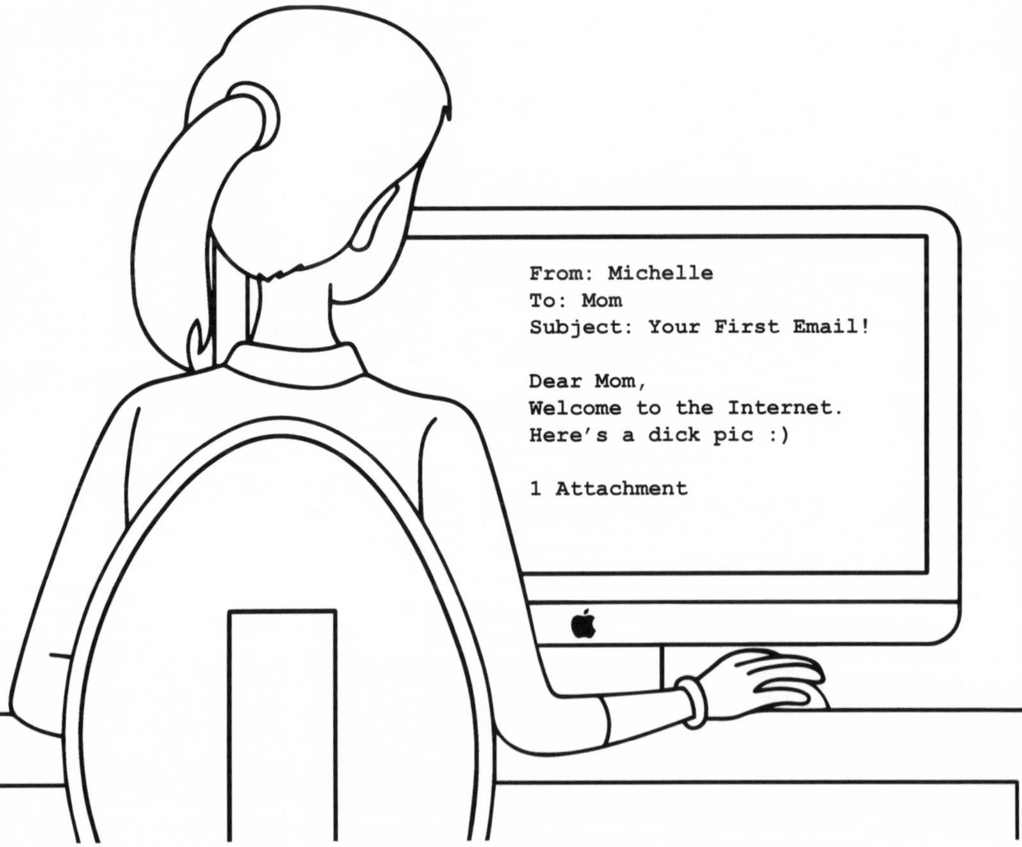
From: Michelle
To: Mom
Subject: Your First Email!
Dear Mom,
Welcome to the Internet.
Here's a dick pic :)
1 Attachment

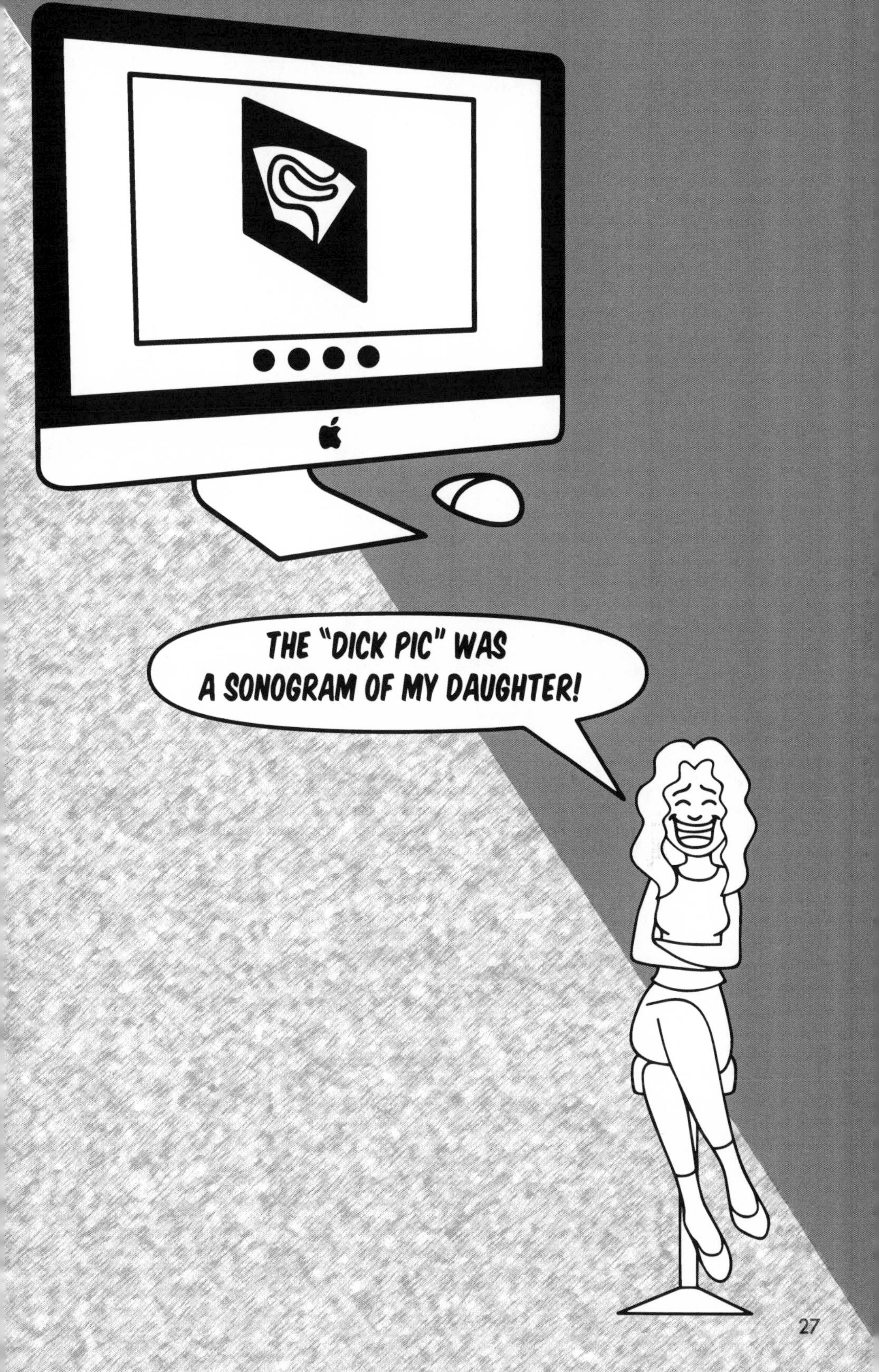
THE "DICK PIC" WAS
A SONOGRAM OF MY DAUGHTER!

PREGNANCY CARD

I LOVED PLAYING THE PREGNANCY CARD BECAUSE IT LET ME CUT LINES: THE CAFETERIA, THE BATHROOM, COCAINE.

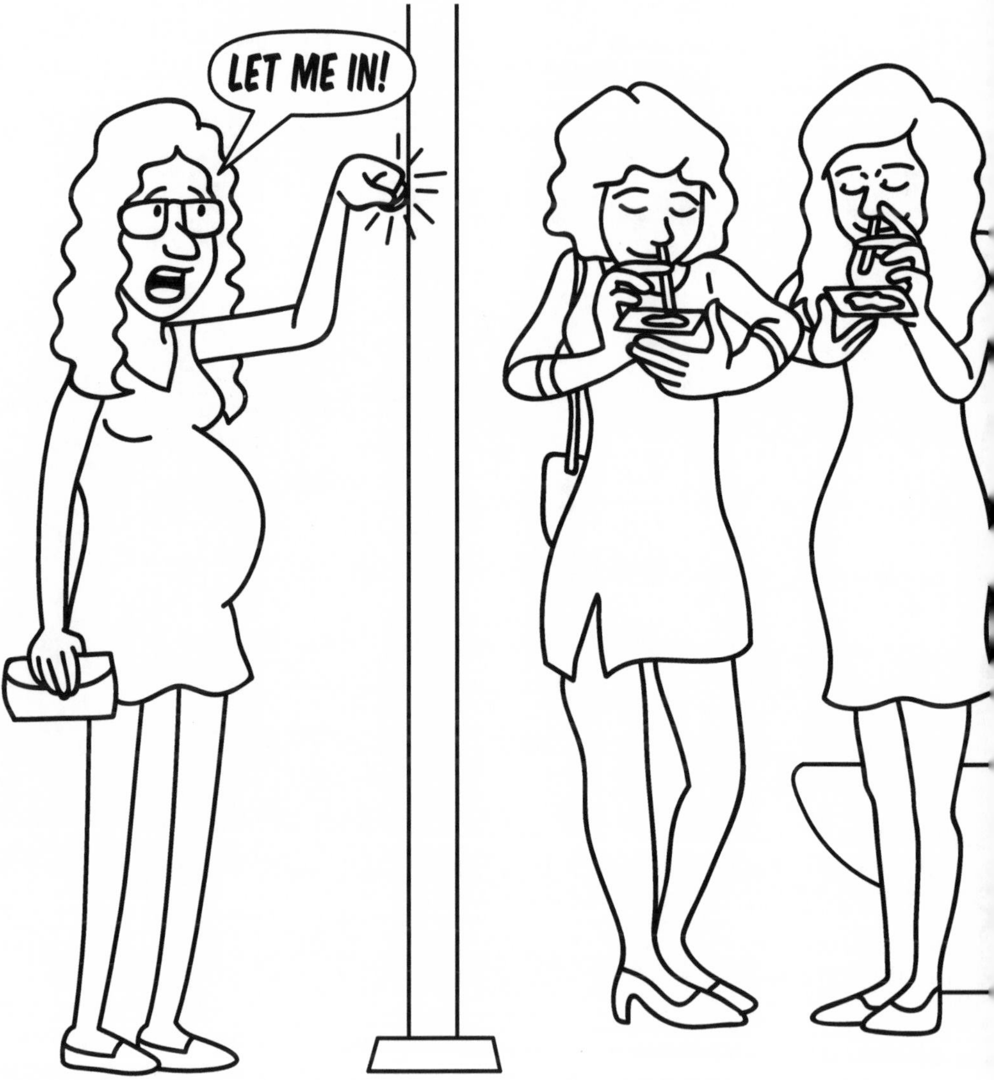
LET ME IN!

CRAIGSLIST

WHILE PREGNANT, WE BOUGHT THE BABY $300 WORTH OF USED CLOTHING ON CRAIGSLIST... SO WE NAMED HER CRAIG.

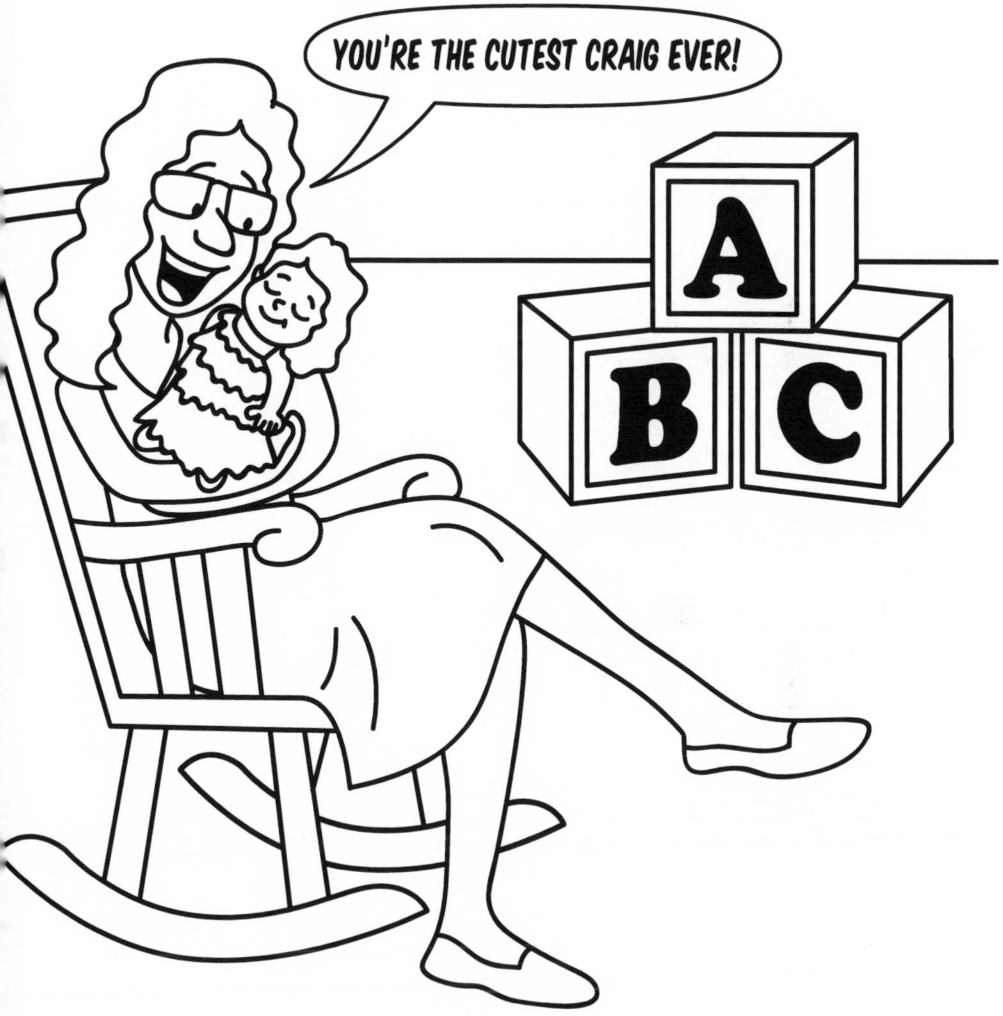
YOU'RE THE CUTEST CRAIG EVER!
A
B
C

FRUITS

EVERY WEEK I'D GET AN EMAIL TELLING ME ABOUT THE GROWTH OF MY BABY.

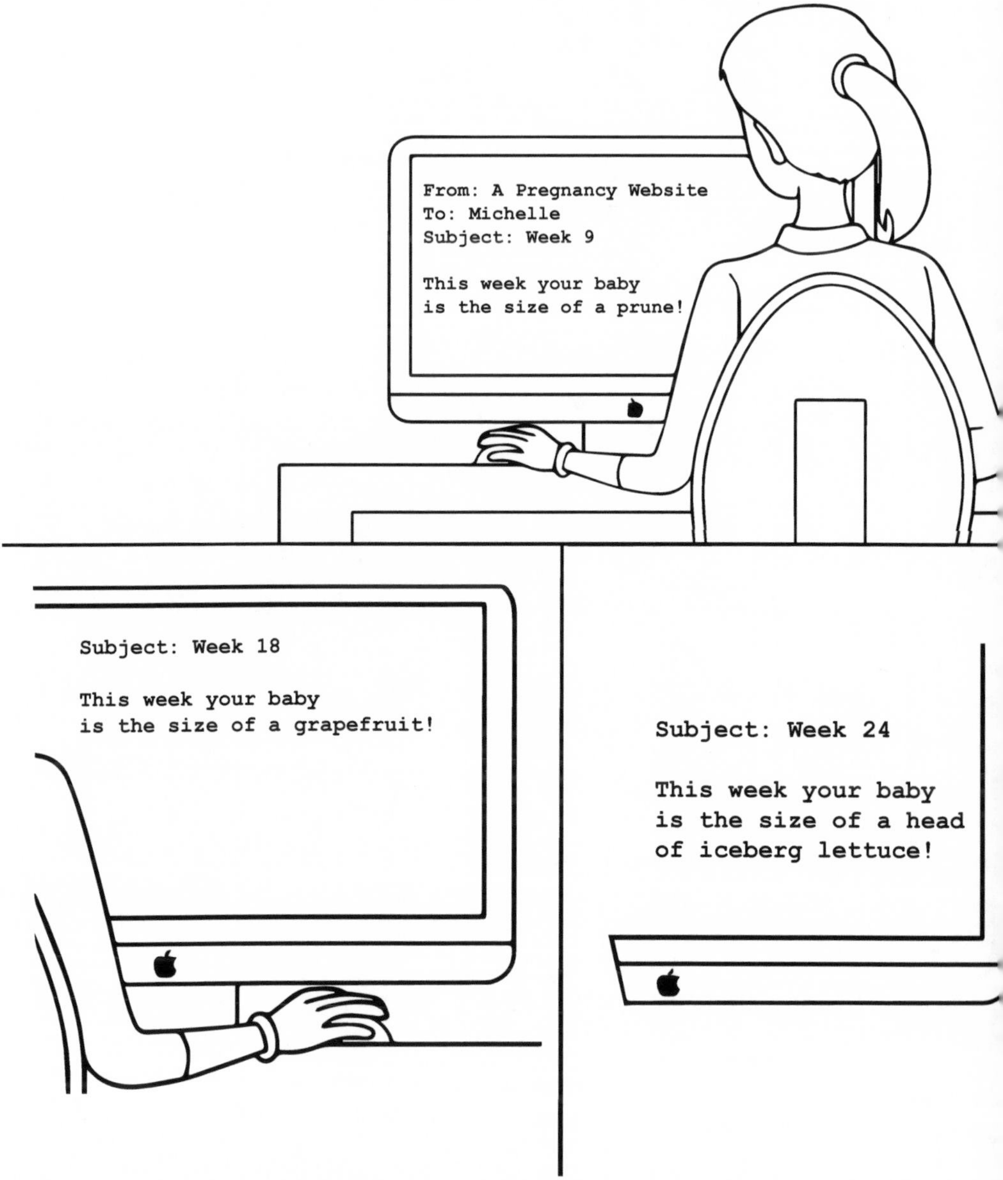
From: A Pregnancy Website
To: Michelle
Subject: Week 9
This week your baby is the size of a prune!
Subject: Week 18
This week your baby is the size of a grapefruit!
Subject: Week 24
This week your baby is the size of a head of iceberg lettuce!

BUT THEY DON'T DO THAT COMPARISON FOR MOTHERS...

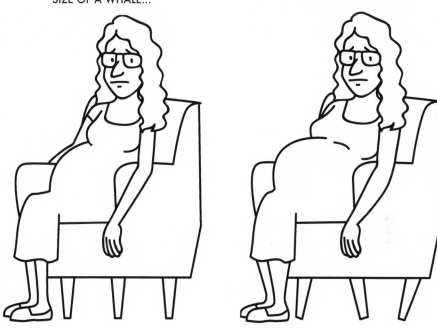

THIS WEEK YOU'RE THE SIZE OF A WHALE...

THIS WEEK YOU'RE A HIPPO...

THIS WEEK YOU'RE A WHALE THAT ATE A HIPPO THAT DIDN'T EAT ICEBERG LETTUCE.

BEN'S PREGNANCY JOKES

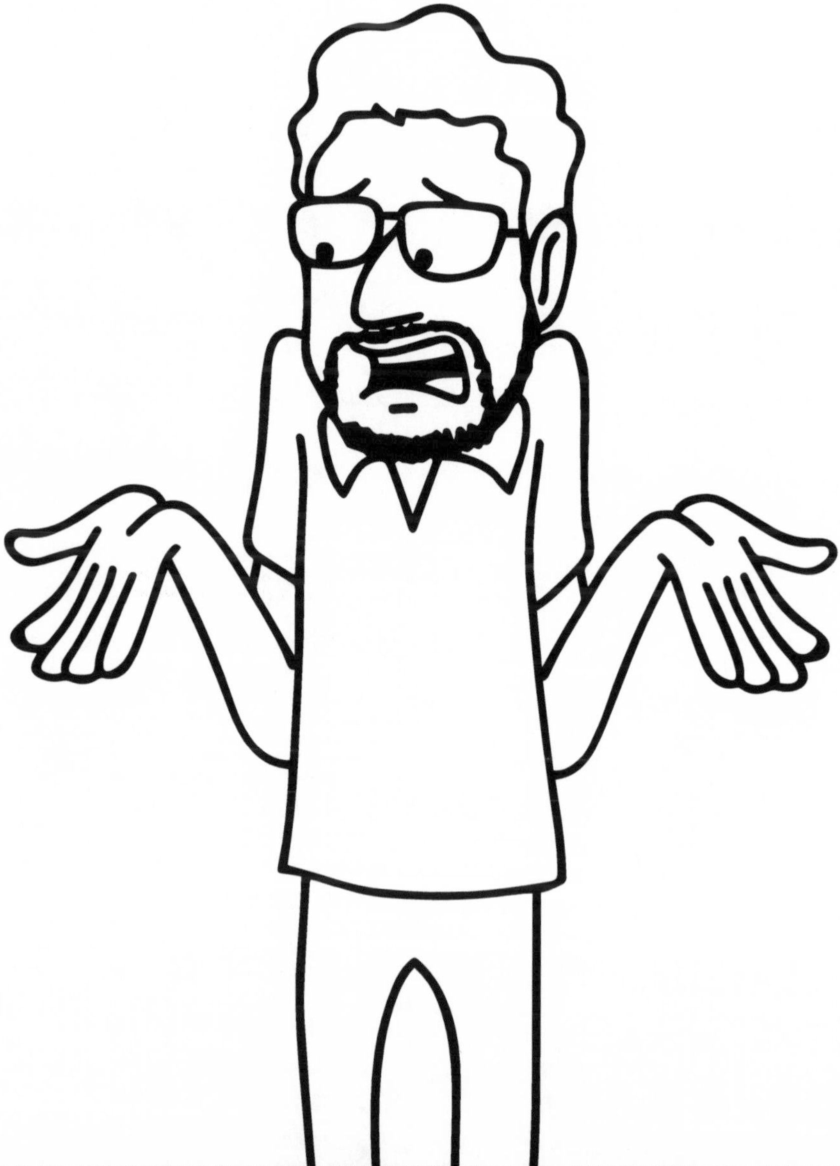

STROLLER

I WAS COMPLAINING TO MY SINGLE FRIEND...

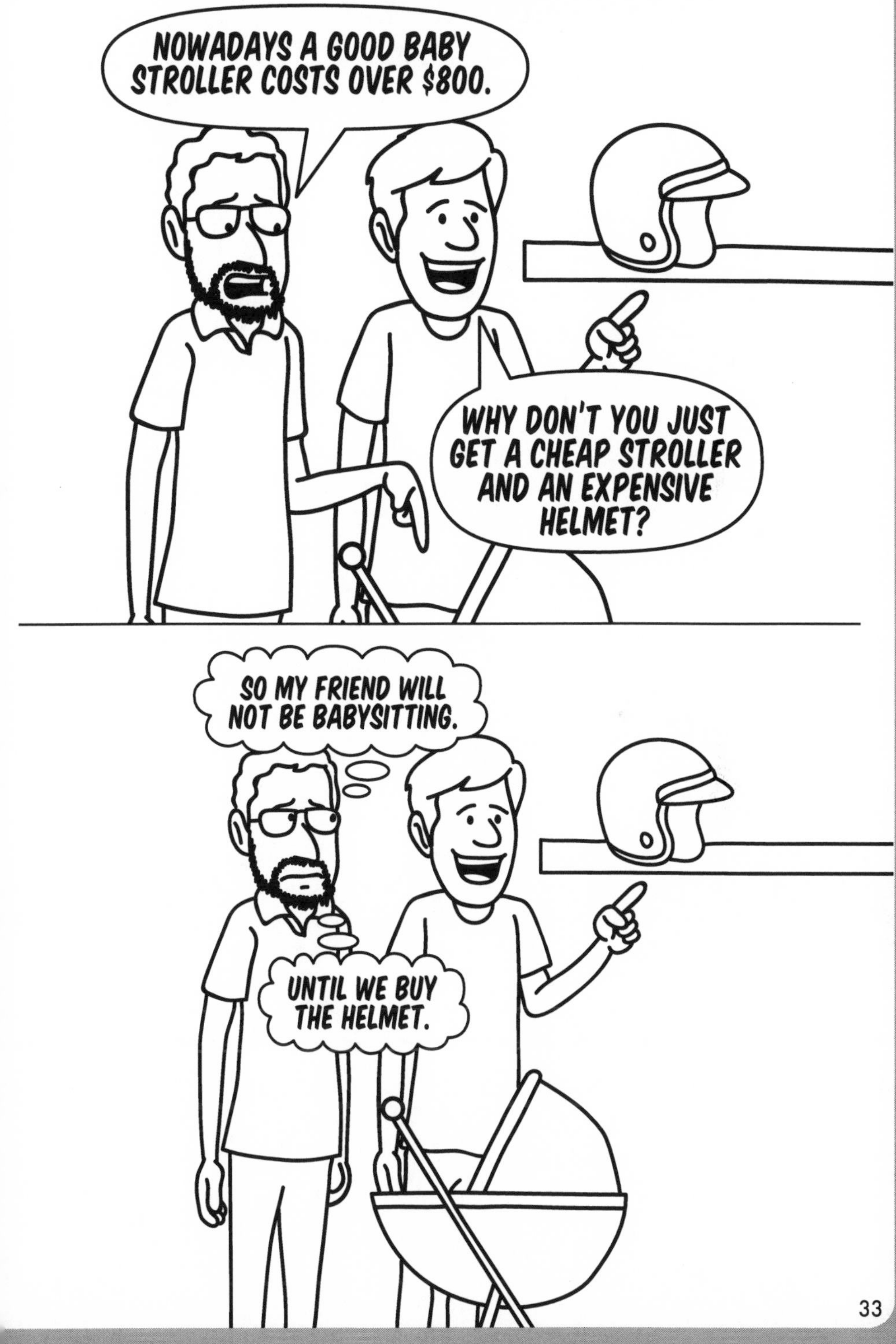

NOWADAYS A GOOD BABY STROLLER COSTS OVER $800.
WHY DON'T YOU JUST GET A CHEAP STROLLER AND AN EXPENSIVE HELMET?
SO MY FRIEND WILL NOT BE BABYSITTING.
UNTIL WE BUY THE HELMET.

BOY OR GIRL

THE SAME FRIEND ASKED...

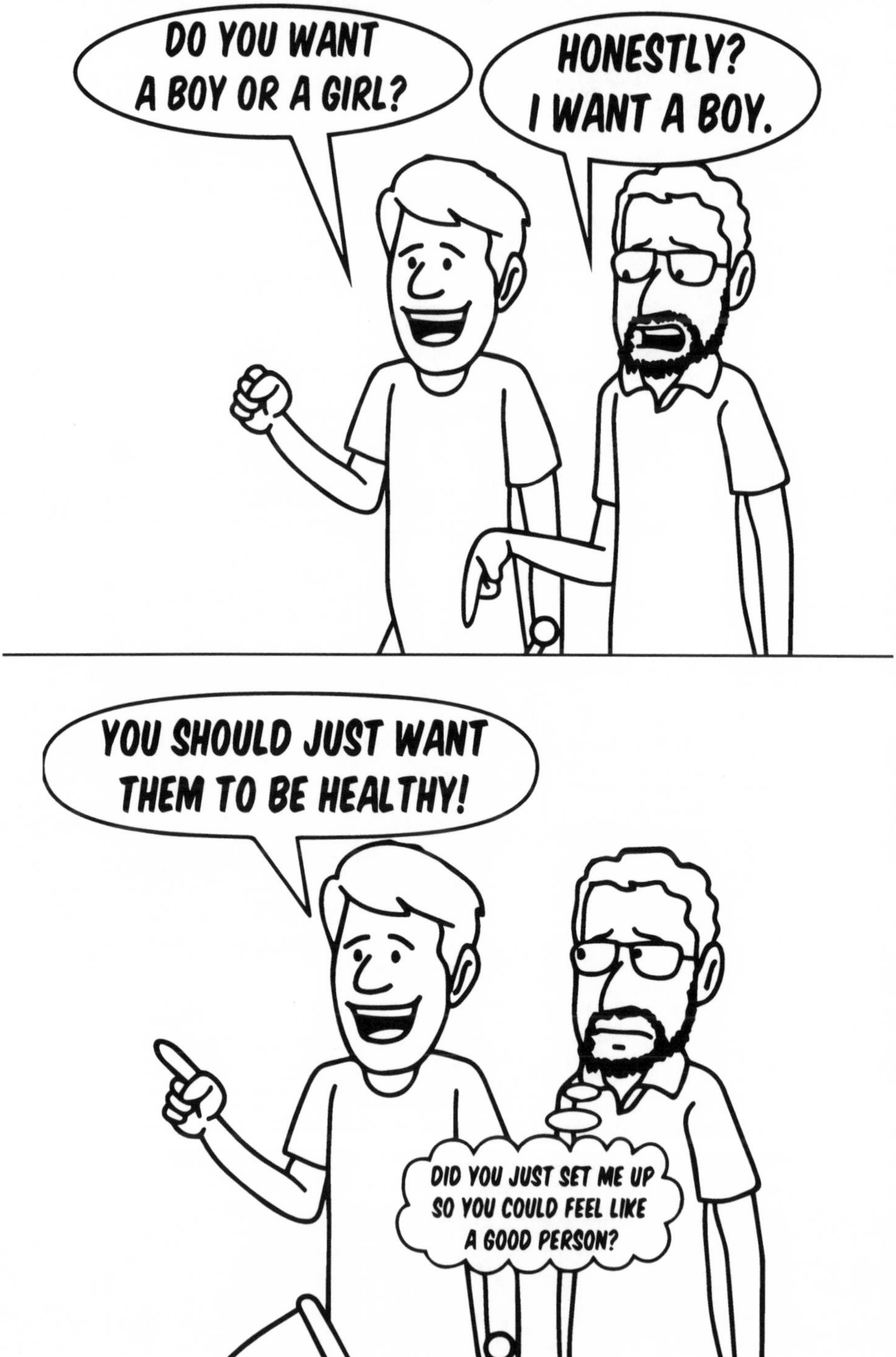

DO YOU WANT A BOY OR A GIRL?
HONESTLY? I WANT A BOY.
YOU SHOULD JUST WANT THEM TO BE HEALTHY!
DID YOU JUST SET ME UP SO YOU COULD FEEL LIKE A GOOD PERSON?

AFTER THAT INCIDENT, WHEN SOMEONE WOULD ASK ME WHAT I WANTED, I'D ANSWER IN CODE...

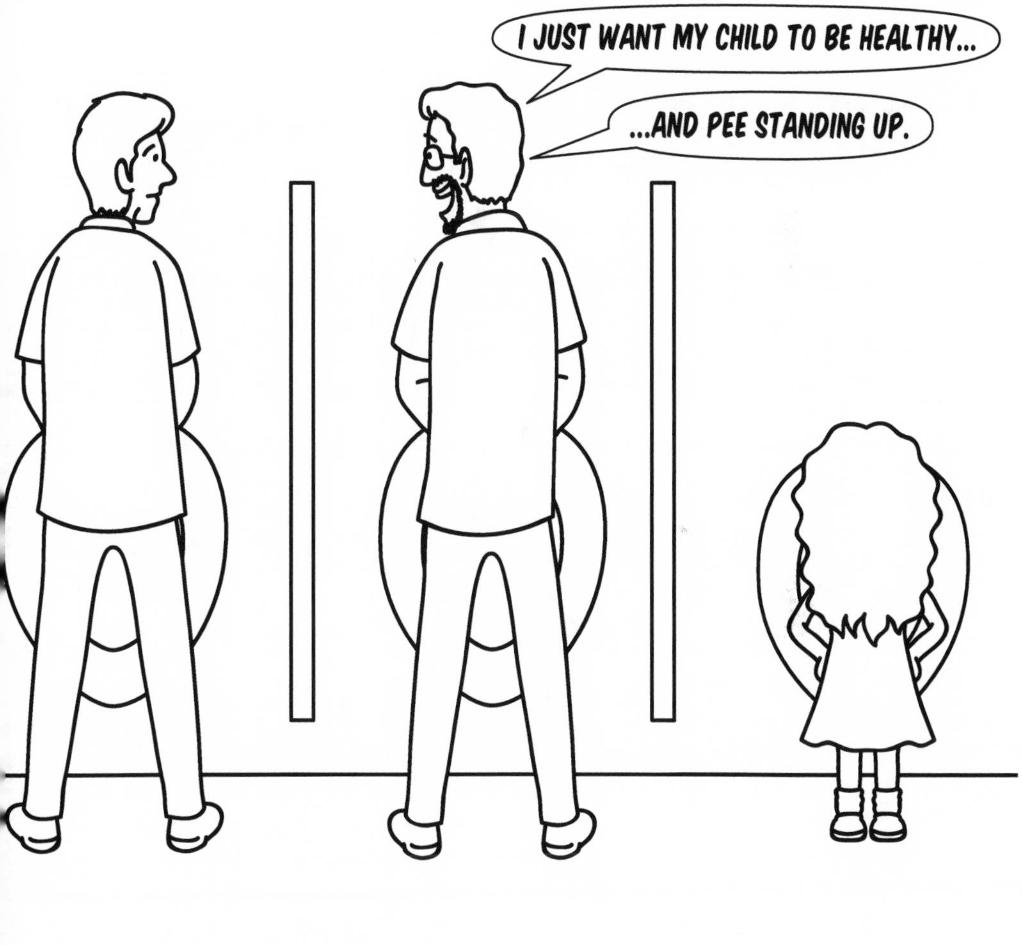
I JUST WANT MY CHILD TO BE HEALTHY...
...AND PEE STANDING UP.

ULTRASOUND

AT A PRENATAL CHECKUP...

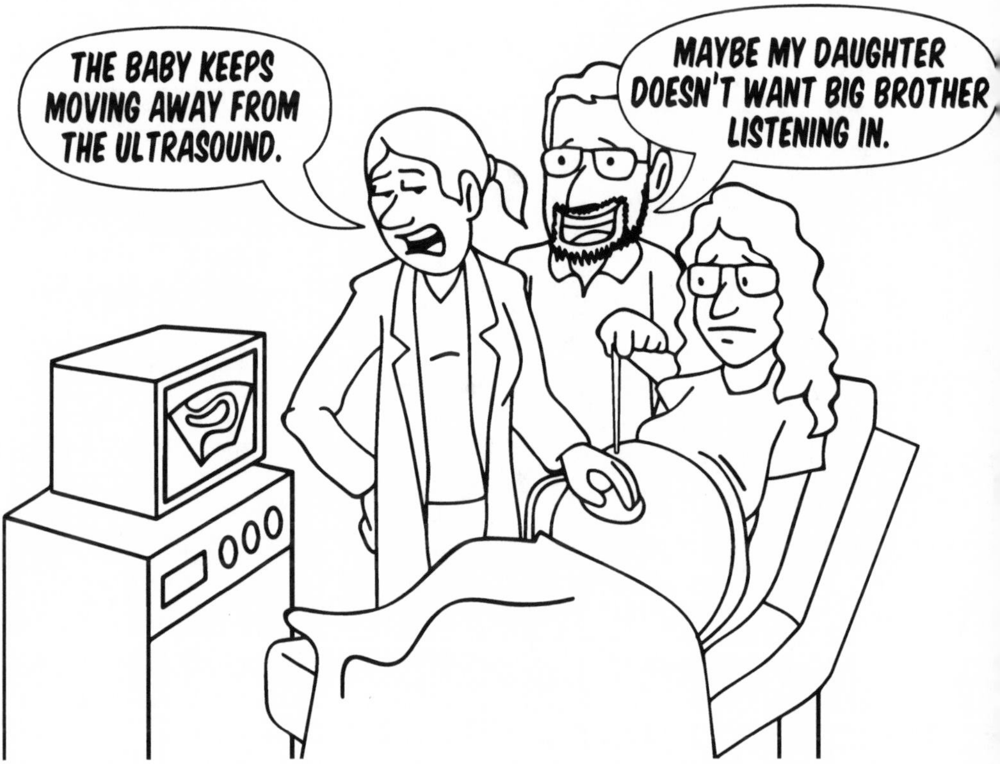
THE BABY KEEPS MOVING AWAY FROM THE ULTRASOUND.
MAYBE MY DAUGHTER DOESN'T WANT BIG BROTHER LISTENING IN.

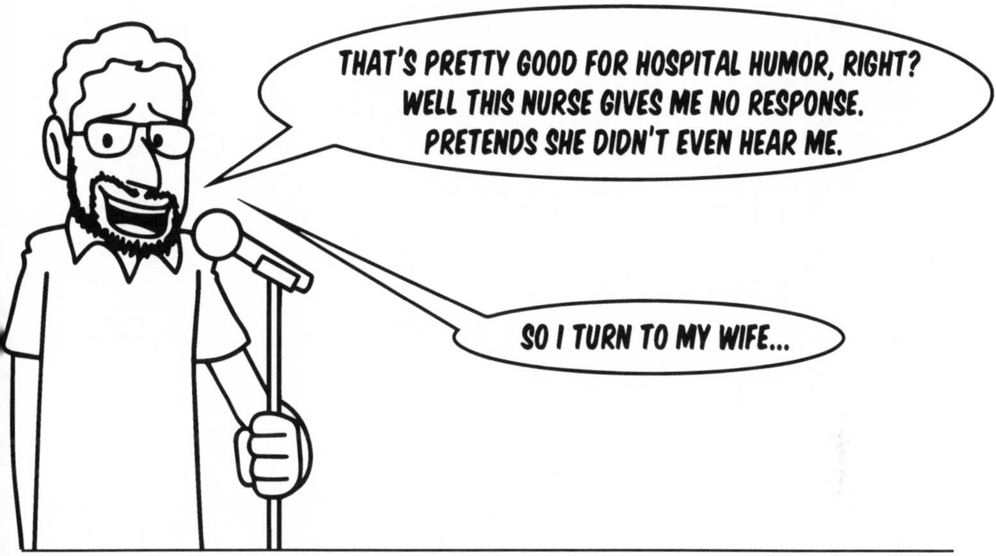
THAT'S PRETTY GOOD FOR HOSPITAL HUMOR, RIGHT? WELL THIS NURSE GIVES ME NO RESPONSE. PRETENDS SHE DIDN'T EVEN HEAR ME.
SO I TURN TO MY WIFE...

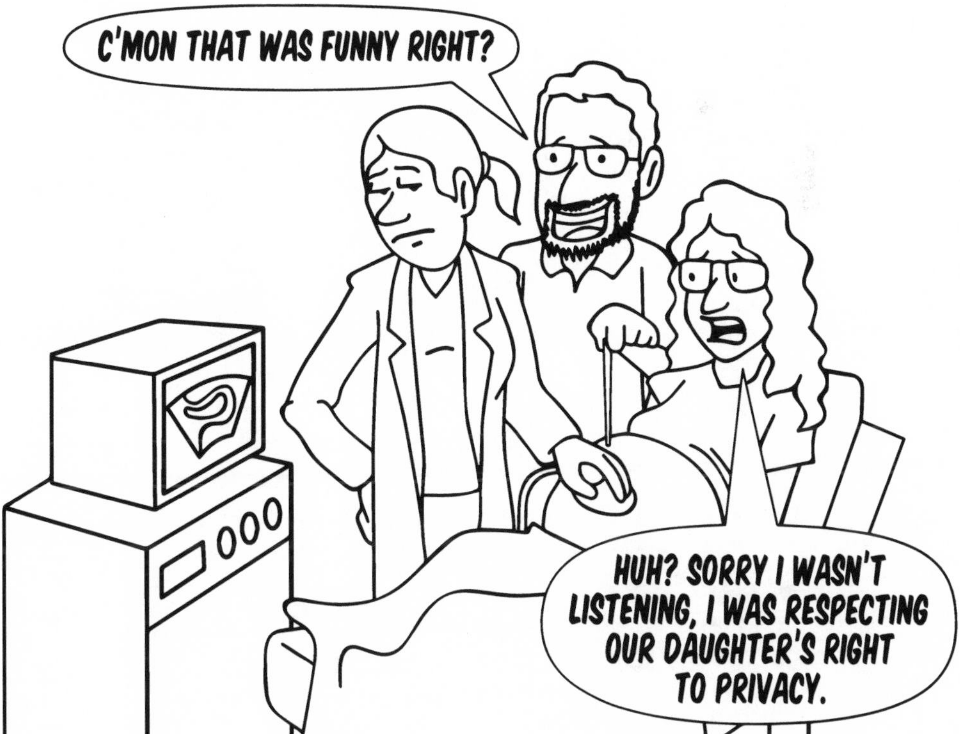
C'MON THAT WAS FUNNY RIGHT?
HUH? SORRY I WASN'T LISTENING, I WAS RESPECTING OUR DAUGHTER'S RIGHT TO PRIVACY.

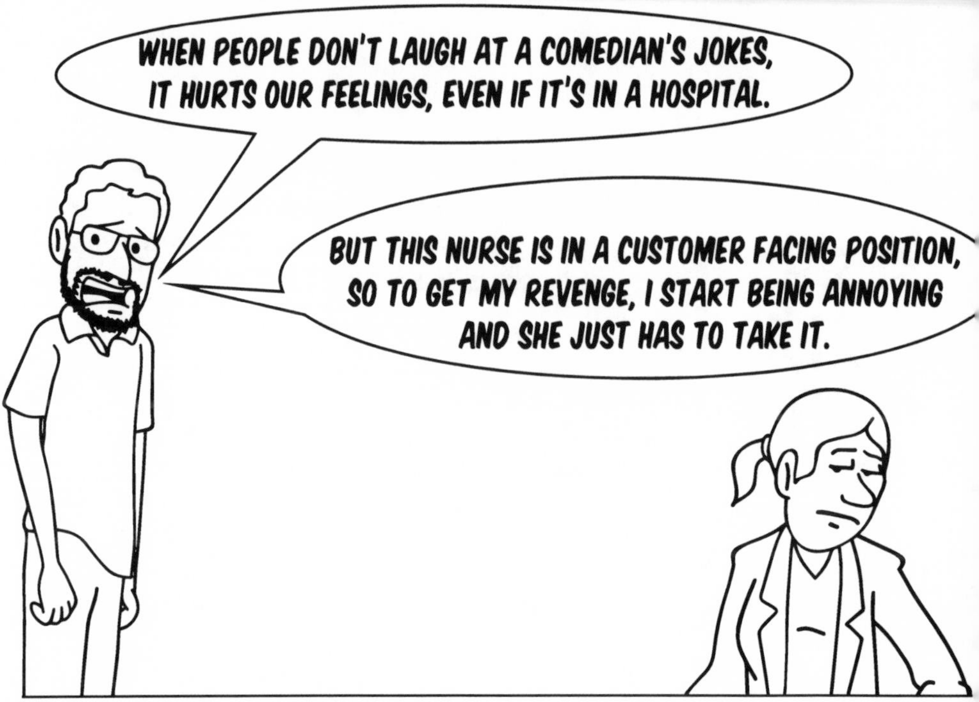
WHEN PEOPLE DON'T LAUGH AT A COMEDIAN'S JOKES, IT HURTS OUR FEELINGS, EVEN IF IT'S IN A HOSPITAL.
BUT THIS NURSE IS IN A CUSTOMER FACING POSITION, SO TO GET MY REVENGE, I START BEING ANNOYING AND SHE JUST HAS TO TAKE IT.

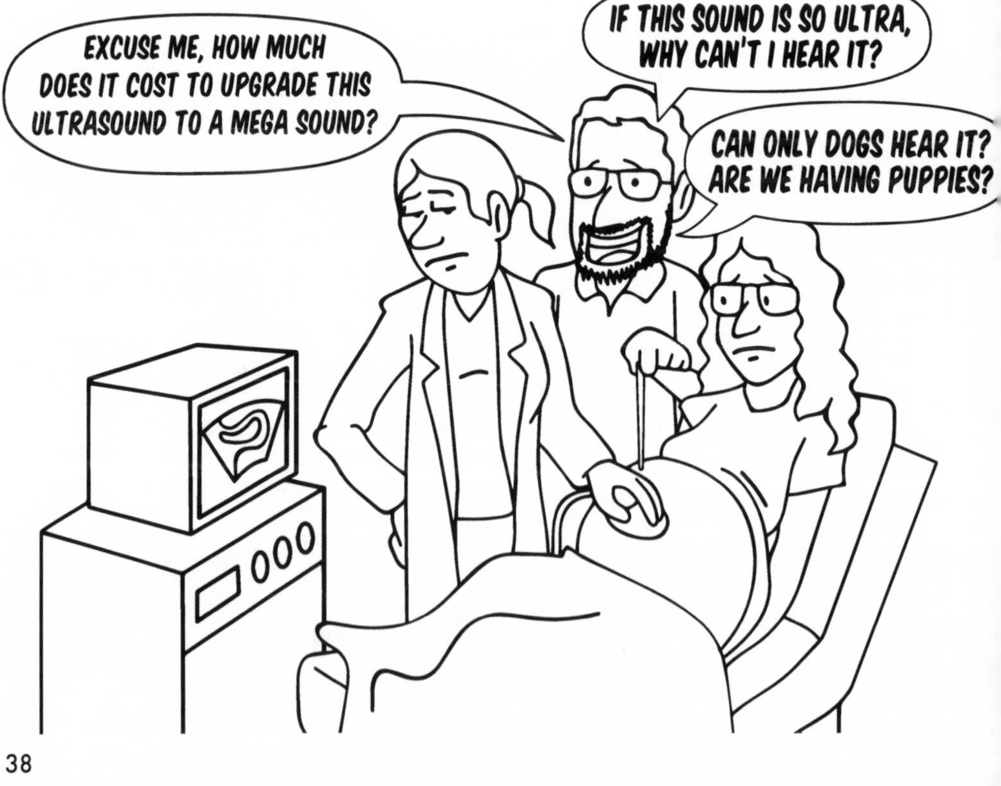
EXCUSE ME, HOW MUCH DOES IT COST TO UPGRADE THIS ULTRASOUND TO A MEGA SOUND?
IF THIS SOUND IS SO ULTRA, WHY CAN'T I HEAR IT?
CAN ONLY DOGS HEAR IT? ARE WE HAVING PUPPIES?

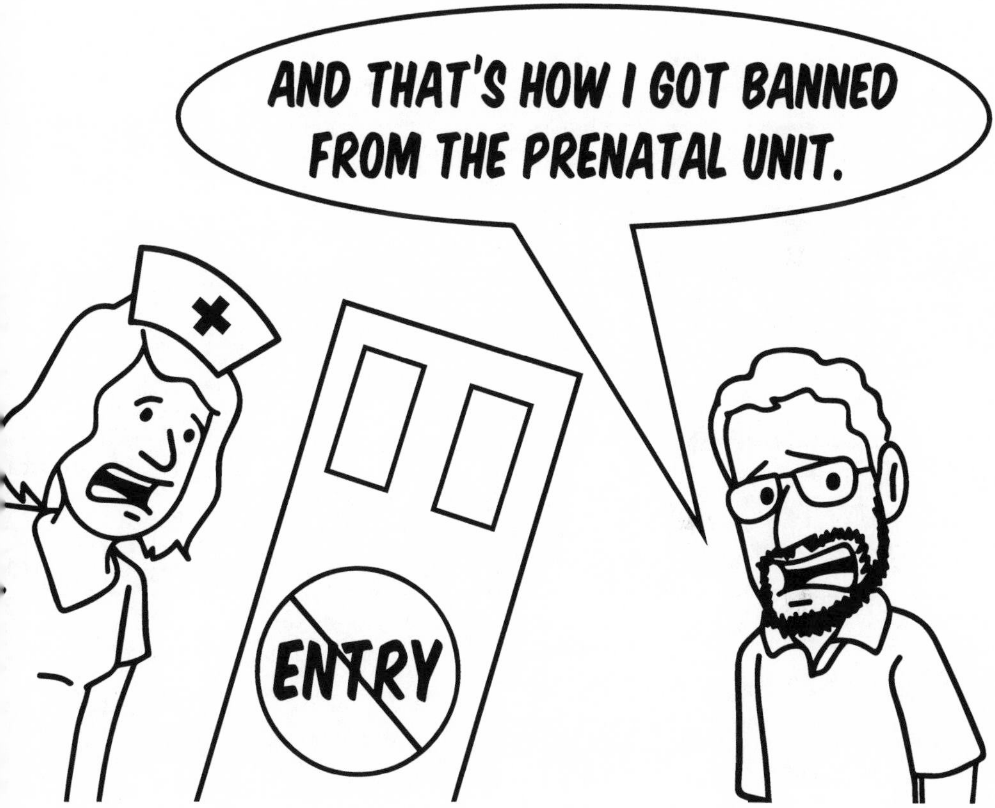
AND THAT'S HOW I GOT BANNED FROM THE PRENATAL UNIT.
ENTRY

NEIGHBORS FIGHT

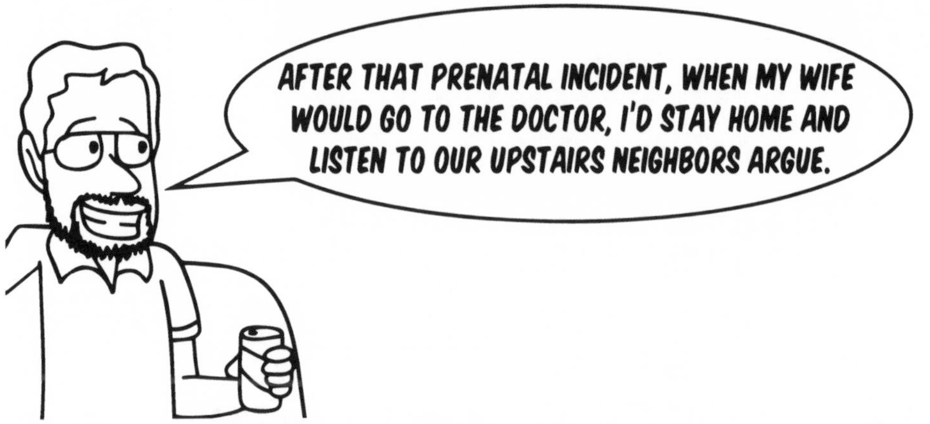
AFTER THAT PRENATAL INCIDENT, WHEN MY WIFE WOULD GO TO THE DOCTOR, I'D STAY HOME AND LISTEN TO OUR UPSTAIRS NEIGHBORS ARGUE.

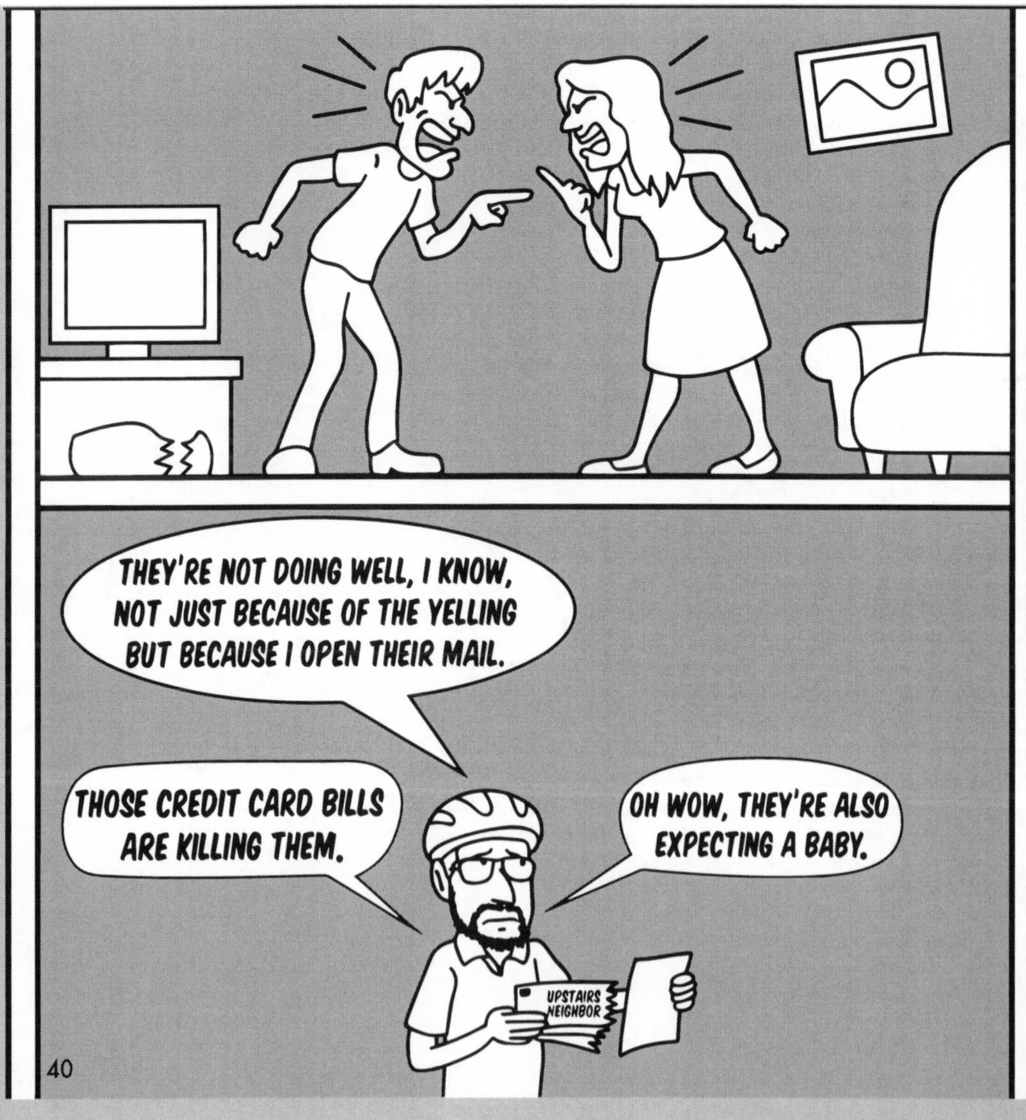
THEY'RE NOT DOING WELL, I KNOW, NOT JUST BECAUSE OF THE YELLING BUT BECAUSE I OPEN THEIR MAIL.
THOSE CREDIT CARD BILLS ARE KILLING THEM.
OH WOW, THEY'RE ALSO EXPECTING A BABY.
UPSTAIRS NEIGHBOR

I GOOGLED THEIR BABY REGISTRY...

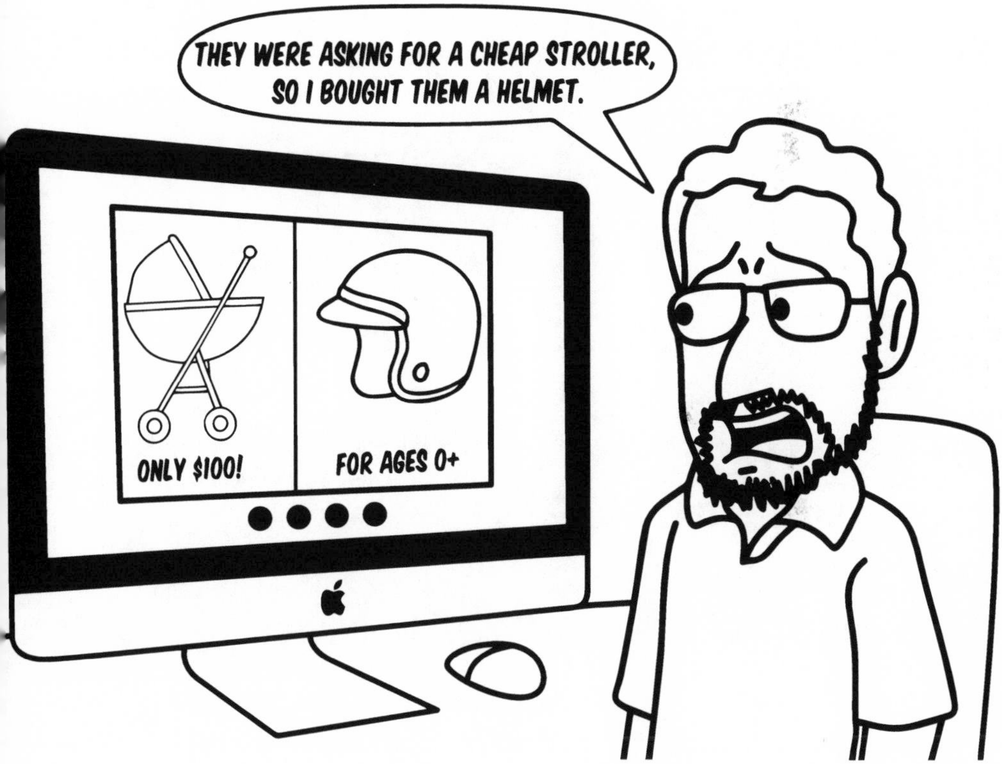
THEY WERE ASKING FOR A CHEAP STROLLER, SO I BOUGHT THEM A HELMET.
ONLY $100!
FOR AGES 0+

BIRTH CLASS

WE ACTUALLY TOOK A BIRTHING CLASS, AND, WE FAILED IT.

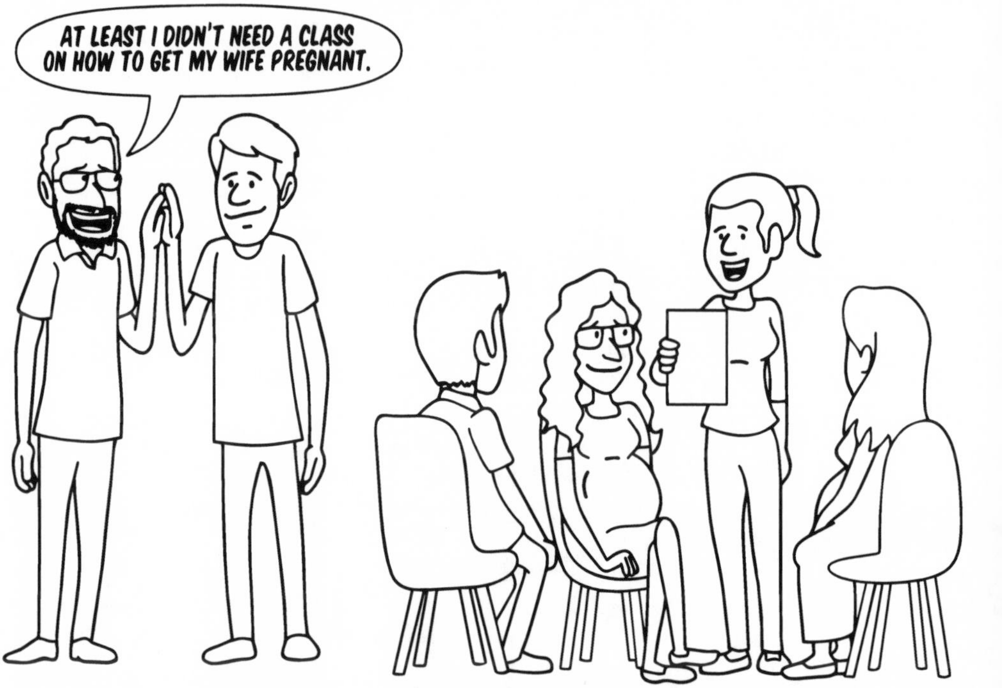
AT LEAST I DIDN'T NEED A CLASS ON HOW TO GET MY WIFE PREGNANT.

THE BIRTH INSTRUCTOR GAVE LOTS OF USELESS TIPS.

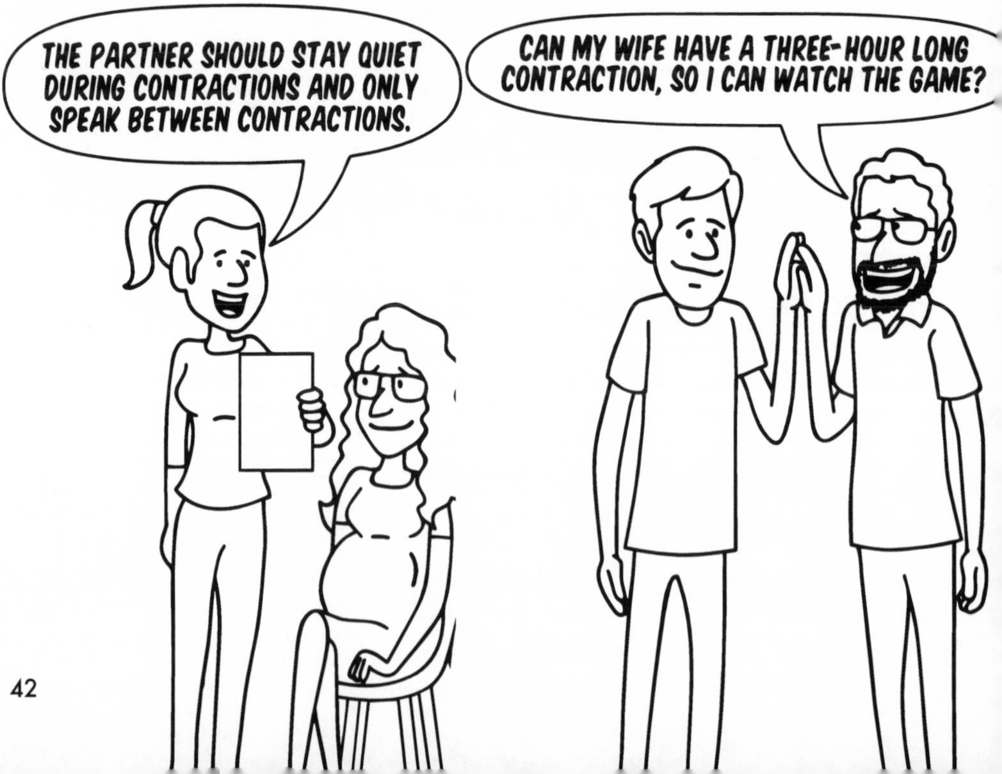
THE PARTNER SHOULD STAY QUIET DURING CONTRACTIONS AND ONLY SPEAK BETWEEN CONTRACTIONS.
CAN MY WIFE HAVE A THREE-HOUR LONG CONTRACTION, SO I CAN WATCH THE GAME?

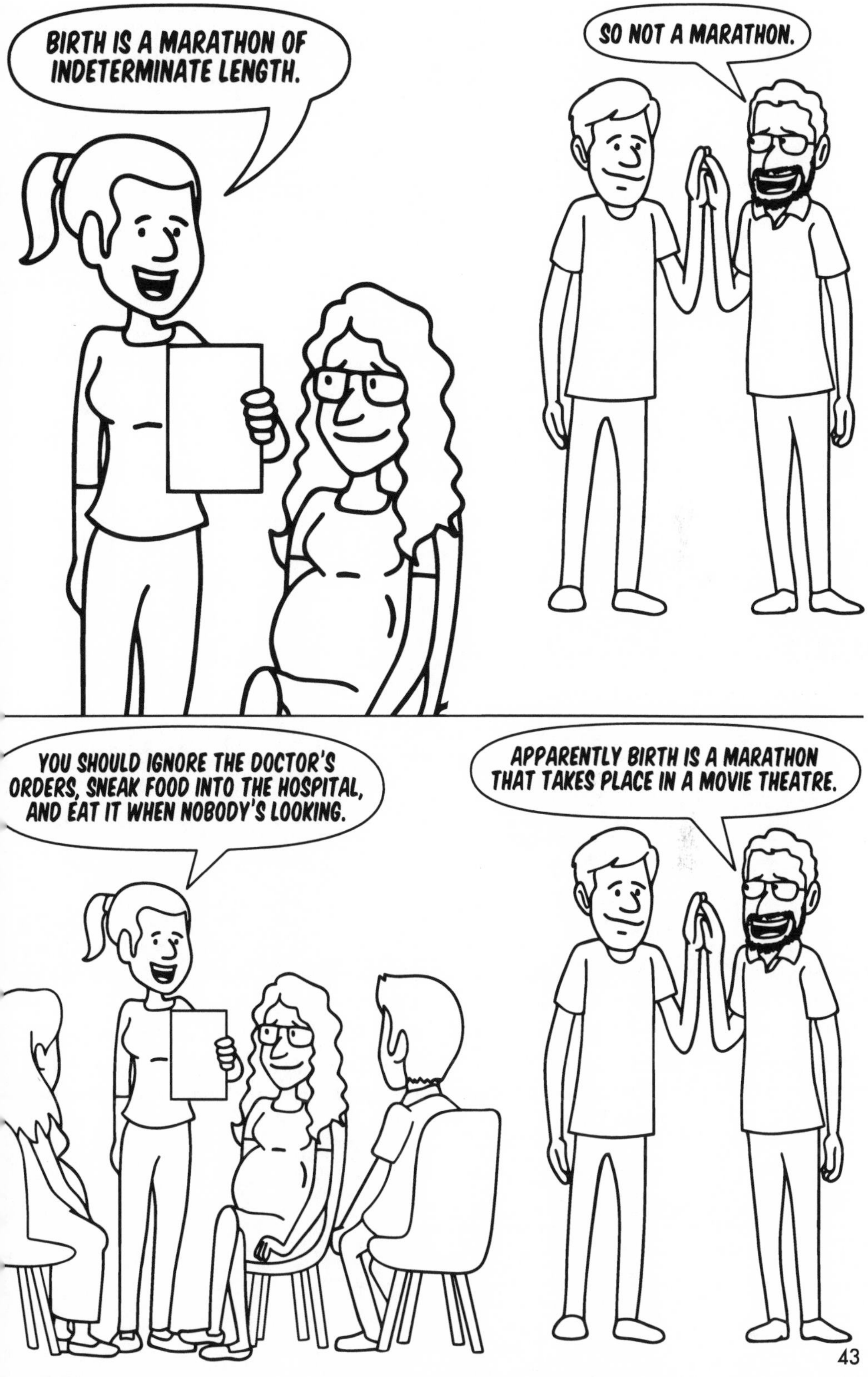
BIRTH IS A MARATHON OF INDETERMINATE LENGTH.
SO NOT A MARATHON.
YOU SHOULD IGNORE THE DOCTOR'S ORDERS, SNEAK FOOD INTO THE HOSPITAL, AND EAT IT WHEN NOBODY'S LOOKING.
APPARENTLY BIRTH IS A MARATHON THAT TAKES PLACE IN A MOVIE THEATRE.

GENETIC TEST

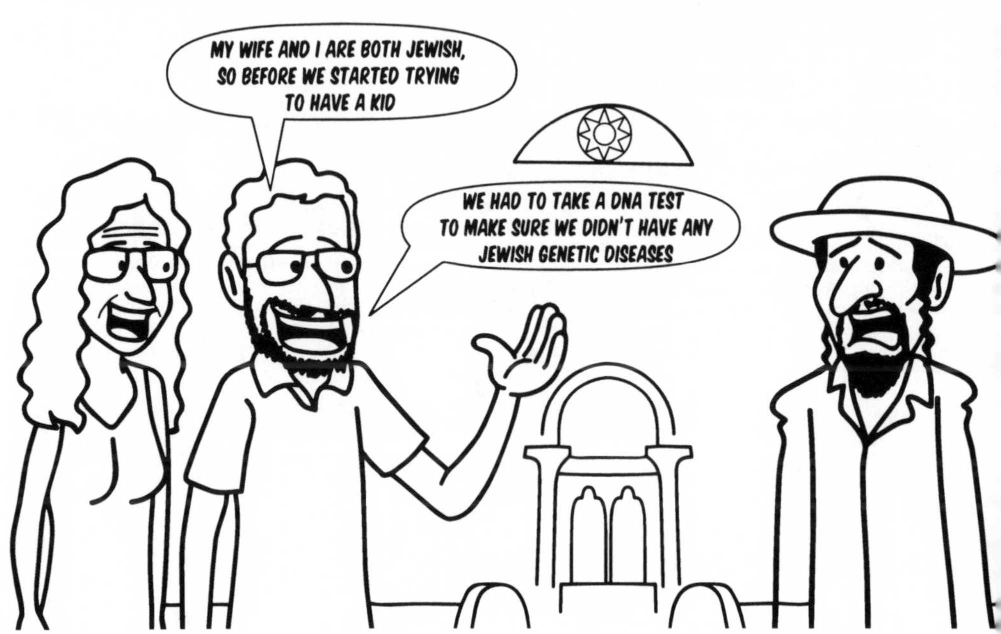
MY WIFE AND I ARE BOTH JEWISH, SO BEFORE WE STARTED TRYING TO HAVE A KID
WE HAD TO TAKE A DNA TEST TO MAKE SURE WE DIDN'T HAVE ANY JEWISH GENETIC DISEASES

HOW THE JEWISH GENETIC TEST WORKS...

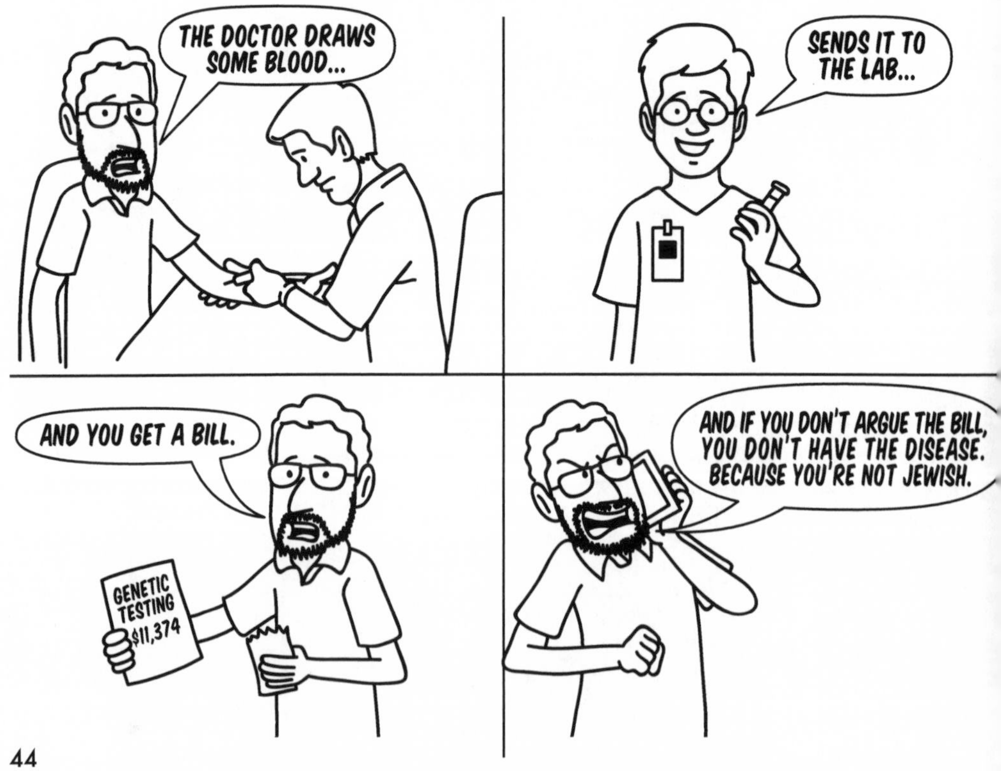
THE DOCTOR DRAWS SOME BLOOD...
SENDS IT TO THE LAB...
AND YOU GET A BILL.
GENETIC TESTING $11,374
AND IF YOU DON'T ARGUE THE BILL, YOU DON'T HAVE THE DISEASE. BECAUSE YOU'RE NOT JEWISH.

CONCERT VIP

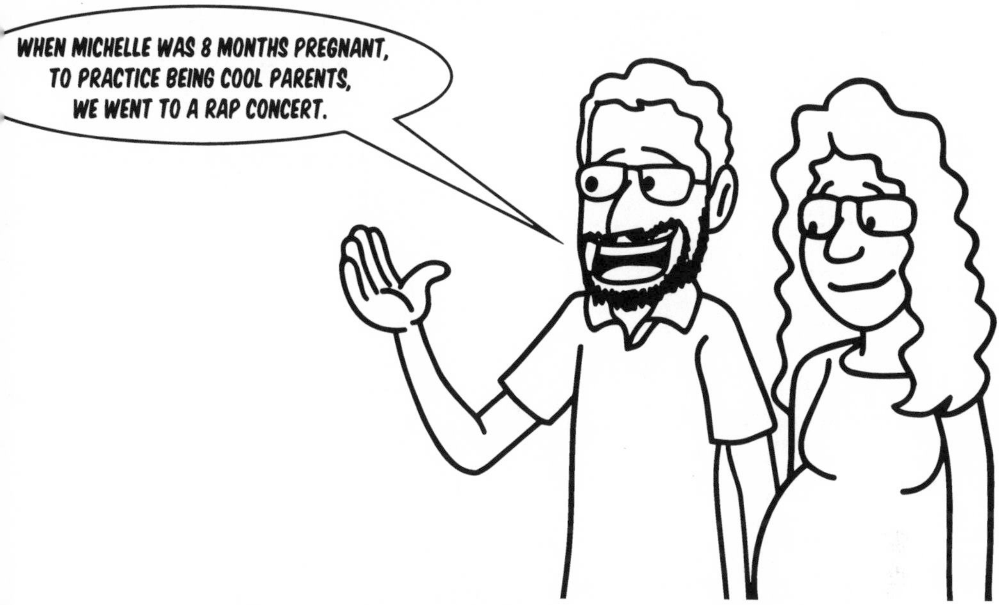
WHEN MICHELLE WAS 8 MONTHS PREGNANT, TO PRACTICE BEING COOL PARENTS, WE WENT TO A RAP CONCERT.

WHEN SECURITY SAW A VERY PREGNANT WOMAN, THEY MOVED US TO THE FRONT ROW, IN VIP SEATING...

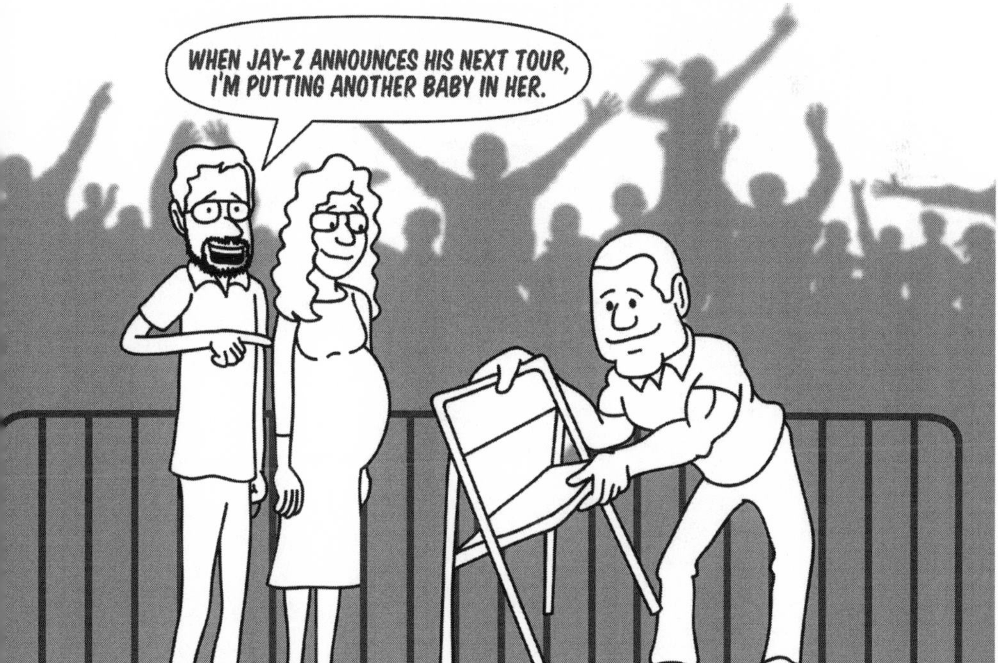
WHEN JAY-Z ANNOUNCES HIS NEXT TOUR, I'M PUTTING ANOTHER BABY IN HER.

HOW NOT TO ANNOUNCE A BABY

A FRIEND OF MINE ANNOUNCED HIS WIFE'S PREGNANCY ON FACEBOOK BY POSTING A SPORTS THEMED SONOGRAM...

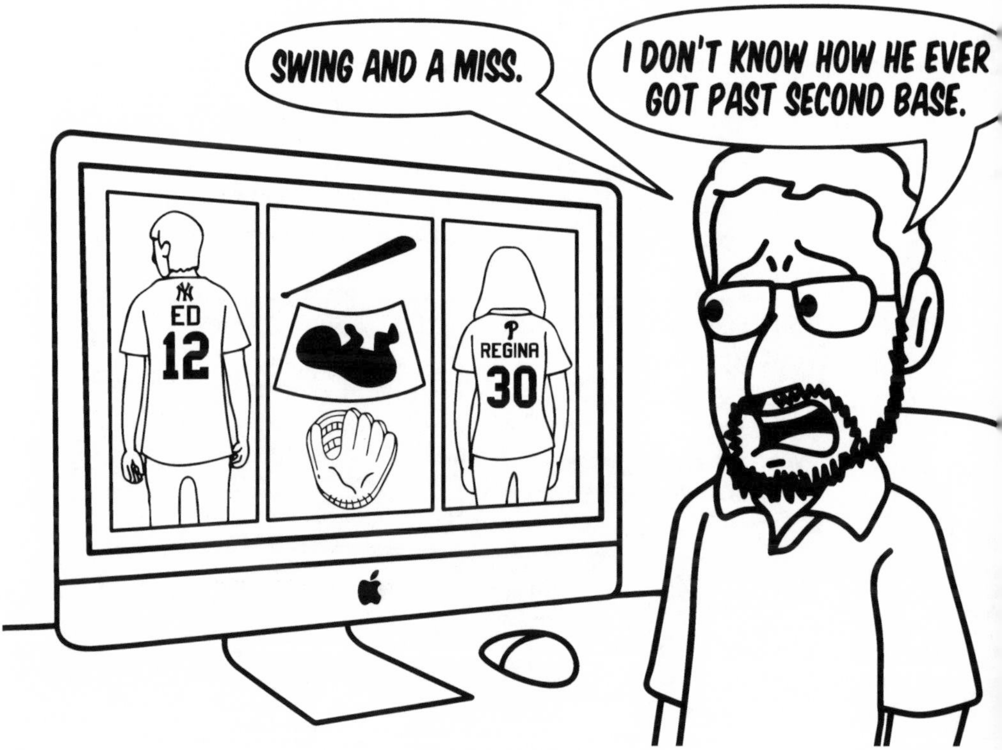

SWING AND A MISS.
I DON'T KNOW HOW HE EVER GOT PAST SECOND BASE.
ED
12
REGINA
30

INSPIRED, I POSTED SOMETHING TOO...

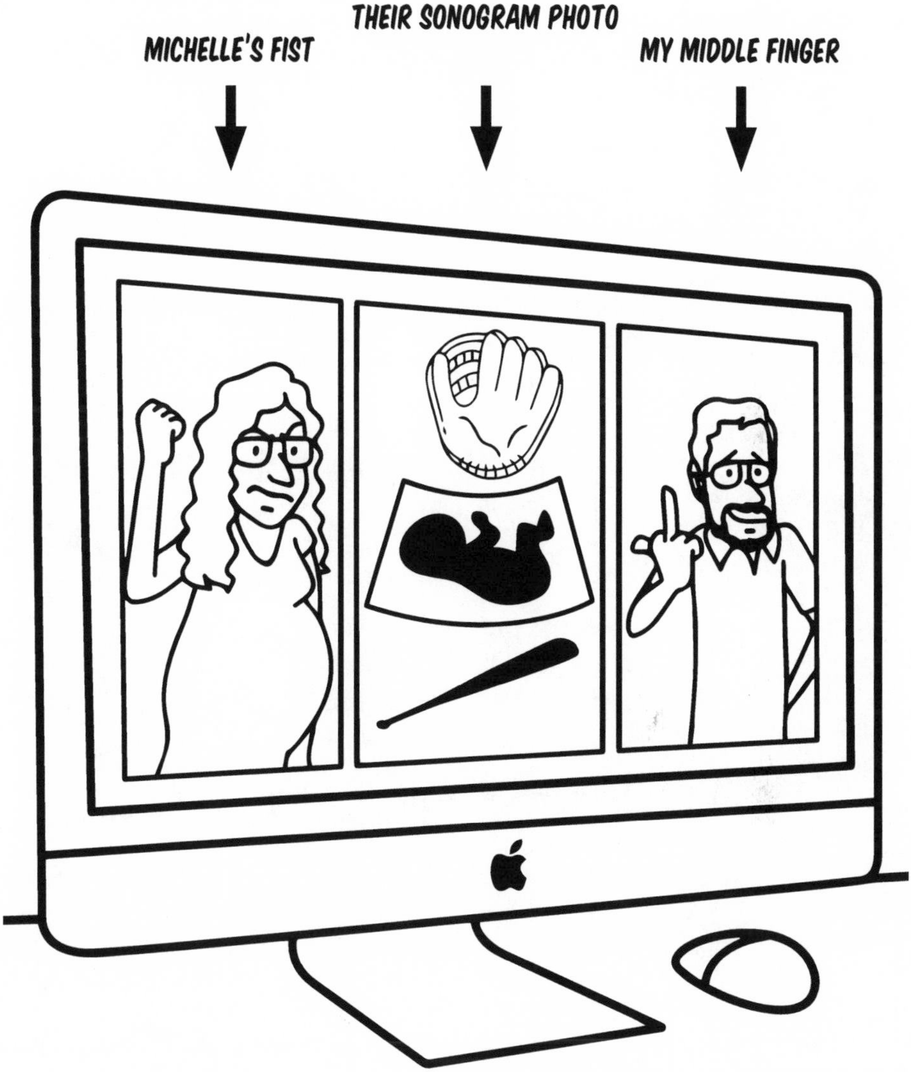

MICHELLE'S FIST
THEIR SONOGRAM PHOTO
MY MIDDLE FINGER

GENDER REVEAL

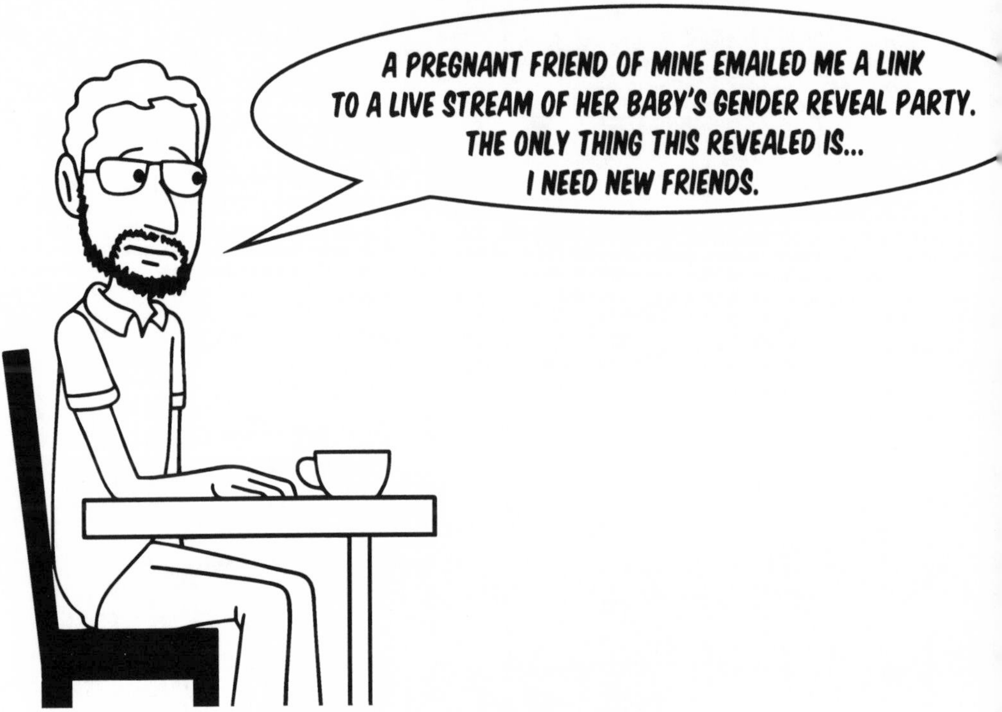
A PREGNANT FRIEND OF MINE EMAILED ME A LINK TO A LIVE STREAM OF HER BABY'S GENDER REVEAL PARTY. THE ONLY THING THIS REVEALED IS... I NEED NEW FRIENDS.

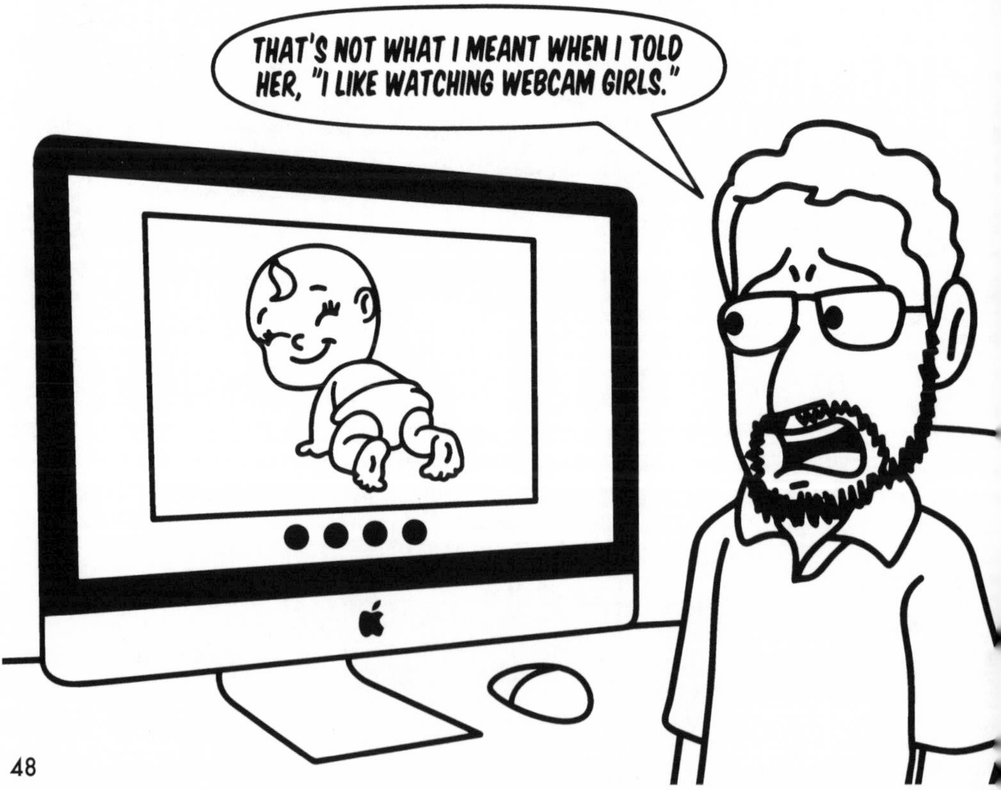
THAT'S NOT WHAT I MEANT WHEN I TOLD HER, "I LIKE WATCHING WEBCAM GIRLS."

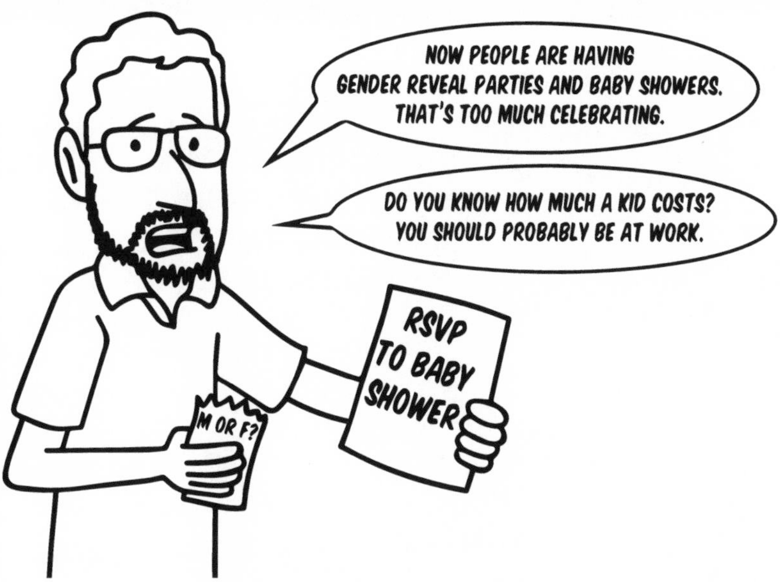
NOW PEOPLE ARE HAVING GENDER REVEAL PARTIES AND BABY SHOWERS. THAT'S TOO MUCH CELEBRATING.
DO YOU KNOW HOW MUCH A KID COSTS? YOU SHOULD PROBABLY BE AT WORK.
RSVP TO BABY SHOWER
M OR F?

SO I'M WATCHING THIS LIVE STREAM, AND AT ONE POINT MY PREGNANT FRIEND SAYS...

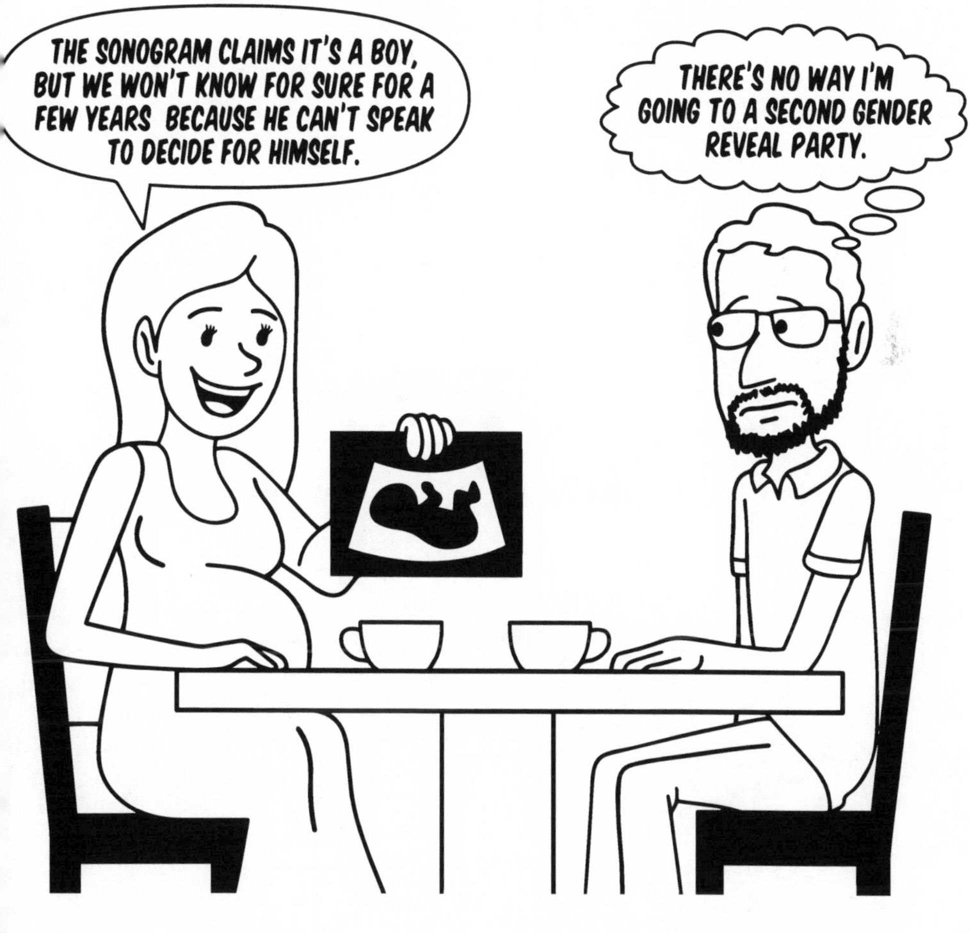
THE SONOGRAM CLAIMS IT'S A BOY, BUT WE WON'T KNOW FOR SURE FOR A FEW YEARS BECAUSE HE CAN'T SPEAK TO DECIDE FOR HIMSELF.
THERE'S NO WAY I'M GOING TO A SECOND GENDER REVEAL PARTY.

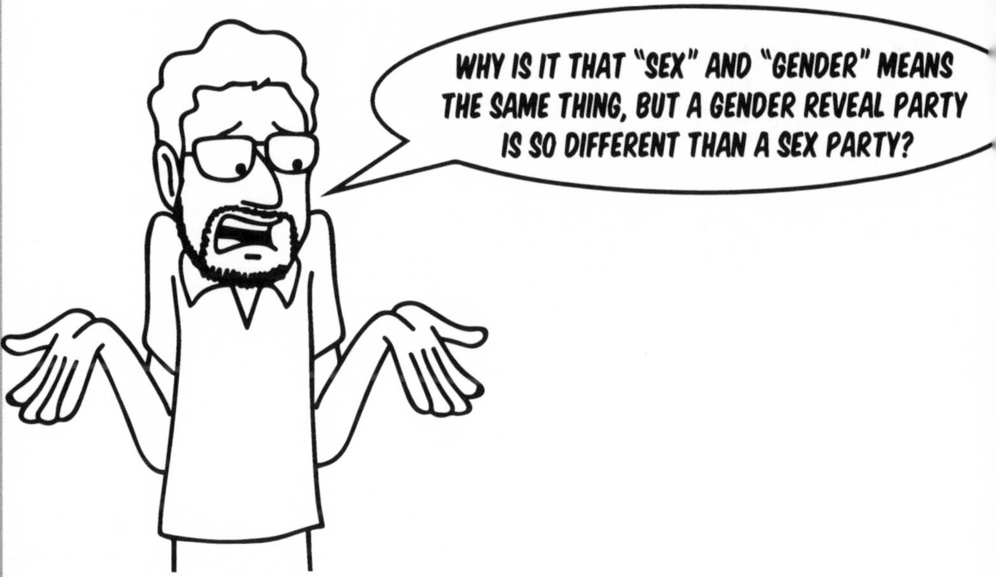
WHY IS IT THAT "SEX" AND "GENDER" MEANS THE SAME THING, BUT A GENDER REVEAL PARTY IS SO DIFFERENT THAN A SEX PARTY?

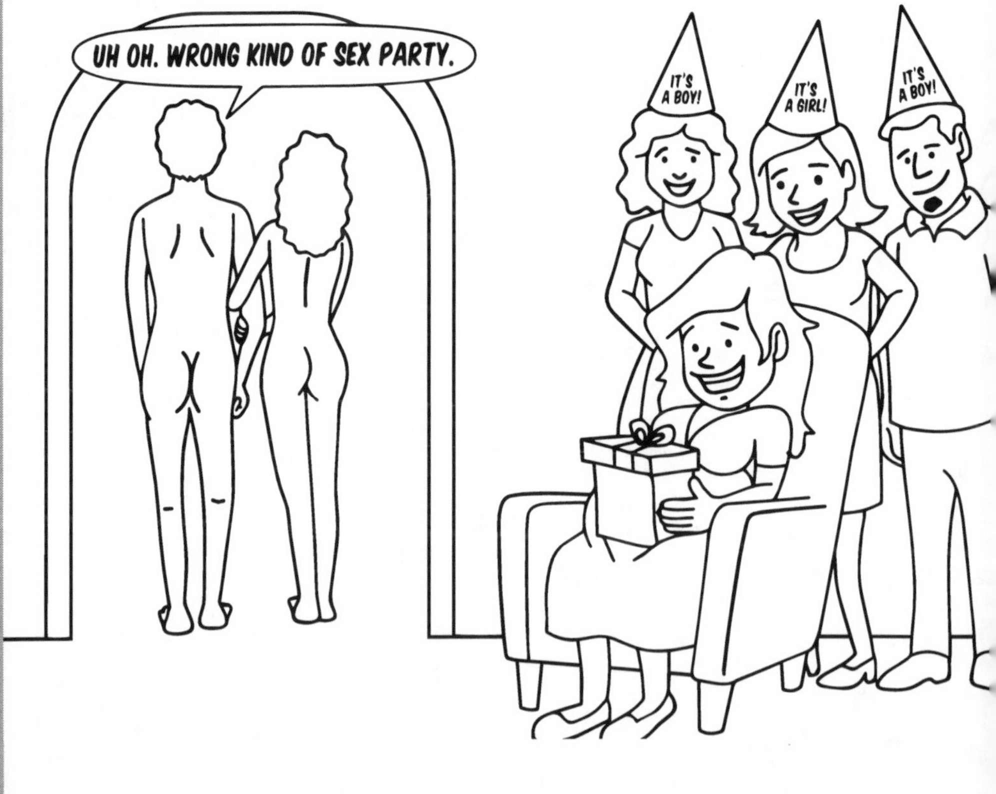
UH OH. WRONG KIND OF SEX PARTY.
IT'S A BOY!
IT'S A GIRL!
IT'S A BOY!

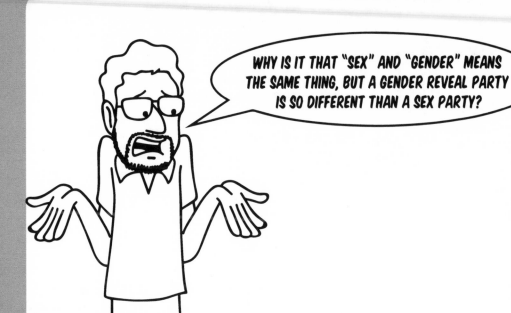

LABOR BIRTH AND THE HOSPITAL

MICHELLE'S BIRTH JOKES

CLOTHING THAT FITS

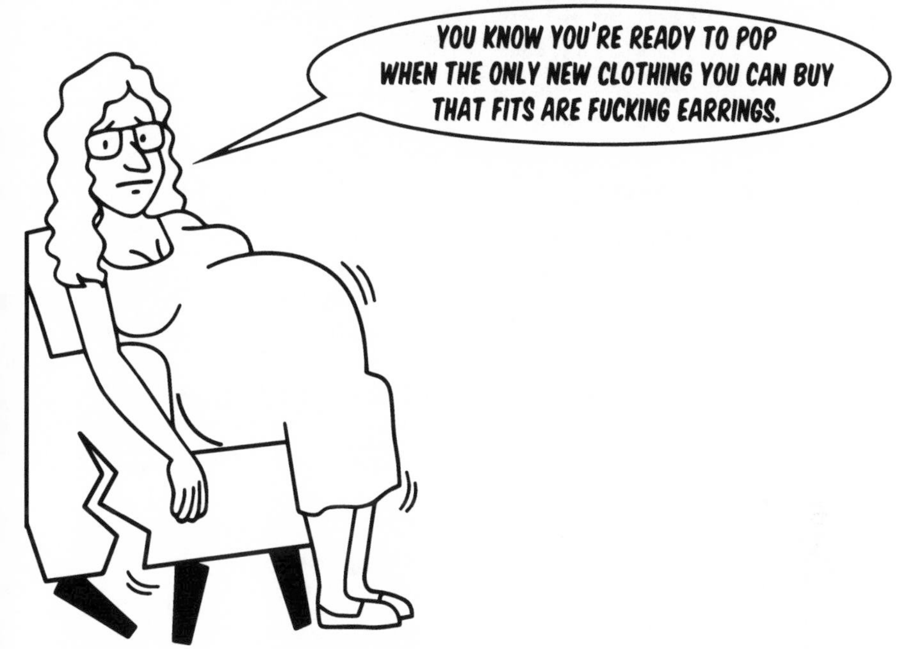

YOU KNOW YOU'RE READY TO POP WHEN THE ONLY NEW CLOTHING YOU CAN BUY THAT FITS ARE FUCKING EARRINGS.

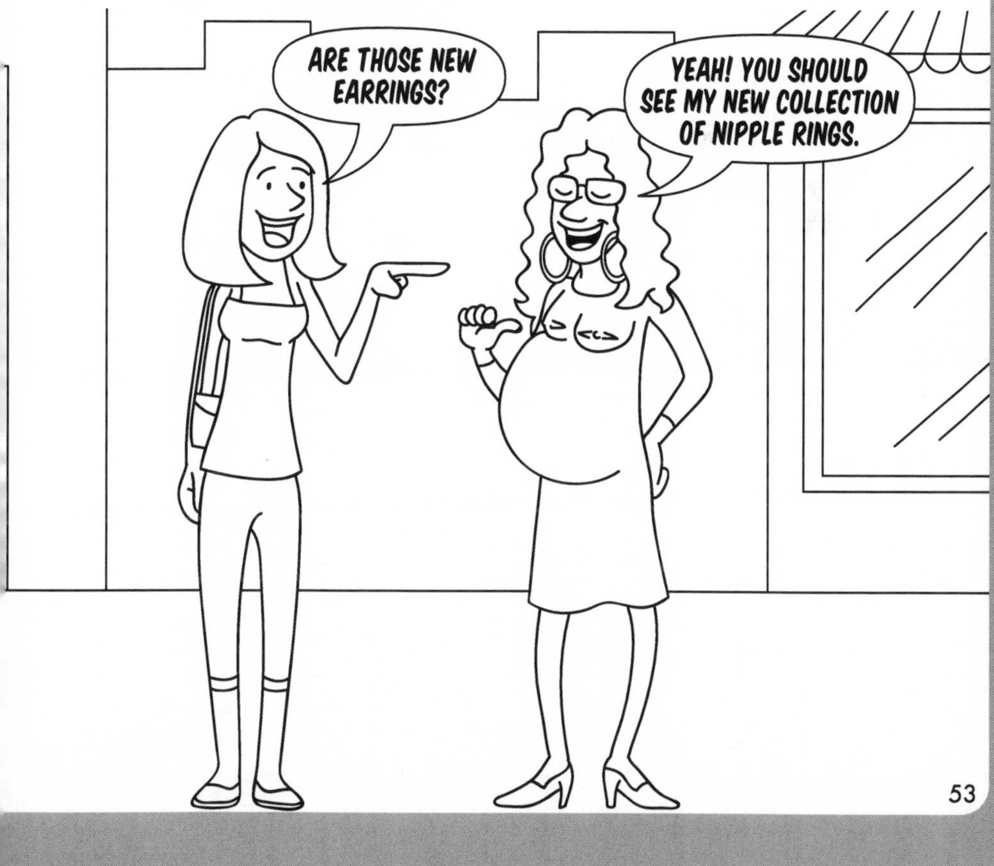

ARE THOSE NEW EARRINGS?
YEAH! YOU SHOULD SEE MY NEW COLLECTION OF NIPPLE RINGS.

PRINCESS

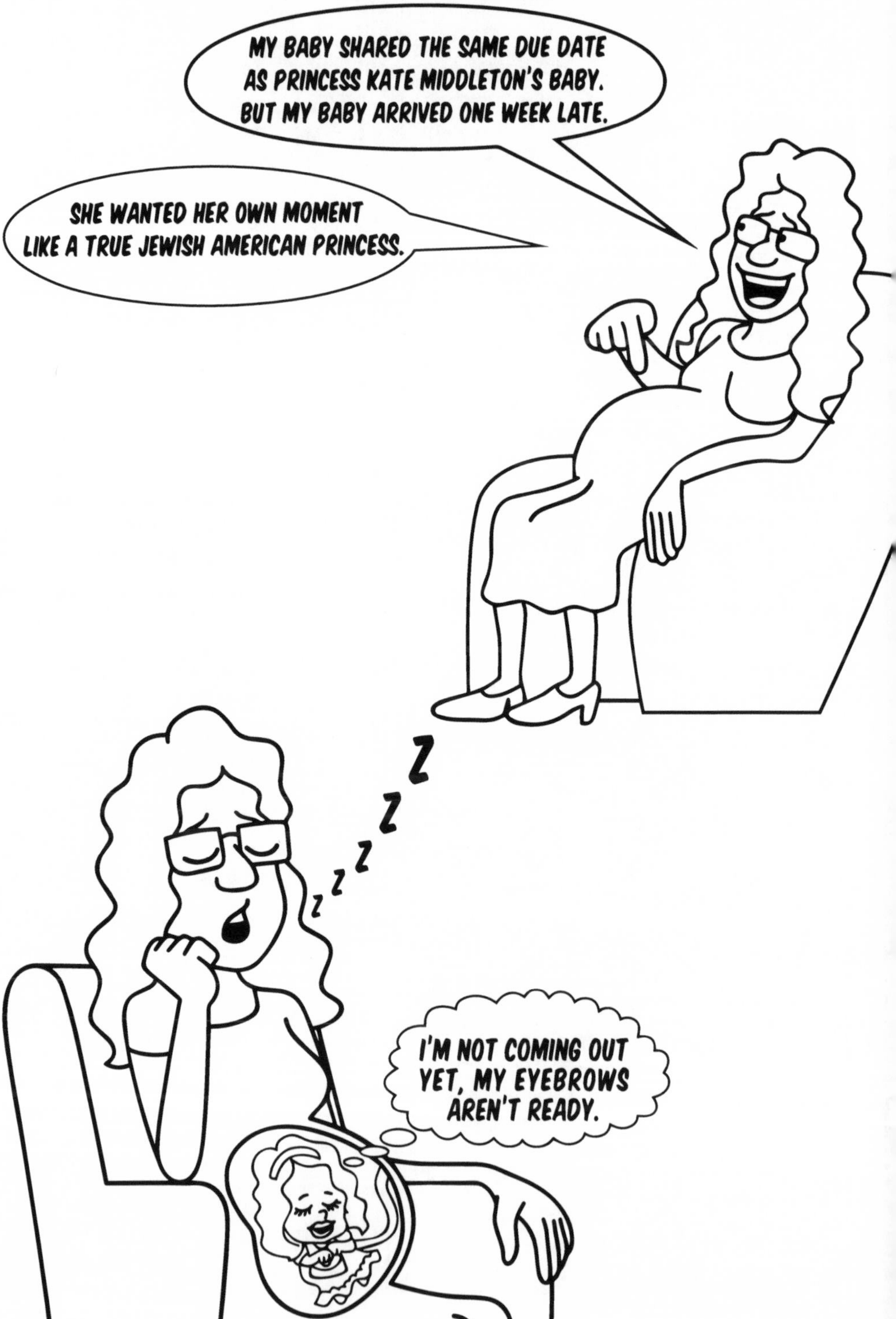

MY BABY SHARED THE SAME DUE DATE AS PRINCESS KATE MIDDLETON'S BABY. BUT MY BABY ARRIVED ONE WEEK LATE.
SHE WANTED HER OWN MOMENT LIKE A TRUE JEWISH AMERICAN PRINCESS.
Z Z Z Z Z
I'M NOT COMING OUT YET, MY EYEBROWS AREN'T READY.

NATURAL BIRTH

SOME PEOPLE WANT A NATURAL BIRTH, WITH INCENSE AND A DOULA. NOT ME...

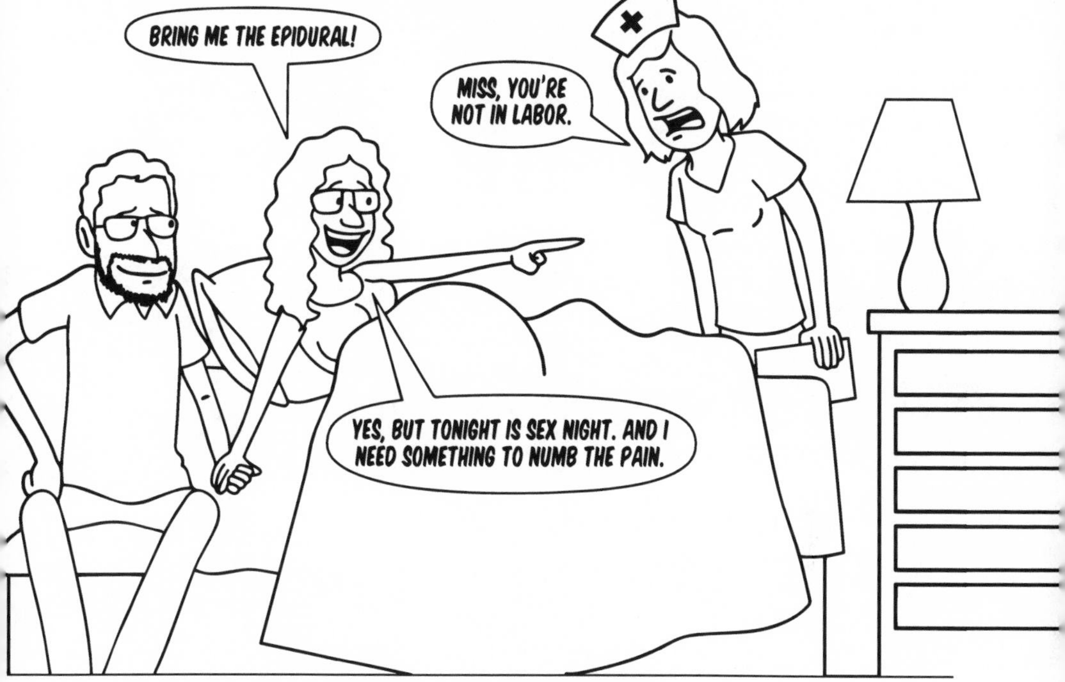
BRING ME THE EPIDURAL!
MISS, YOU'RE NOT IN LABOR.
YES, BUT TONIGHT IS SEX NIGHT. AND I NEED SOMETHING TO NUMB THE PAIN.

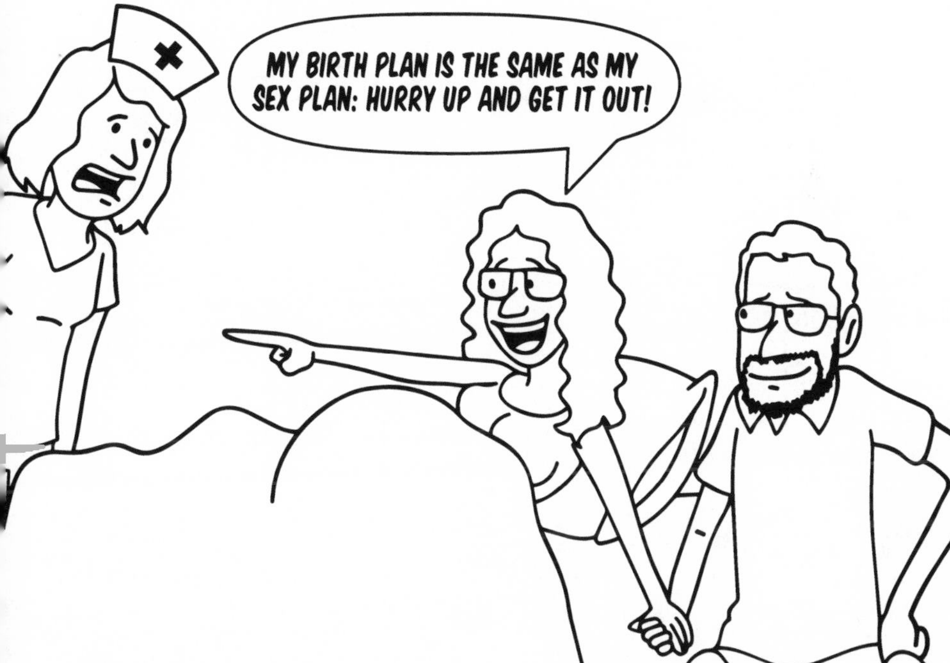
MY BIRTH PLAN IS THE SAME AS MY SEX PLAN: HURRY UP AND GET IT OUT!

ROCK STAR

RIGHT AFTER MY DAUGHTER WAS BORN, MY FRIEND CALLED ME...

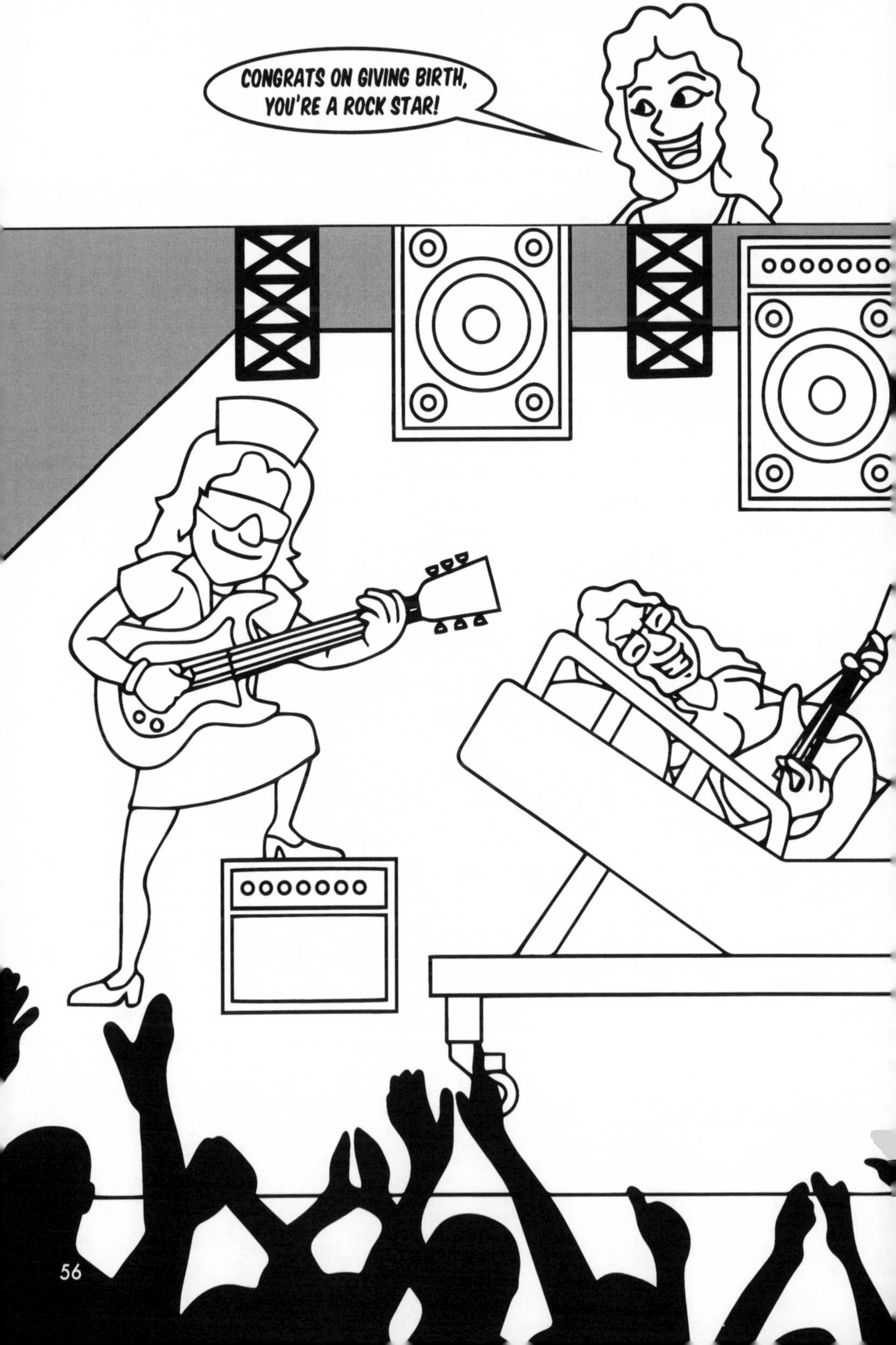
CONGRATS ON GIVING BIRTH, YOU'RE A ROCK STAR!

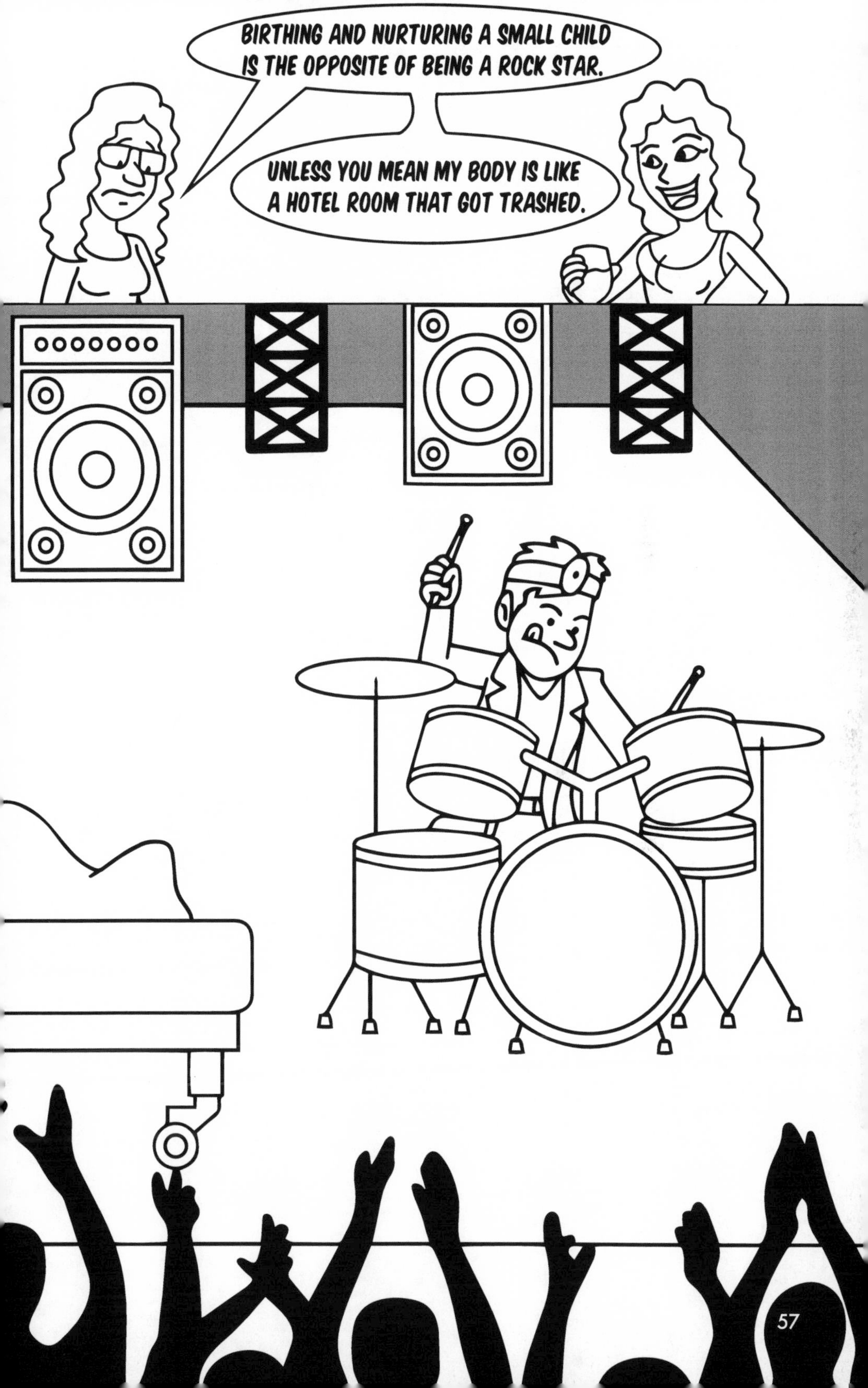
BIRTHING AND NURTURING A SMALL CHILD IS THE OPPOSITE OF BEING A ROCK STAR.
UNLESS YOU MEAN MY BODY IS LIKE A HOTEL ROOM THAT GOT TRASHED.

INSURANCE

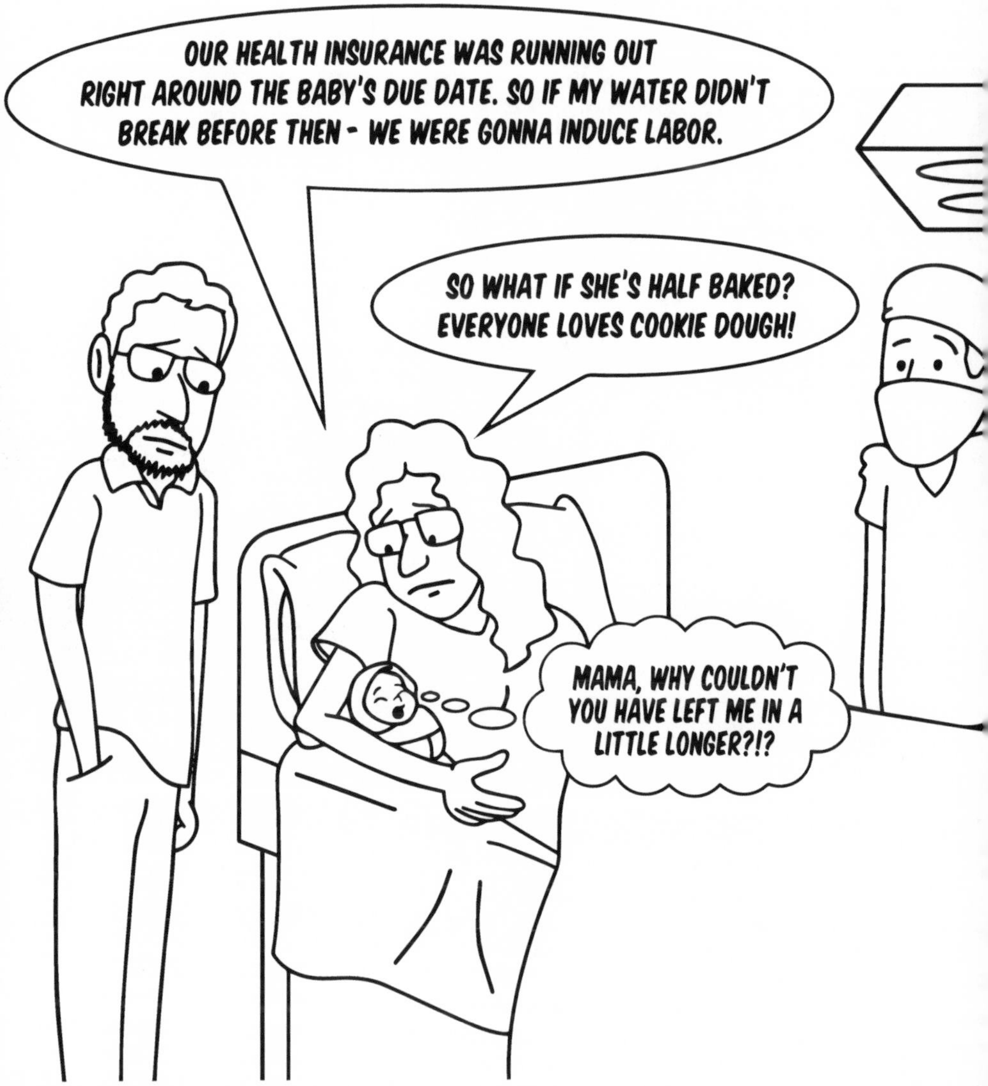
OUR HEALTH INSURANCE WAS RUNNING OUT RIGHT AROUND THE BABY'S DUE DATE. SO IF MY WATER DIDN'T BREAK BEFORE THEN - WE WERE GONNA INDUCE LABOR.
SO WHAT IF SHE'S HALF BAKED? EVERYONE LOVES COOKIE DOUGH!
MAMA, WHY COULDN'T YOU HAVE LEFT ME IN A LITTLE LONGER?!?

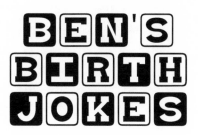

BEN'S BIRTH JOKES

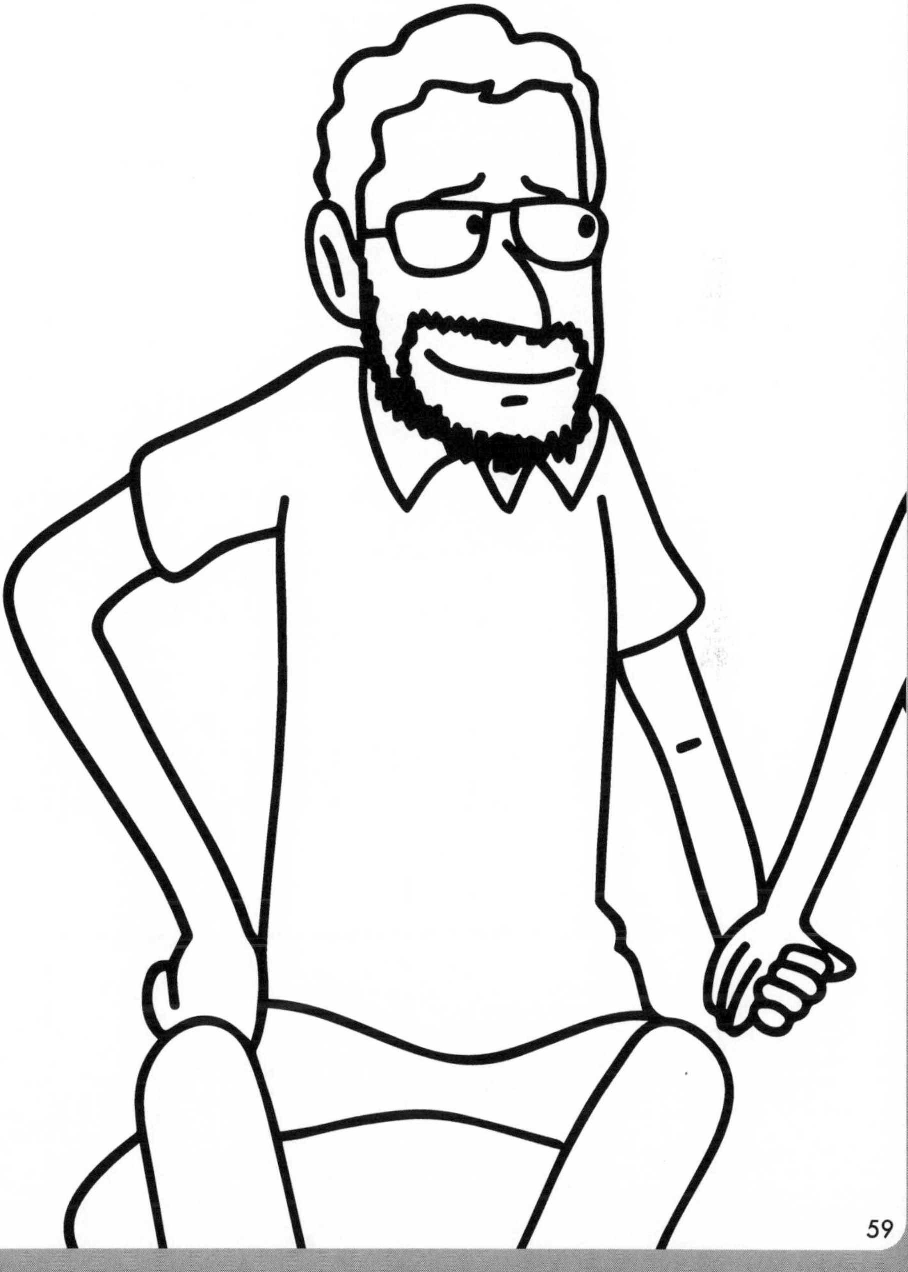

BABY 2.0

MOMENTS AFTER MY WIFE GAVE BIRTH, A NURSE CAME IN, ASKING US TO DONATE OUR BABY'S UMBILICAL CORD TO SCIENCE.

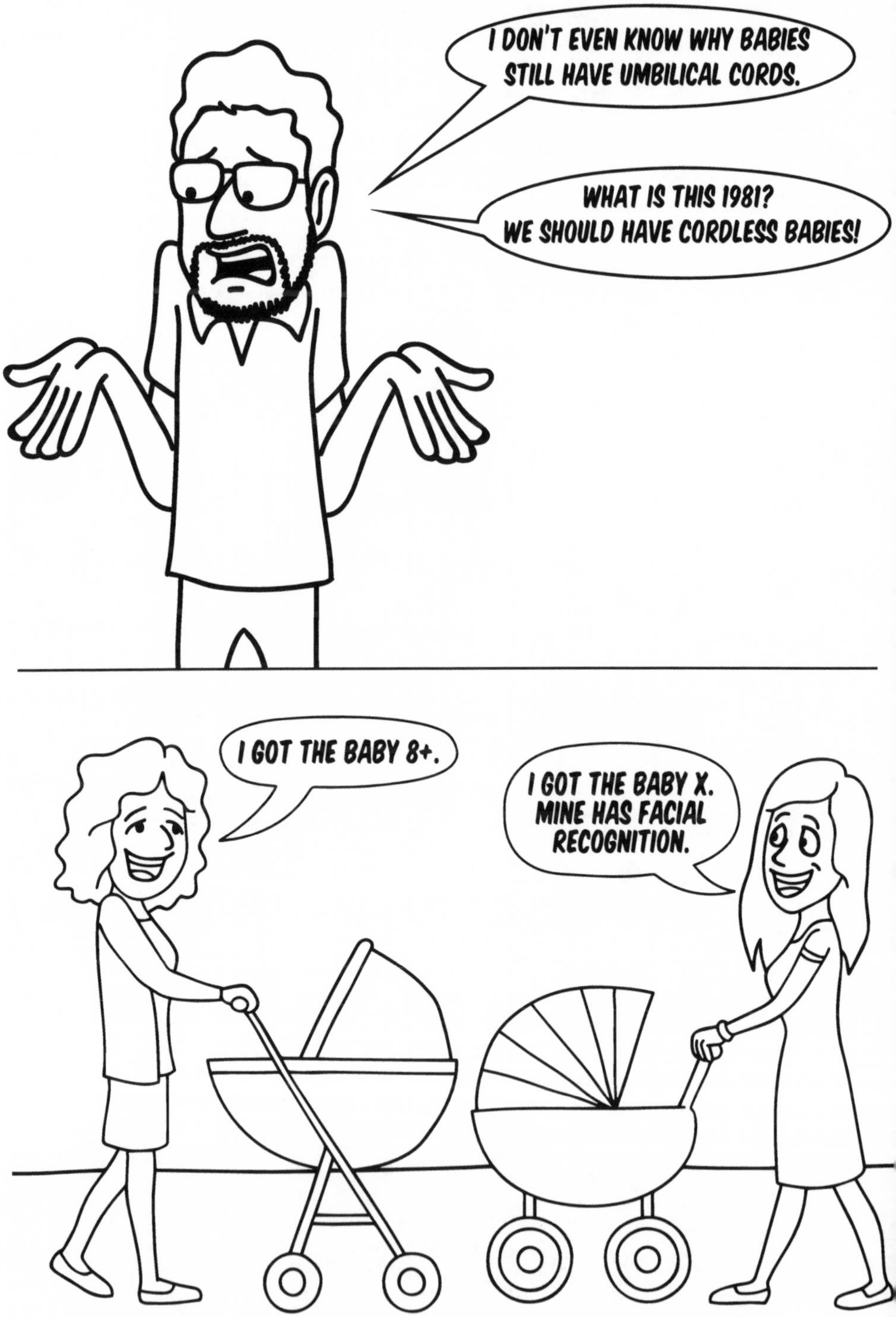
I DON'T EVEN KNOW WHY BABIES STILL HAVE UMBILICAL CORDS.
WHAT IS THIS 1981? WE SHOULD HAVE CORDLESS BABIES!
I GOT THE BABY 8+.
I GOT THE BABY X. MINE HAS FACIAL RECOGNITION.

HOSPITALS ARE OBSESSED WITH YOUR DONATING THE BABY'S UMBILICAL CORD. THEY'RE LIKE THE SALVATION ARMY OF PLACENTA.

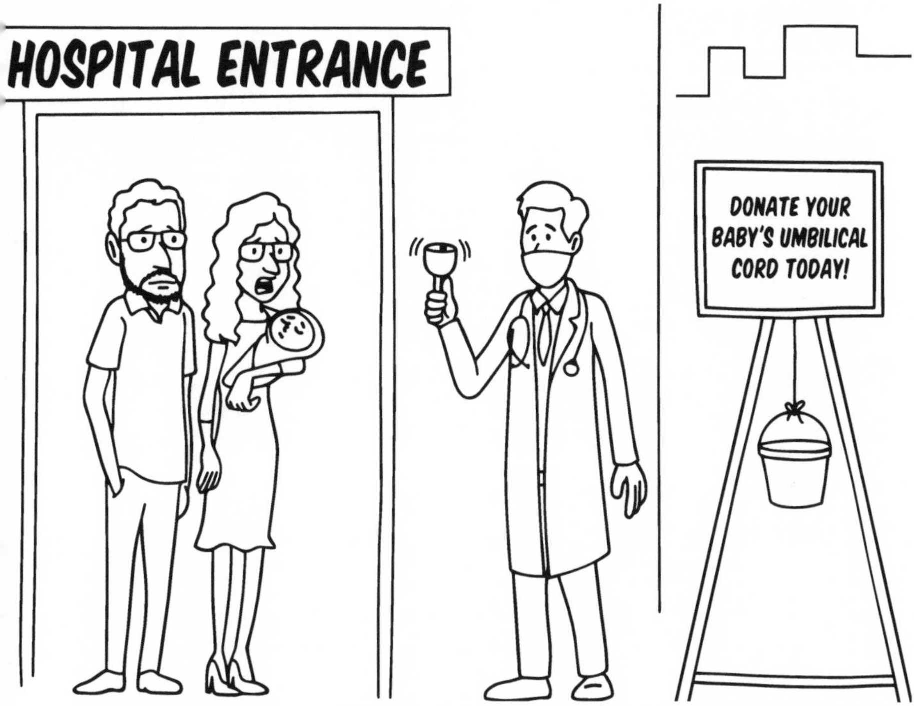

HOSPITAL ENTRANCE
DONATE YOUR BABY'S UMBILICAL CORD TODAY!

THE UMBILICAL CORD NURSE KEEPS ASKING FOR A SIGNATURE...

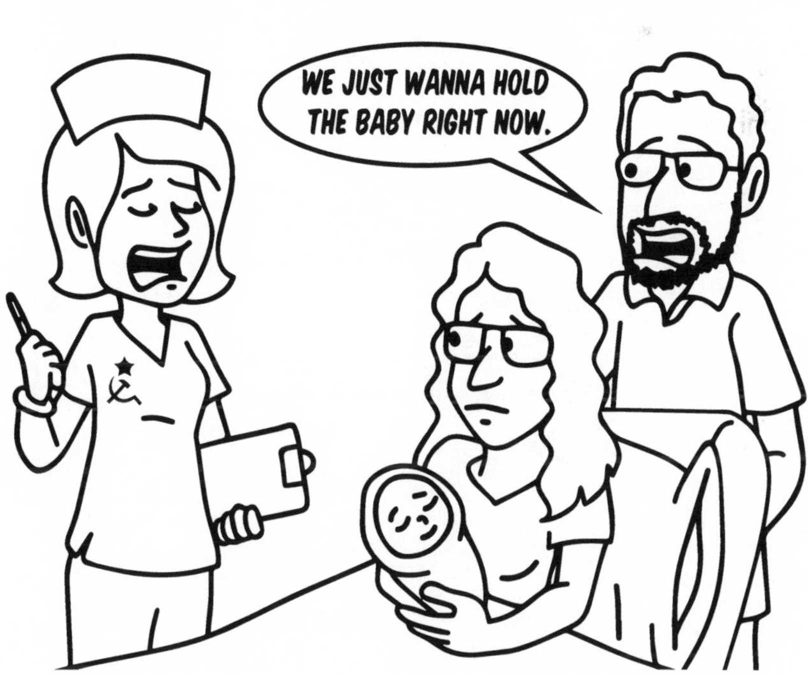

WE JUST WANNA HOLD THE BABY RIGHT NOW.

THE NURSE KEEPS ASKING US TO SIGN, IN HER FRIGHTENING EASTERN EUROPEAN ACCENT....

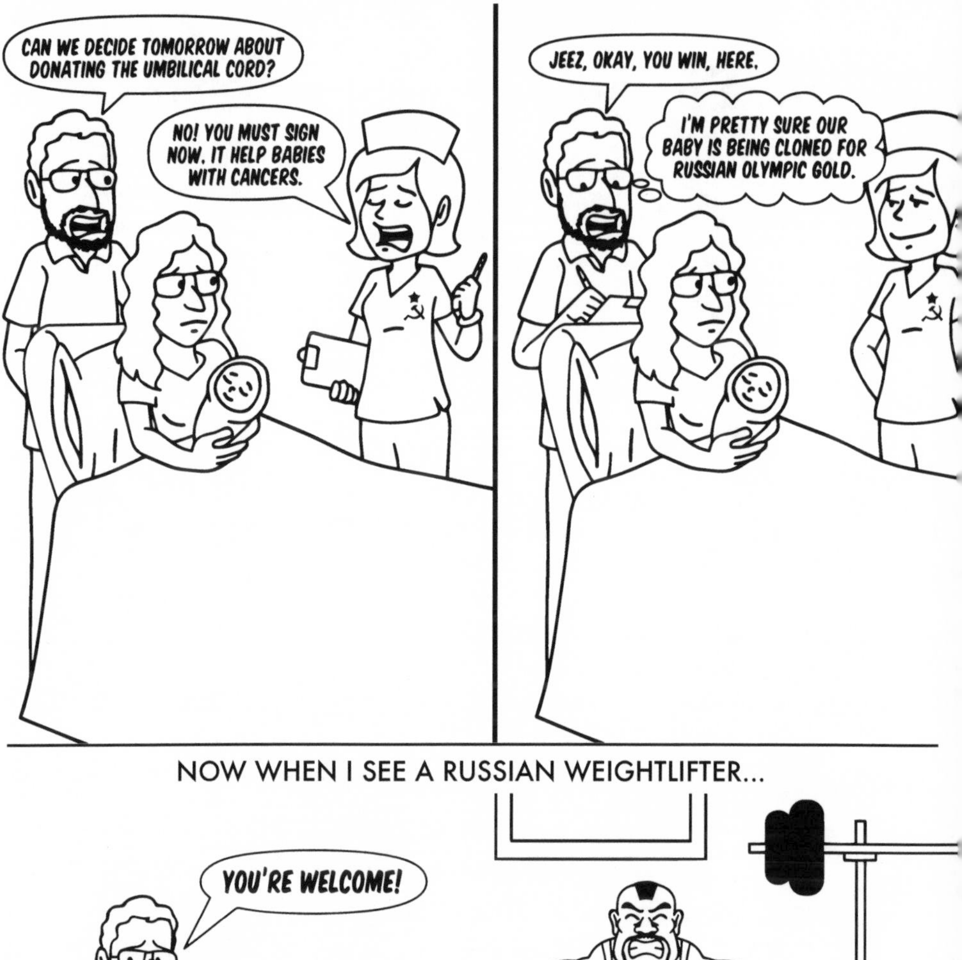

CAN WE DECIDE TOMORROW ABOUT DONATING THE UMBILICAL CORD?
NO! YOU MUST SIGN NOW. IT HELP BABIES WITH CANCERS.
JEEZ, OKAY, YOU WIN, HERE.
I'M PRETTY SURE OUR BABY IS BEING CLONED FOR RUSSIAN OLYMPIC GOLD.

NOW WHEN I SEE A RUSSIAN WEIGHTLIFTER...

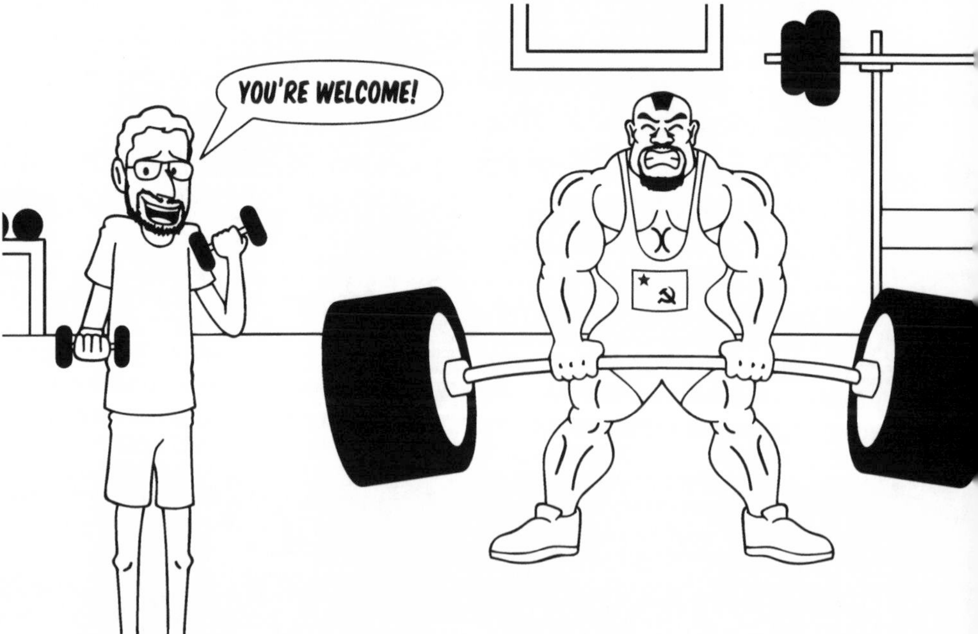

YOU'RE WELCOME!

LATCHING

THE NEXT DAY, A NURSE WAS SHOWING MY WIFE HOW TO BREASTFEED...

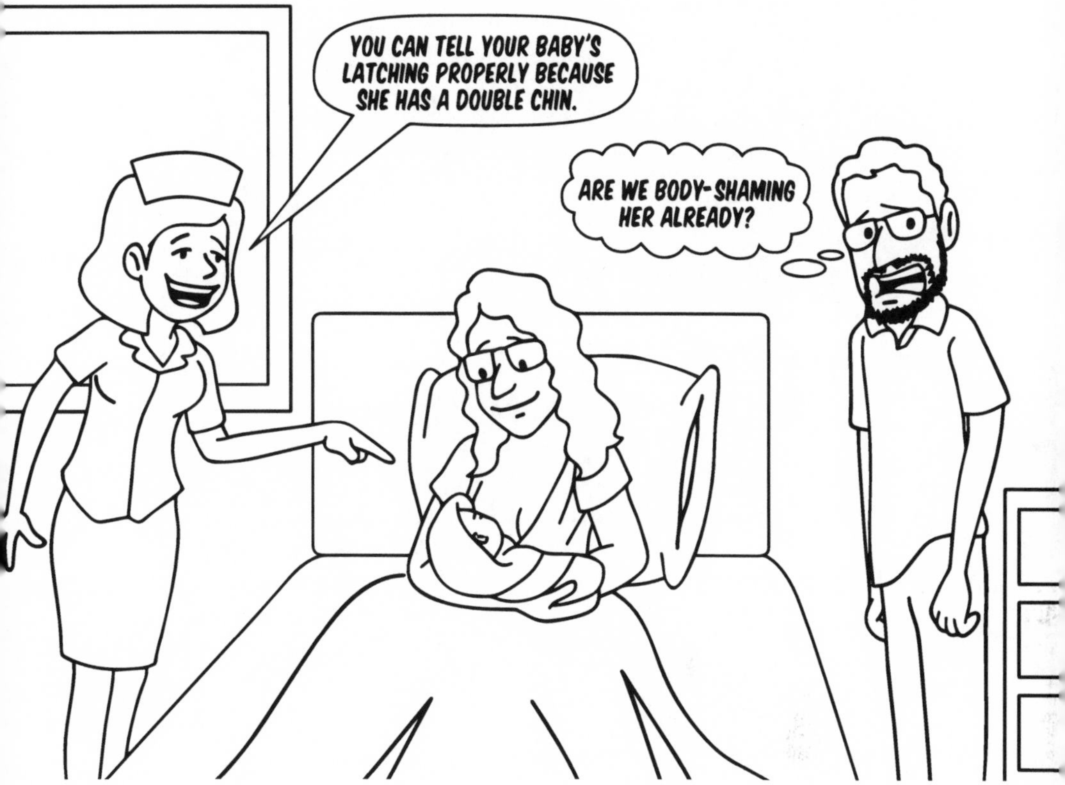
YOU CAN TELL YOUR BABY'S LATCHING PROPERLY BECAUSE SHE HAS A DOUBLE CHIN.
ARE WE BODY-SHAMING HER ALREADY?

NO SLEEP

PEOPLE KEPT TELLING ME...

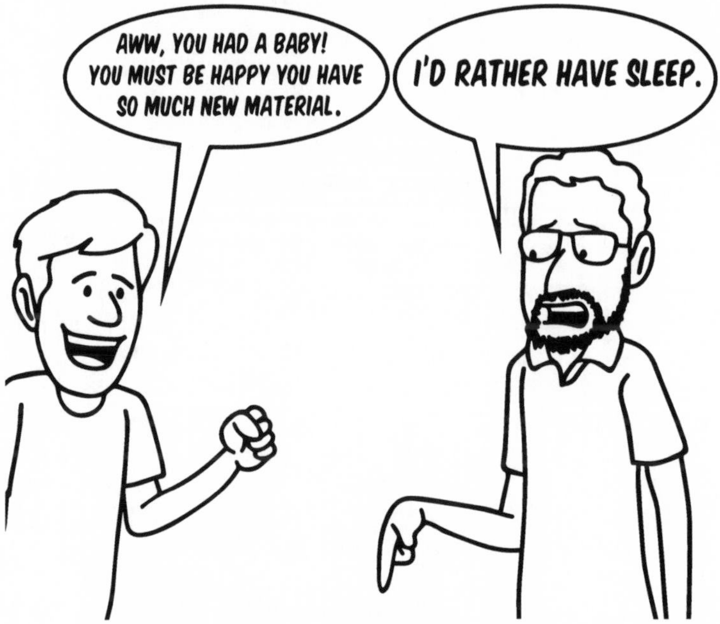
AWW, YOU HAD A BABY! YOU MUST BE HAPPY YOU HAVE SO MUCH NEW MATERIAL.
I'D RATHER HAVE SLEEP.

OUR LAST NIGHT AT THE HOSPITAL...

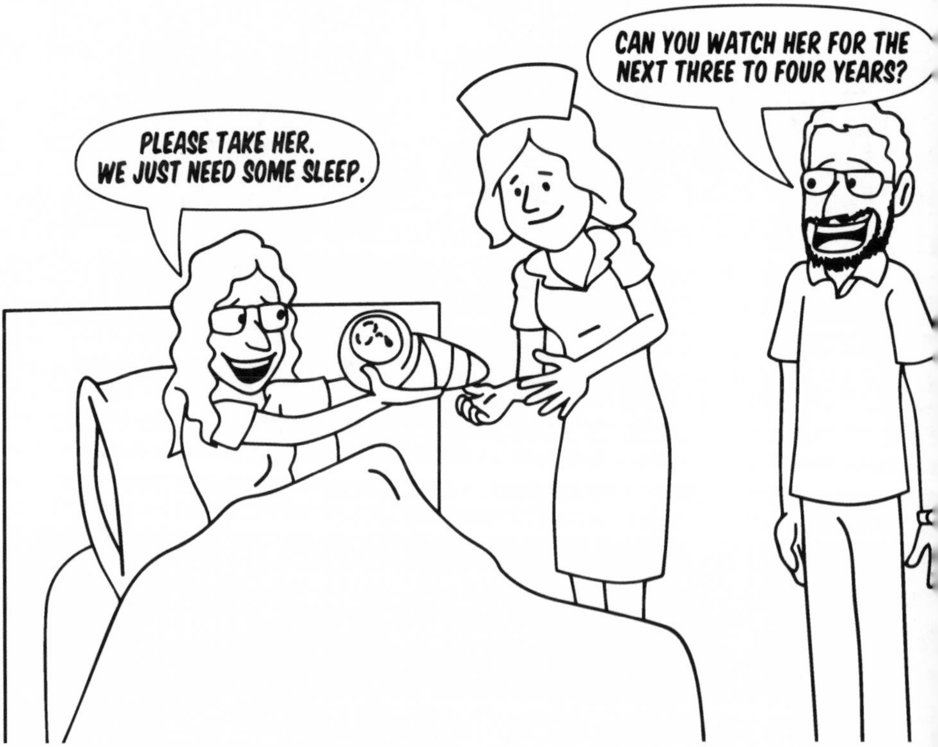
PLEASE TAKE HER. WE JUST NEED SOME SLEEP.
CAN YOU WATCH HER FOR THE NEXT THREE TO FOUR YEARS?

HOLY BABY!

IS HAVING A BABY REALLY A MIRACLE?

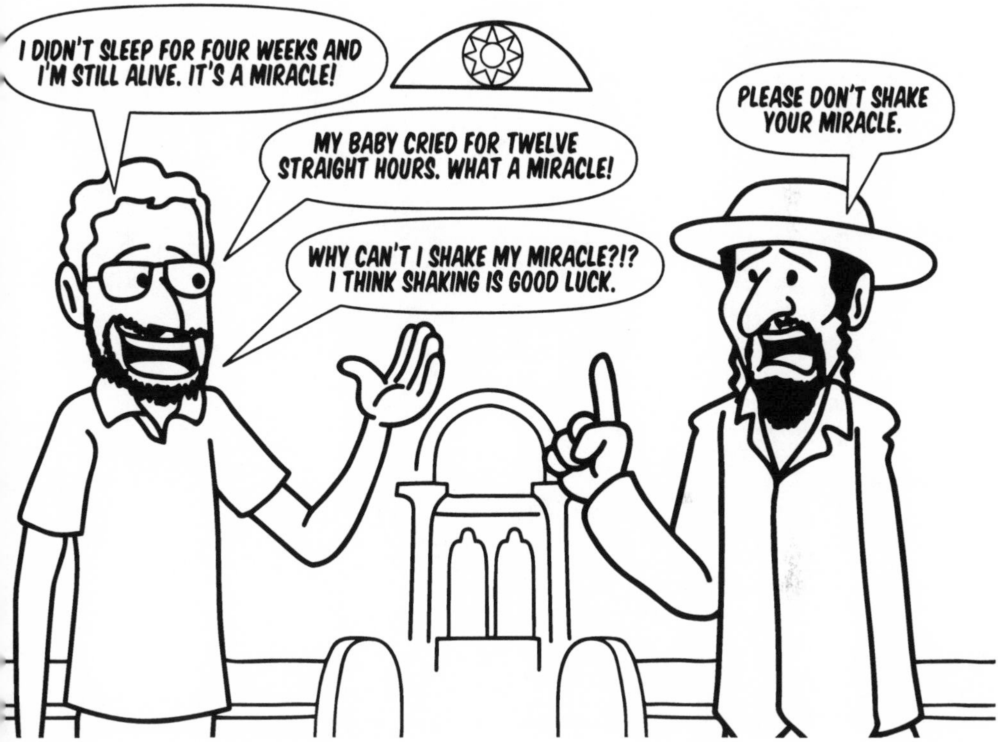

I DIDN'T SLEEP FOR FOUR WEEKS AND I'M STILL ALIVE. IT'S A MIRACLE!
MY BABY CRIED FOR TWELVE STRAIGHT HOURS. WHAT A MIRACLE!
WHY CAN'T I SHAKE MY MIRACLE?!? I THINK SHAKING IS GOOD LUCK.
PLEASE DON'T SHAKE YOUR MIRACLE.

GOOD EATER

MY BABY EATS WELL...

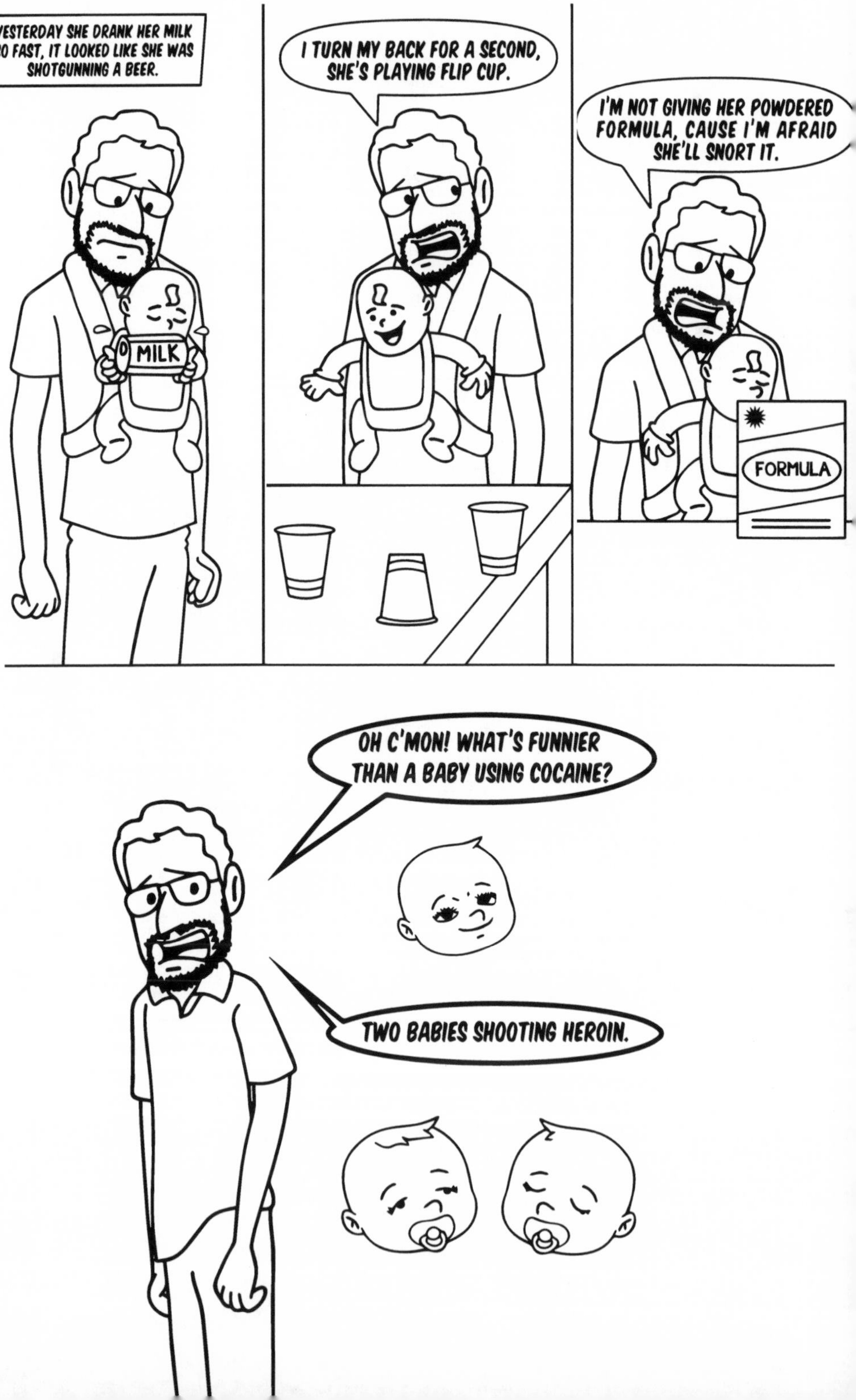

YESTERDAY SHE DRANK HER MILK SO FAST, IT LOOKED LIKE SHE WAS SHOTGUNNING A BEER.
MILK
I TURN MY BACK FOR A SECOND, SHE'S PLAYING FLIP CUP.
I'M NOT GIVING HER POWDERED FORMULA, CAUSE I'M AFRAID SHE'LL SNORT IT.
FORMULA
OH C'MON! WHAT'S FUNNIER THAN A BABY USING COCAINE?
TWO BABIES SHOOTING HEROIN.

HEROIN BABIES

IF YOU THINK ABOUT IT, BABIES LOOK LIKE THEY'RE ON HEROIN...

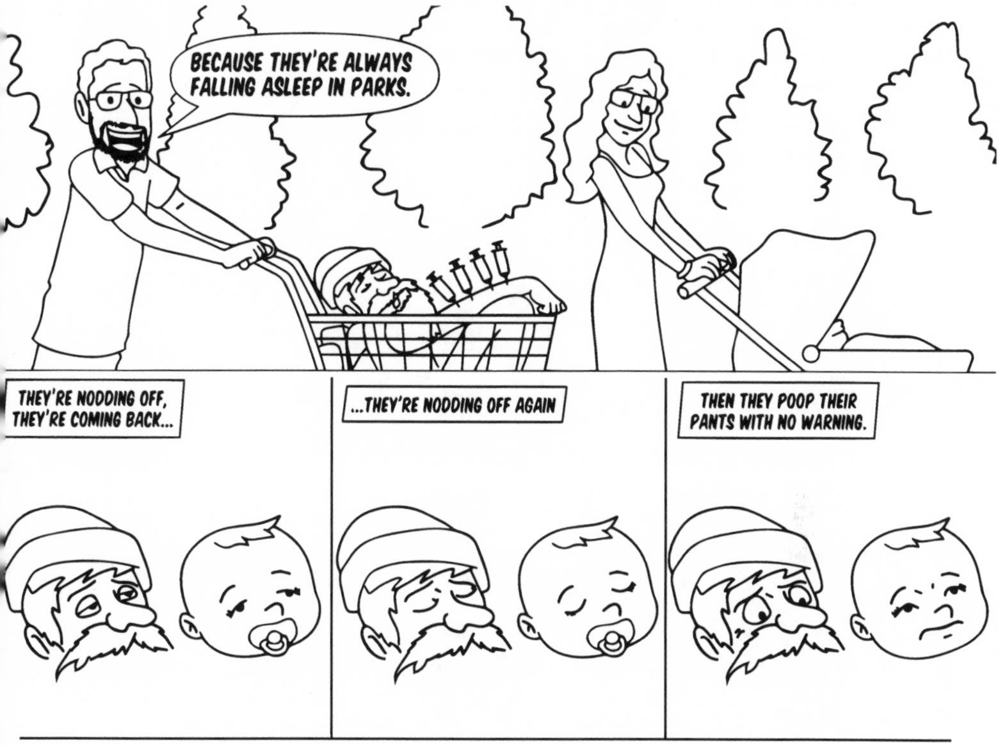
BECAUSE THEY'RE ALWAYS FALLING ASLEEP IN PARKS.
THEY'RE NODDING OFF, THEY'RE COMING BACK...
...THEY'RE NODDING OFF AGAIN
THEN THEY POOP THEIR PANTS WITH NO WARNING.

SOMEONE ONCE CORRECTED ME...

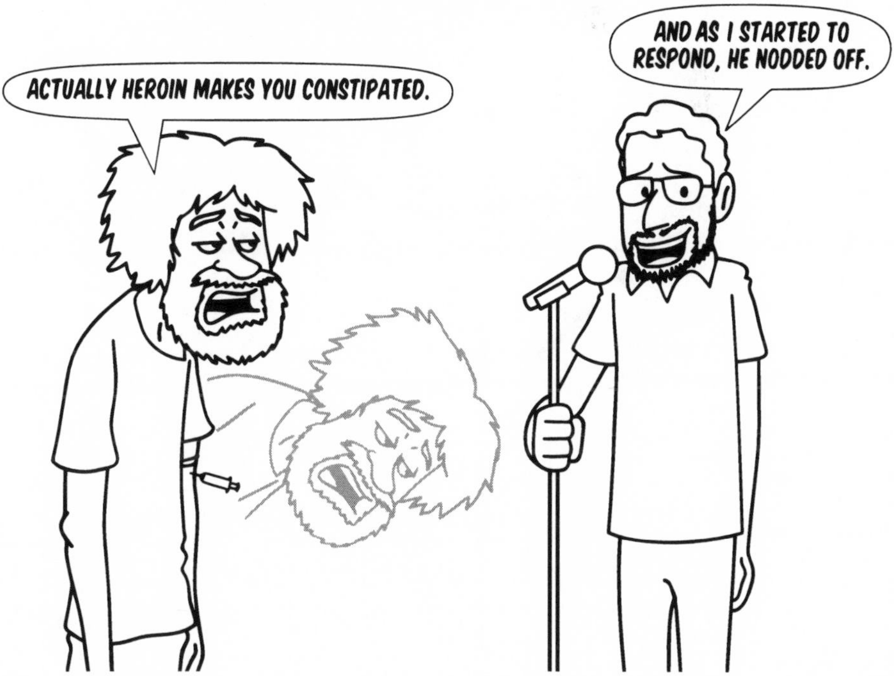
ACTUALLY HEROIN MAKES YOU CONSTIPATED.
AND AS I STARTED TO RESPOND, HE NODDED OFF.

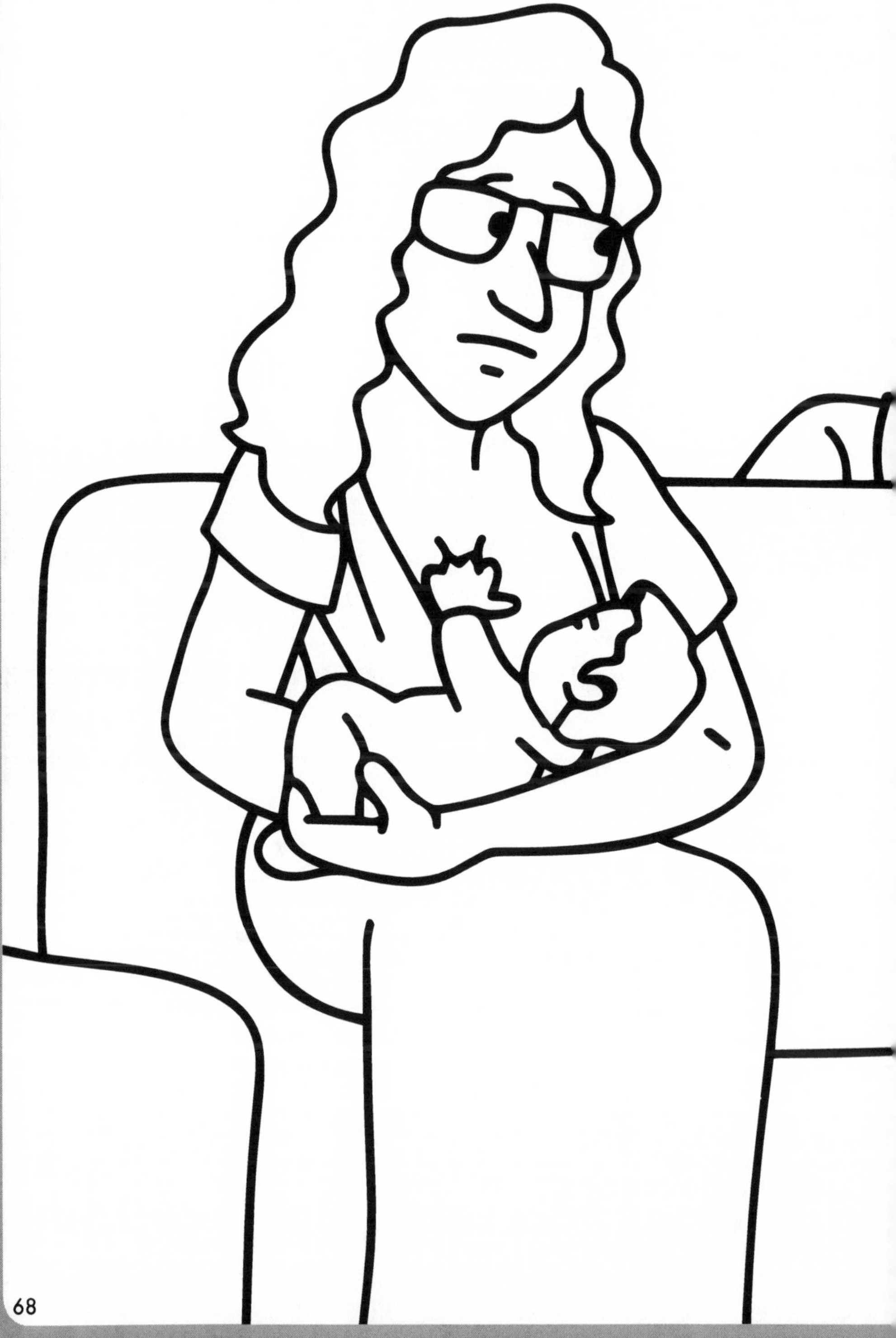

NEWBORNS AND TOTS

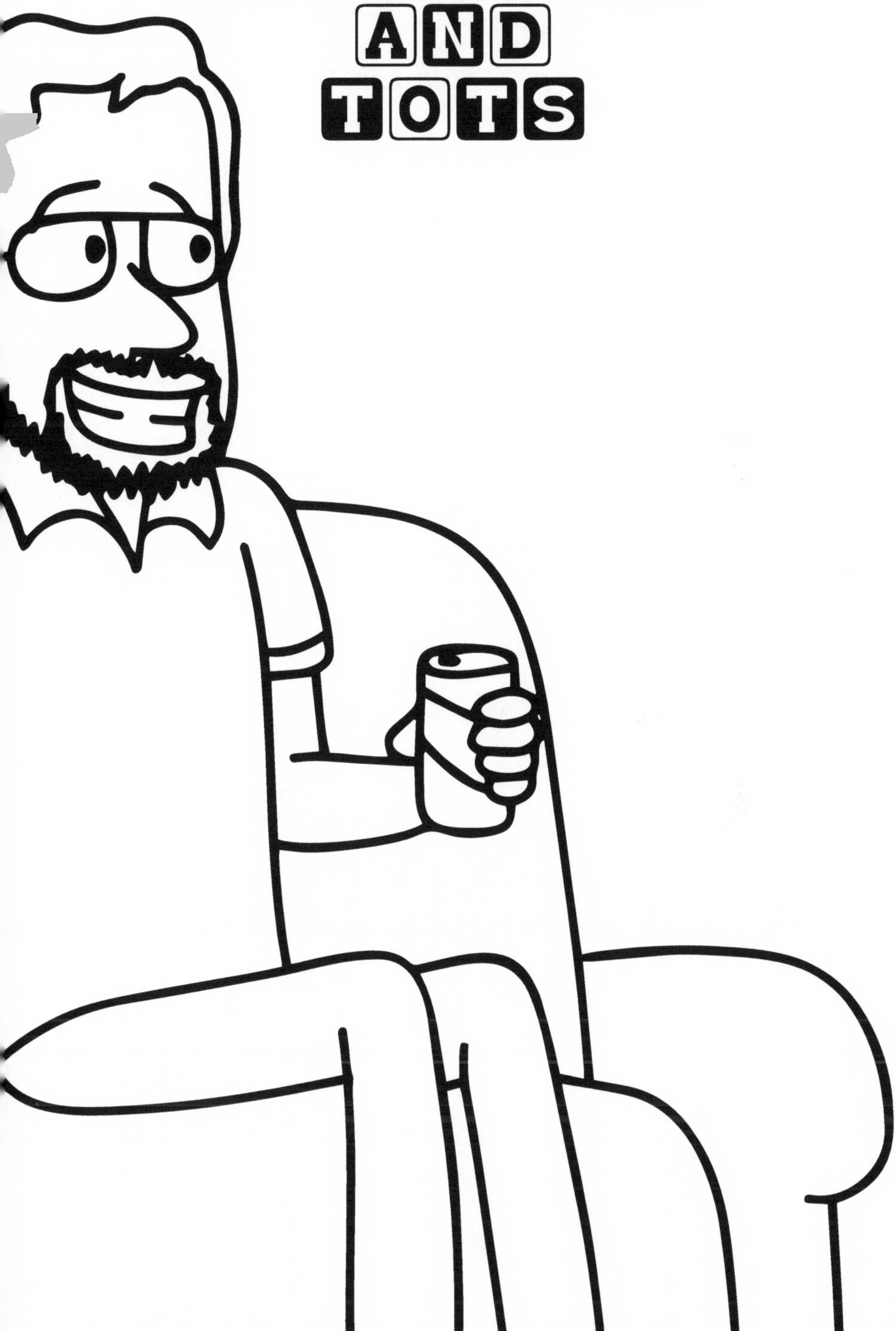

MICHELLE'S BABY JOKES

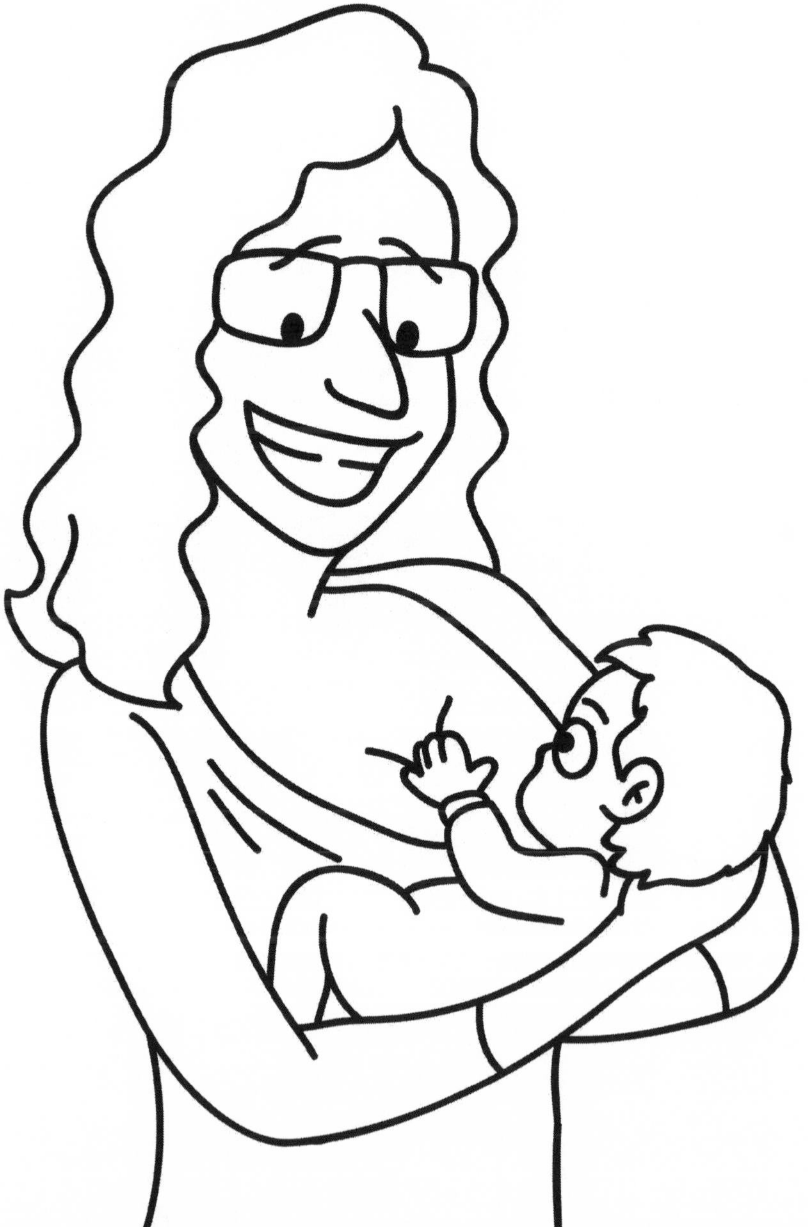

BREASTFEEDING

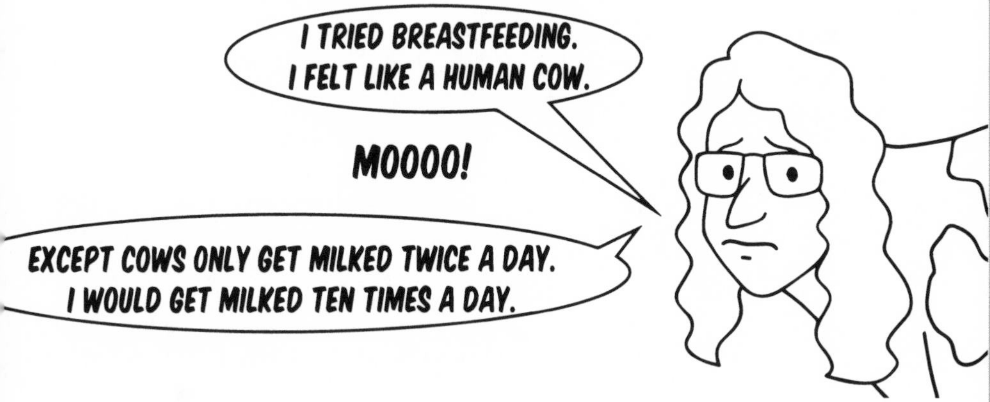
I TRIED BREASTFEEDING.
I FELT LIKE A HUMAN COW.
MOOOO!
EXCEPT COWS ONLY GET MILKED TWICE A DAY.
I WOULD GET MILKED TEN TIMES A DAY.

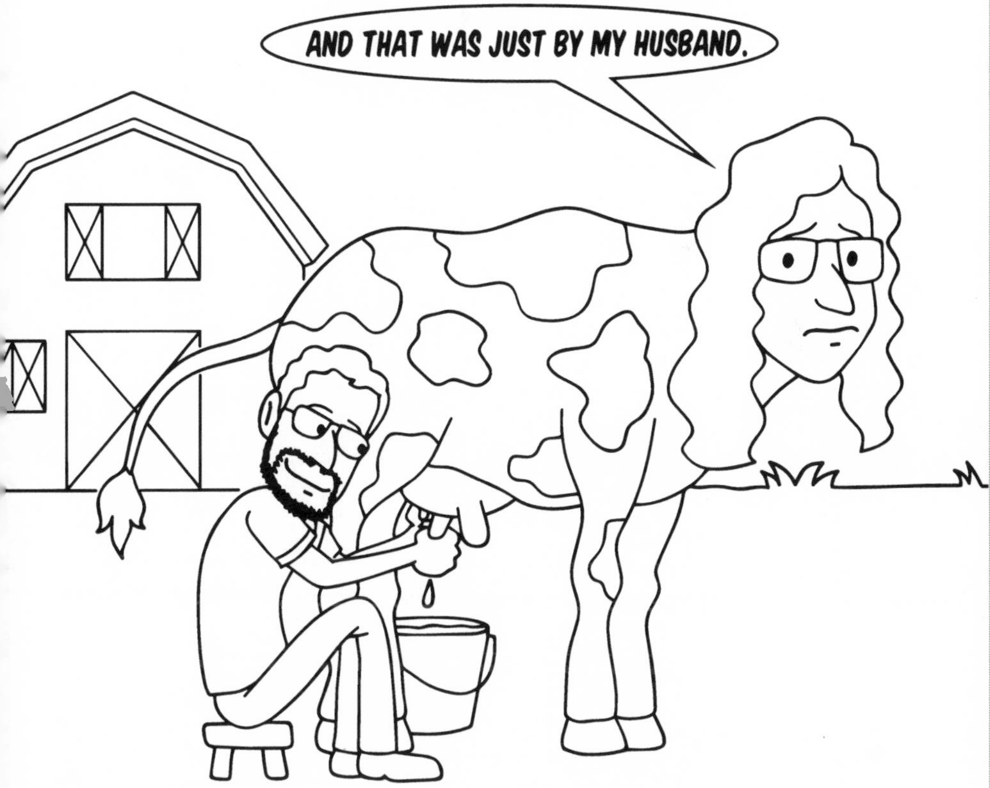
AND THAT WAS JUST BY MY HUSBAND.

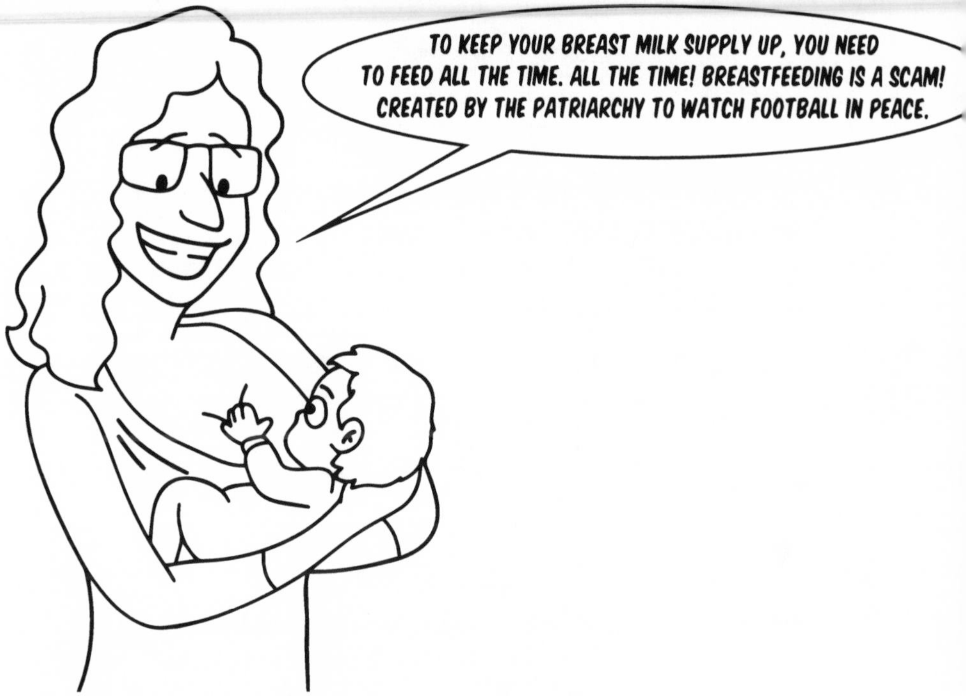
TO KEEP YOUR BREAST MILK SUPPLY UP, YOU NEED TO FEED ALL THE TIME. ALL THE TIME! BREASTFEEDING IS A SCAM! CREATED BY THE PATRIARCHY TO WATCH FOOTBALL IN PEACE.

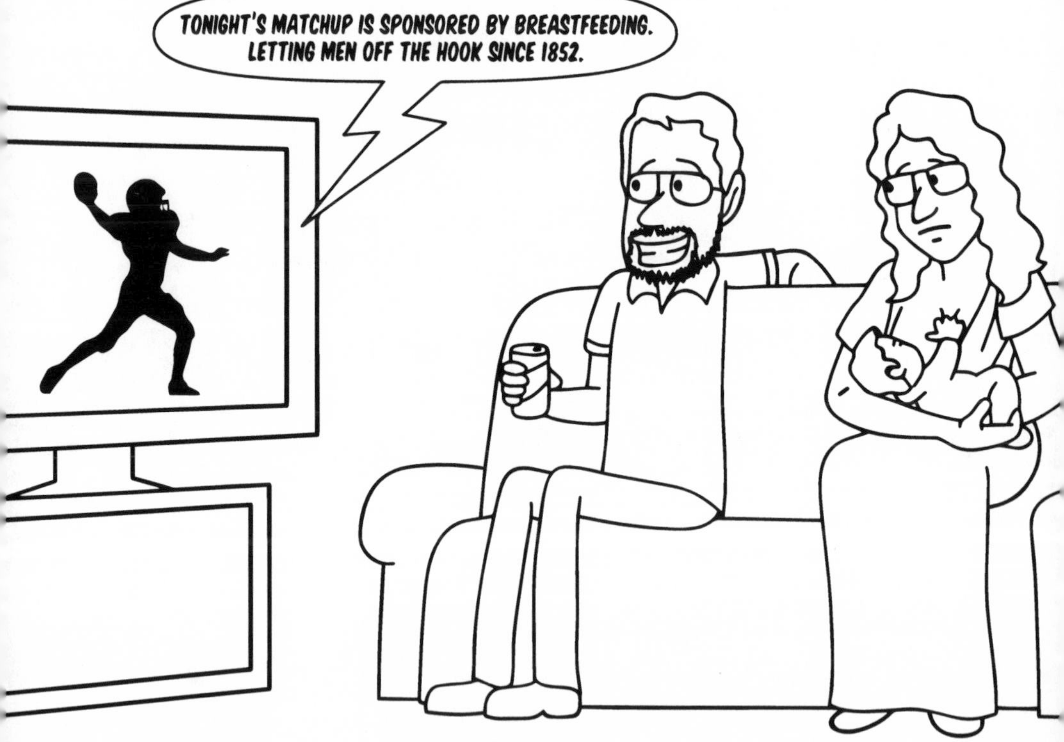
TONIGHT'S MATCHUP IS SPONSORED BY BREASTFEEDING. LETTING MEN OFF THE HOOK SINCE 1852.

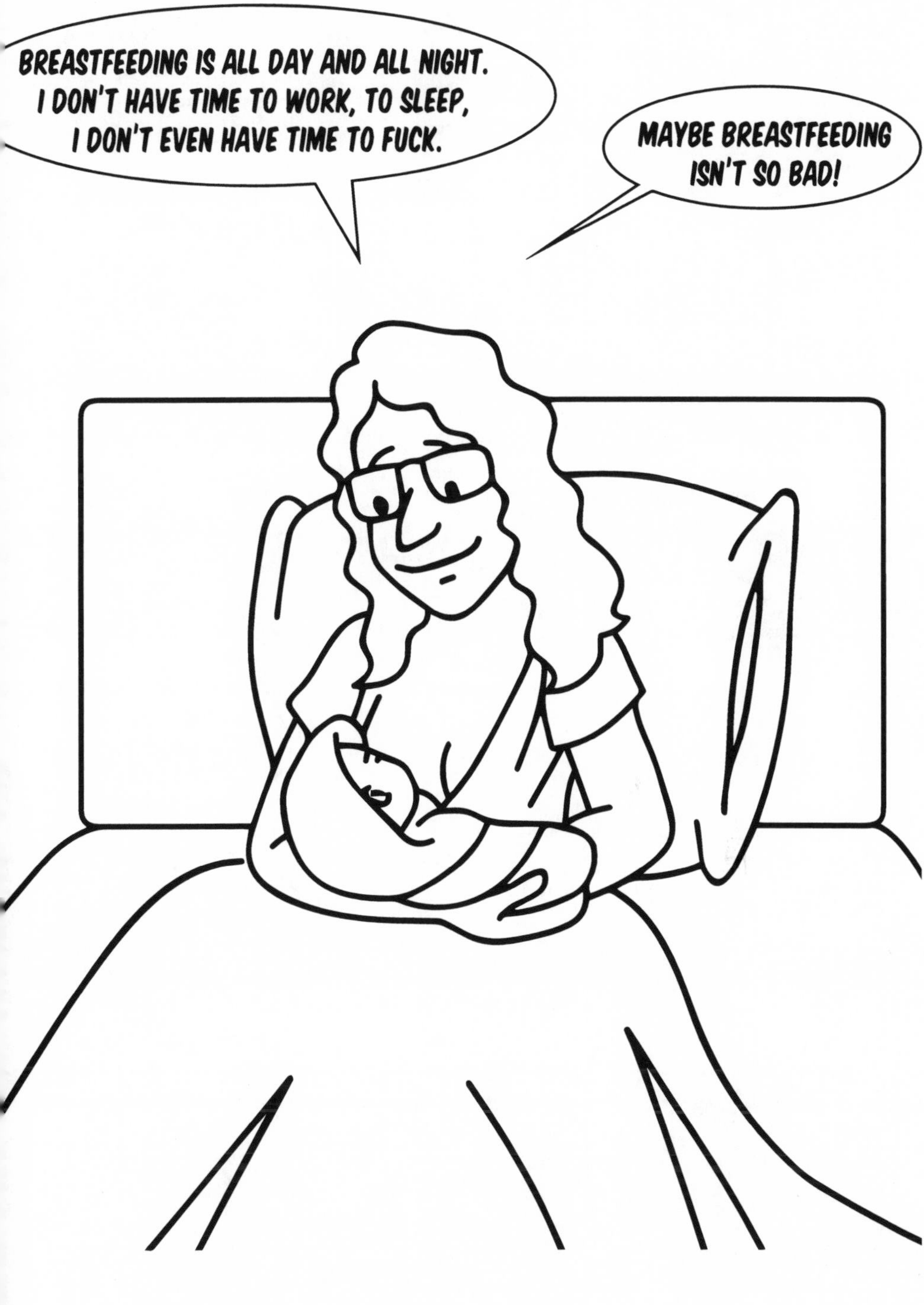
BREASTFEEDING IS ALL DAY AND ALL NIGHT. I DON'T HAVE TIME TO WORK, TO SLEEP, I DON'T EVEN HAVE TIME TO FUCK.
MAYBE BREASTFEEDING ISN'T SO BAD!

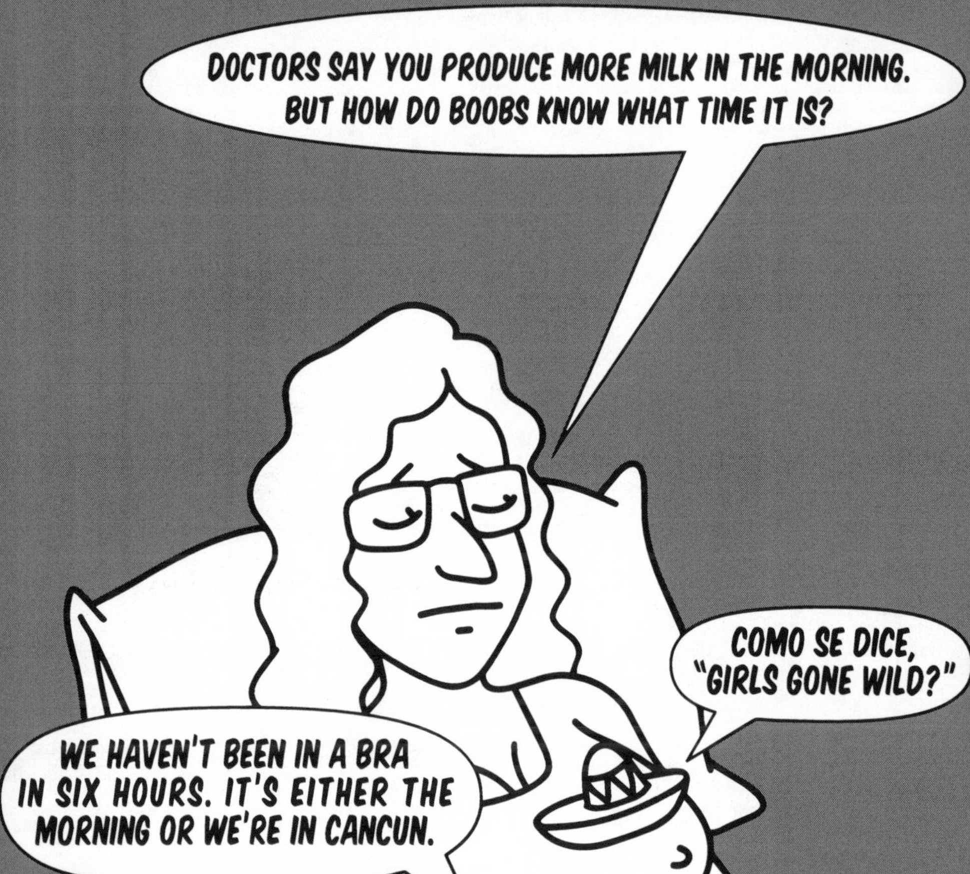
DOCTORS SAY YOU PRODUCE MORE MILK IN THE MORNING. BUT HOW DO BOOBS KNOW WHAT TIME IT IS?
WE HAVEN'T BEEN IN A BRA IN SIX HOURS. IT'S EITHER THE MORNING OR WE'RE IN CANCUN.
COMO SE DICE, "GIRLS GONE WILD?"

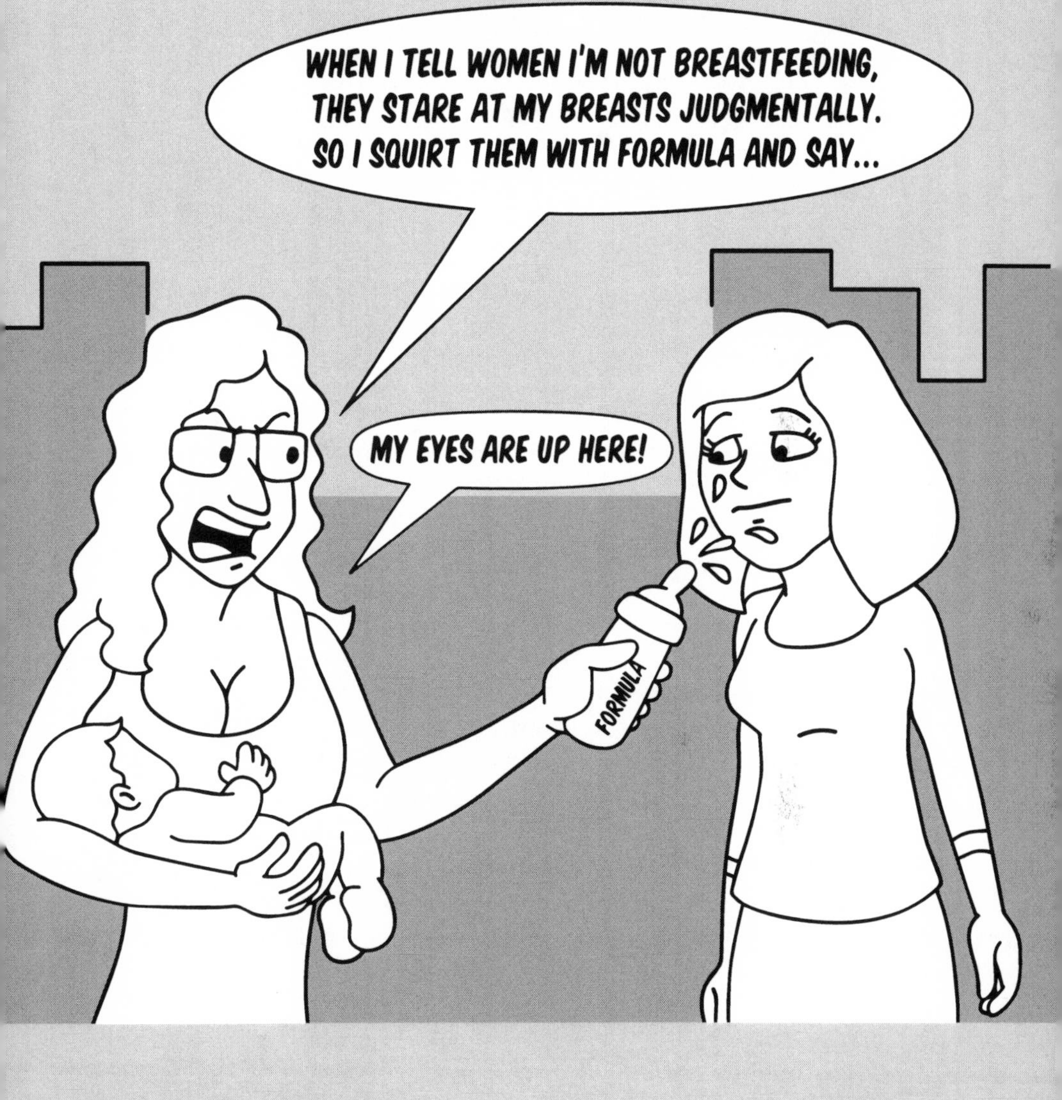
WHEN I TELL WOMEN I'M NOT BREASTFEEDING, THEY STARE AT MY BREASTS JUDGMENTALLY. SO I SQUIRT THEM WITH FORMULA AND SAY...
MY EYES ARE UP HERE!
FORMULA

COFFEE

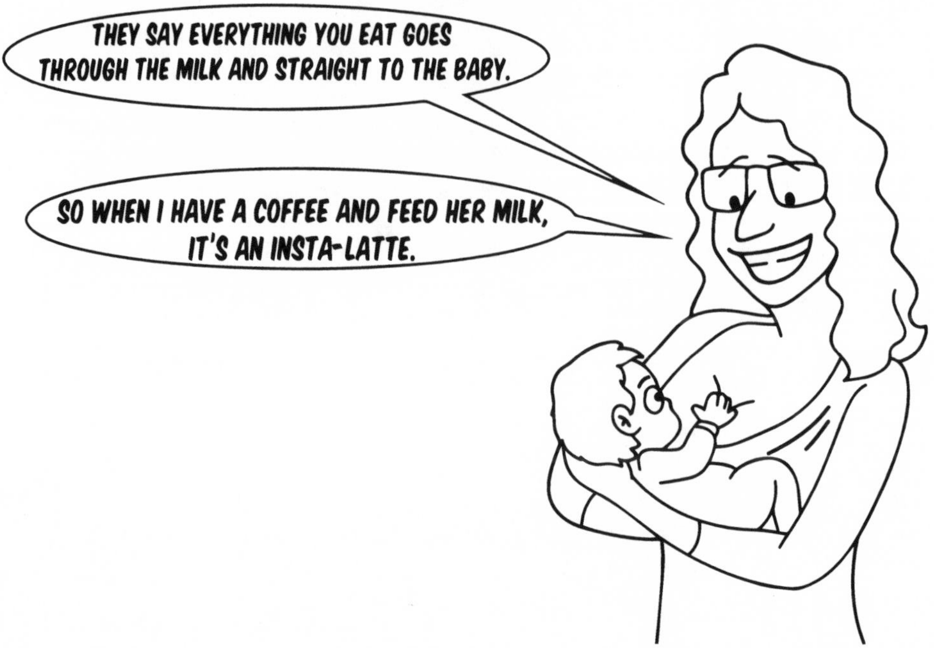
THEY SAY EVERYTHING YOU EAT GOES THROUGH THE MILK AND STRAIGHT TO THE BABY.
SO WHEN I HAVE A COFFEE AND FEED HER MILK, IT'S AN INSTA-LATTE.

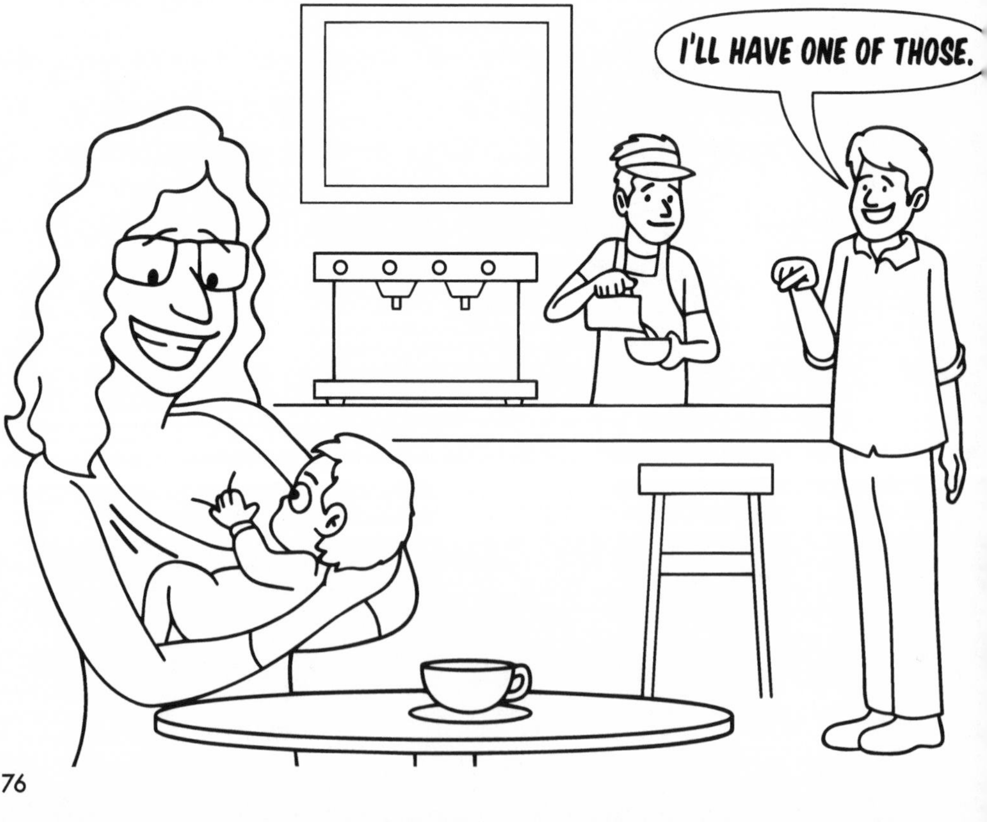
I'LL HAVE ONE OF THOSE.

LACTATION CONSULTANTS

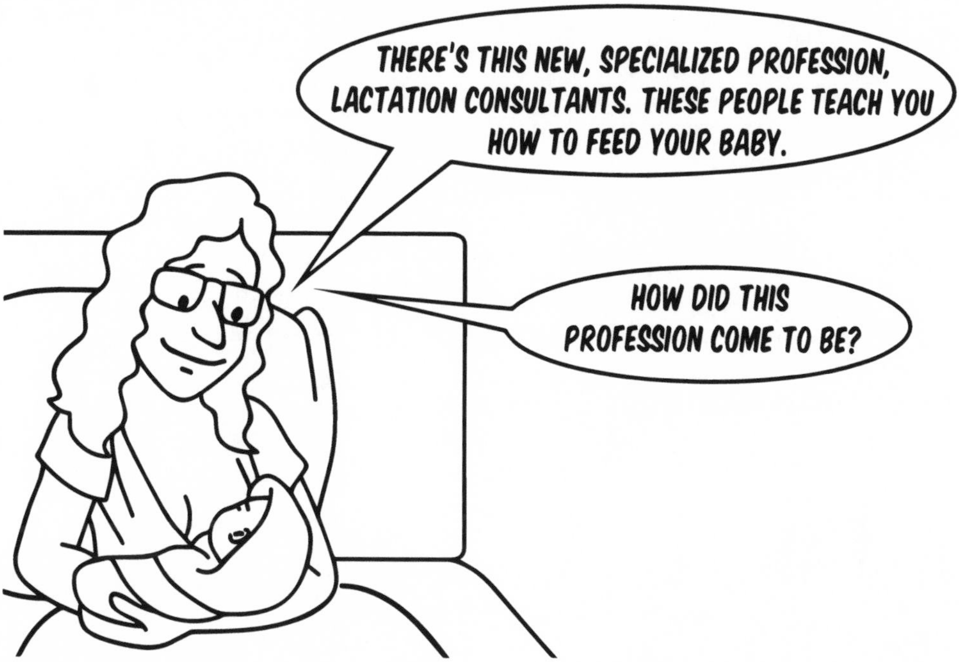
THERE'S THIS NEW, SPECIALIZED PROFESSION, LACTATION CONSULTANTS. THESE PEOPLE TEACH YOU HOW TO FEED YOUR BABY.
HOW DID THIS PROFESSION COME TO BE?

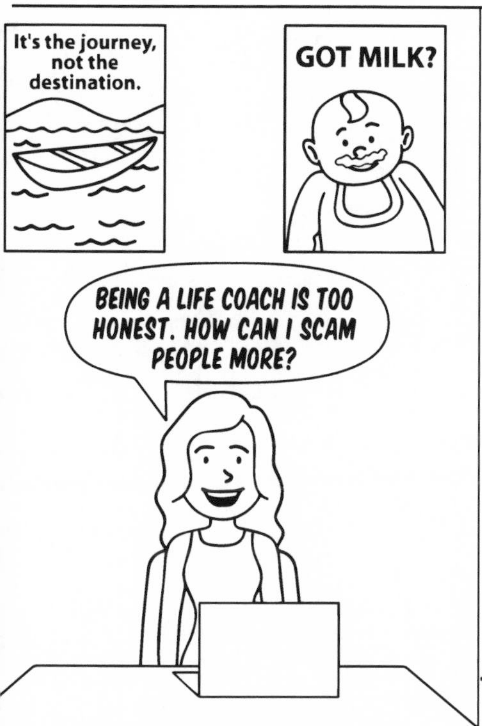
It's the journey, not the destination.
GOT MILK?
BEING A LIFE COACH IS TOO HONEST. HOW CAN I SCAM PEOPLE MORE?

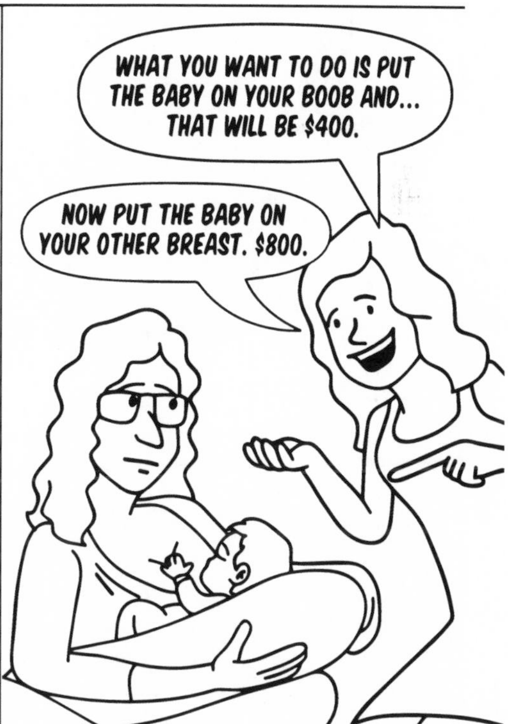
WHAT YOU WANT TO DO IS PUT THE BABY ON YOUR BOOB AND... THAT WILL BE $400.
NOW PUT THE BABY ON YOUR OTHER BREAST. $800.

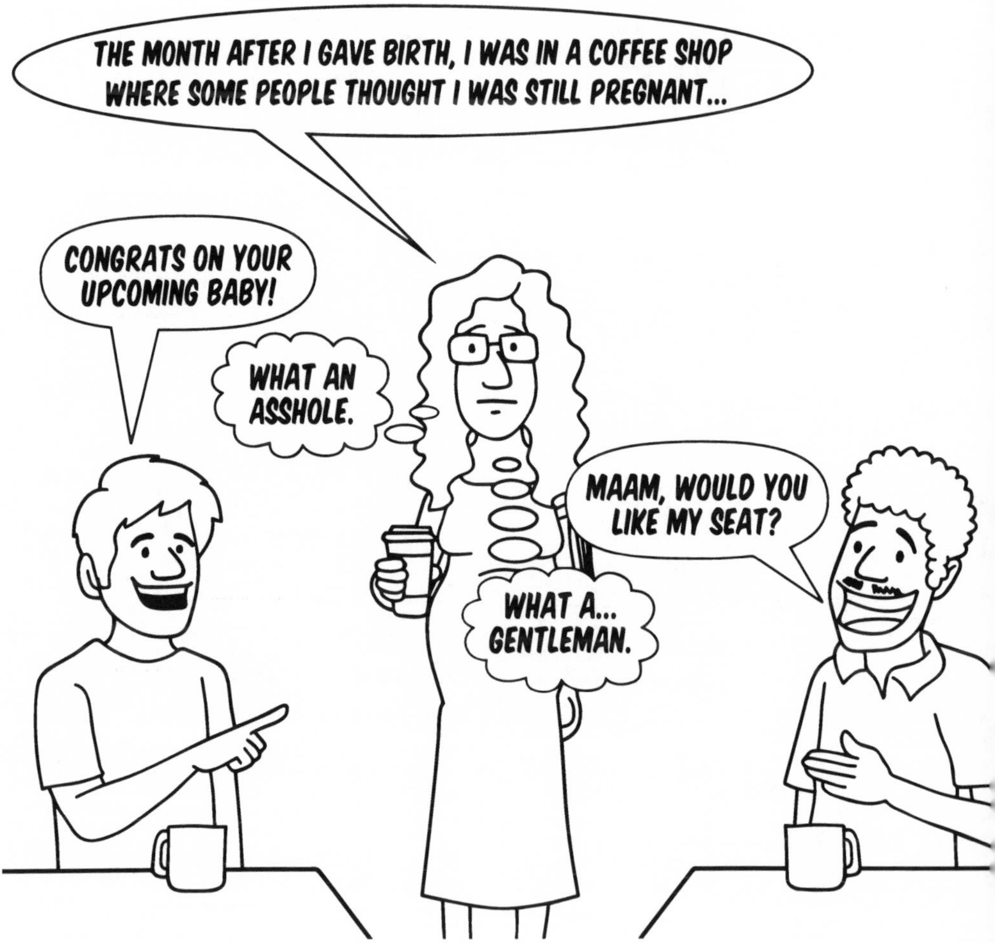
THE MONTH AFTER I GAVE BIRTH, I WAS IN A COFFEE SHOP WHERE SOME PEOPLE THOUGHT I WAS STILL PREGNANT...
CONGRATS ON YOUR UPCOMING BABY!
WHAT AN ASSHOLE.
MAAM, WOULD YOU LIKE MY SEAT?
WHAT A... GENTLEMAN.

THERE'S A FINE LINE BETWEEN BEING AN ASSHOLE AND BEING A GENTLEMAN.

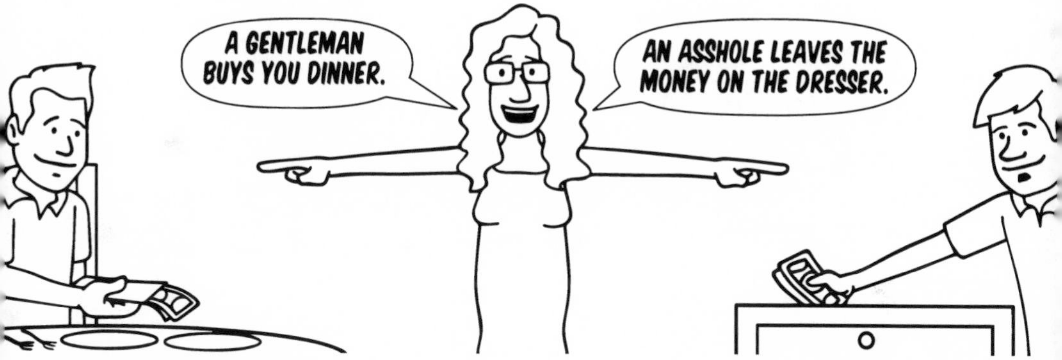
A GENTLEMAN BUYS YOU DINNER.
AN ASSHOLE LEAVES THE MONEY ON THE DRESSER.

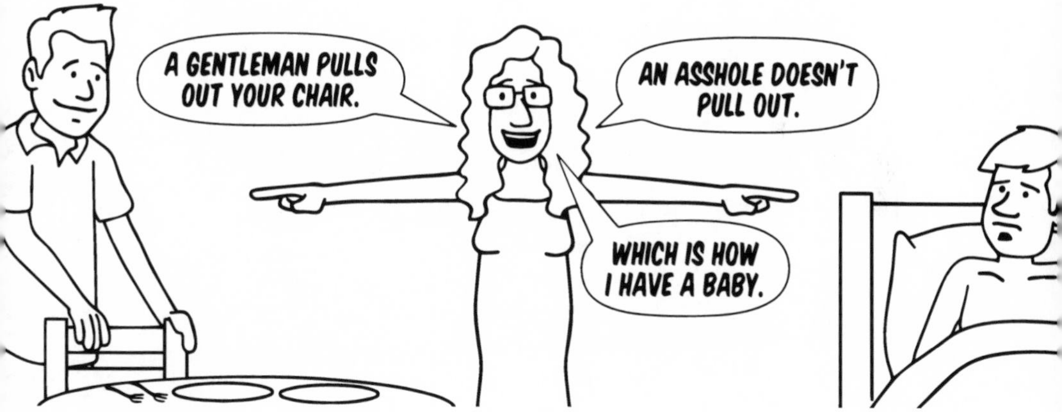
A GENTLEMAN PULLS OUT YOUR CHAIR.
AN ASSHOLE DOESN'T PULL OUT.
WHICH IS HOW I HAVE A BABY.

THE BABY'S AGE

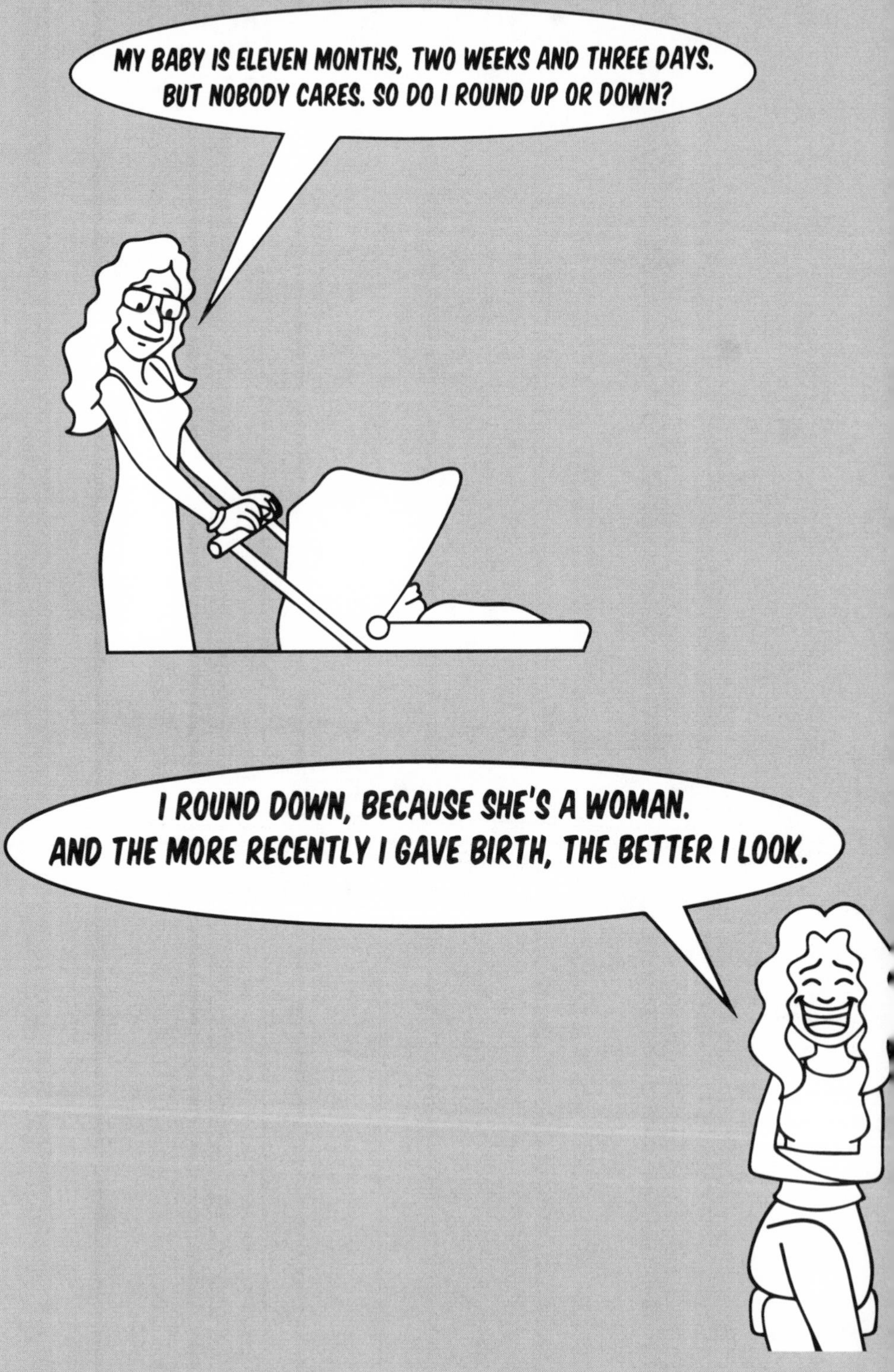
MY BABY IS ELEVEN MONTHS, TWO WEEKS AND THREE DAYS. BUT NOBODY CARES. SO DO I ROUND UP OR DOWN?
I ROUND DOWN, BECAUSE SHE'S A WOMAN. AND THE MORE RECENTLY I GAVE BIRTH, THE BETTER I LOOK.

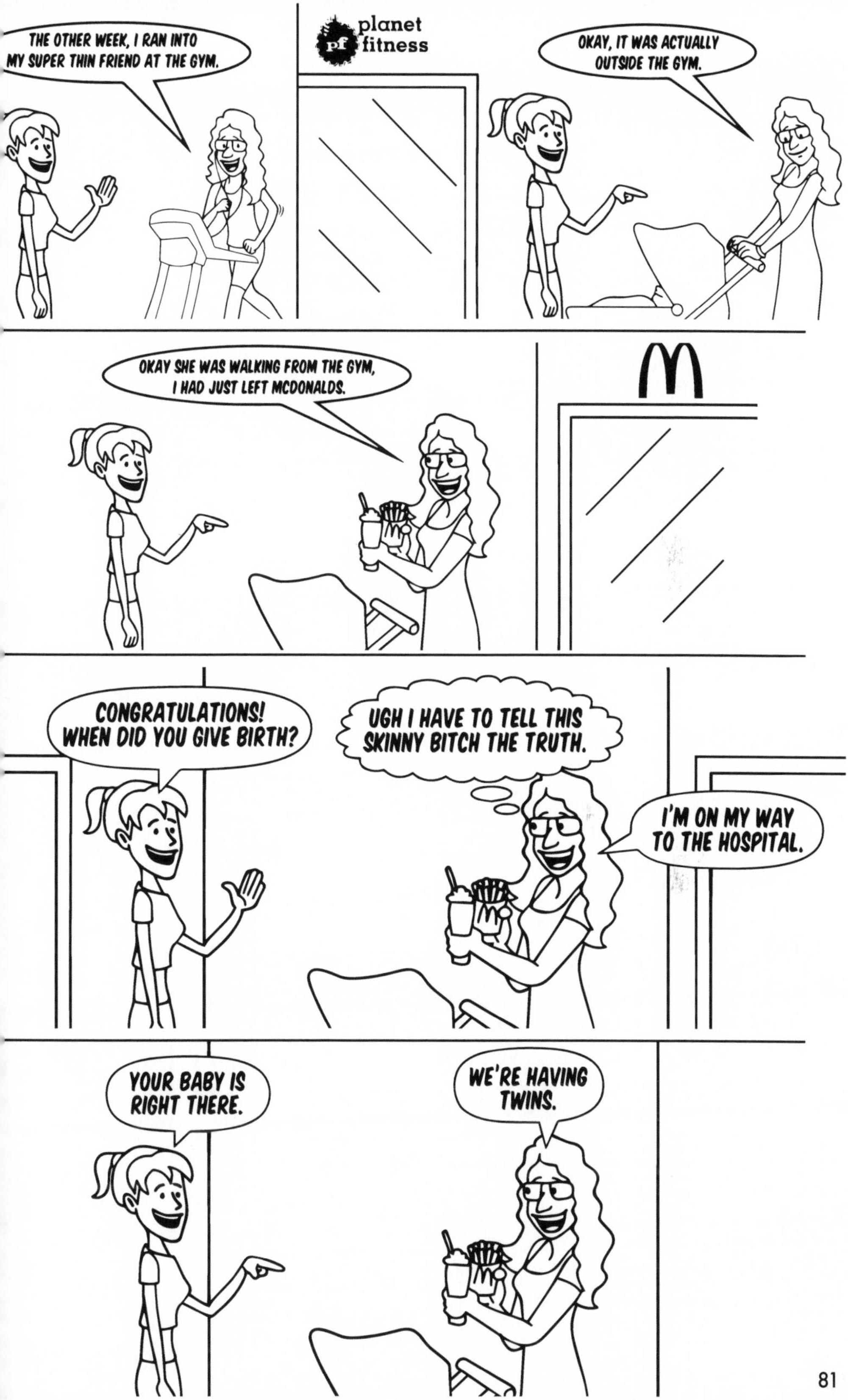
THE OTHER WEEK, I RAN INTO MY SUPER THIN FRIEND AT THE GYM.
planet fitness
OKAY, IT WAS ACTUALLY OUTSIDE THE GYM.
OKAY SHE WAS WALKING FROM THE GYM, I HAD JUST LEFT MCDONALDS.
CONGRATULATIONS! WHEN DID YOU GIVE BIRTH?
UGH I HAVE TO TELL THIS SKINNY BITCH THE TRUTH.
I'M ON MY WAY TO THE HOSPITAL.
YOUR BABY IS RIGHT THERE.
WE'RE HAVING TWINS.

MISSING YOUR CHILD

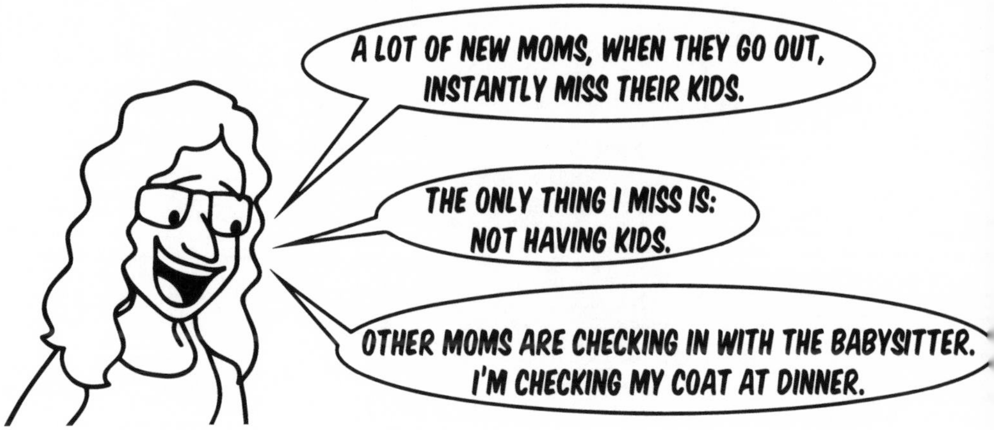
A LOT OF NEW MOMS, WHEN THEY GO OUT, INSTANTLY MISS THEIR KIDS.
THE ONLY THING I MISS IS: NOT HAVING KIDS.
OTHER MOMS ARE CHECKING IN WITH THE BABYSITTER. I'M CHECKING MY COAT AT DINNER.

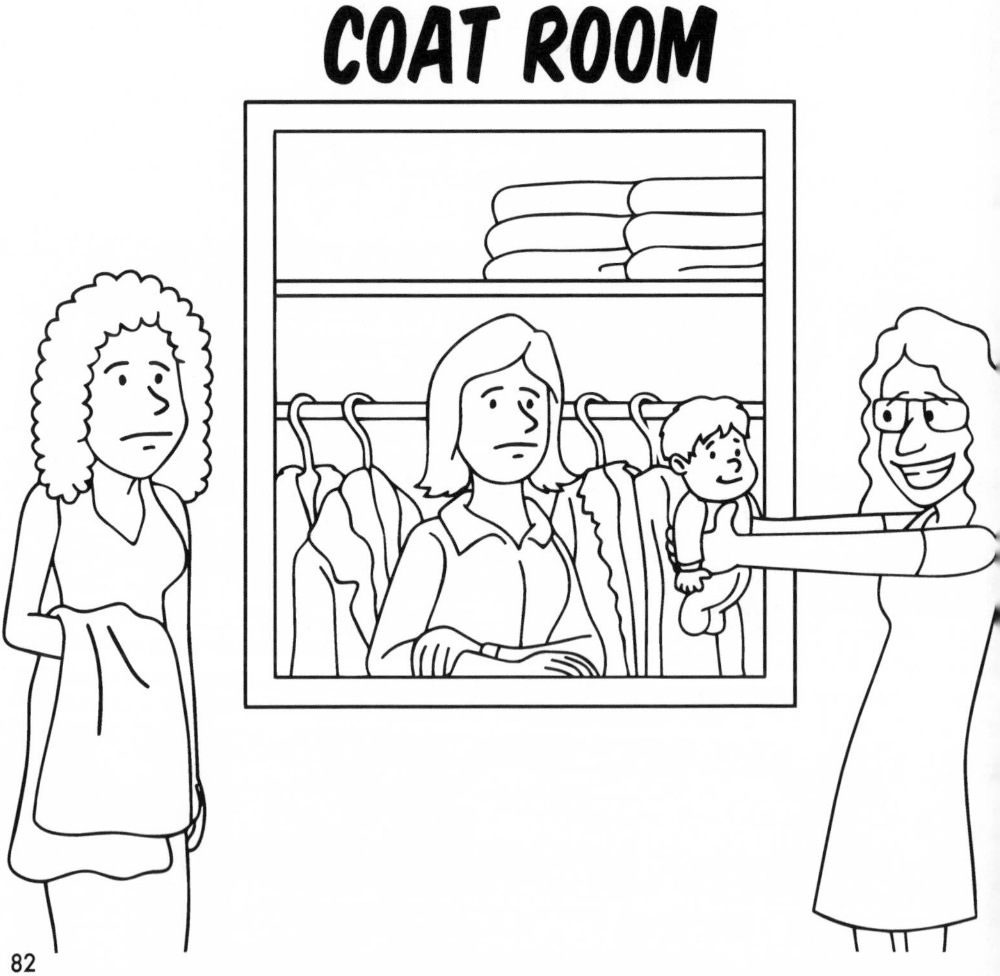
COAT ROOM

HELICOPTER PARENT

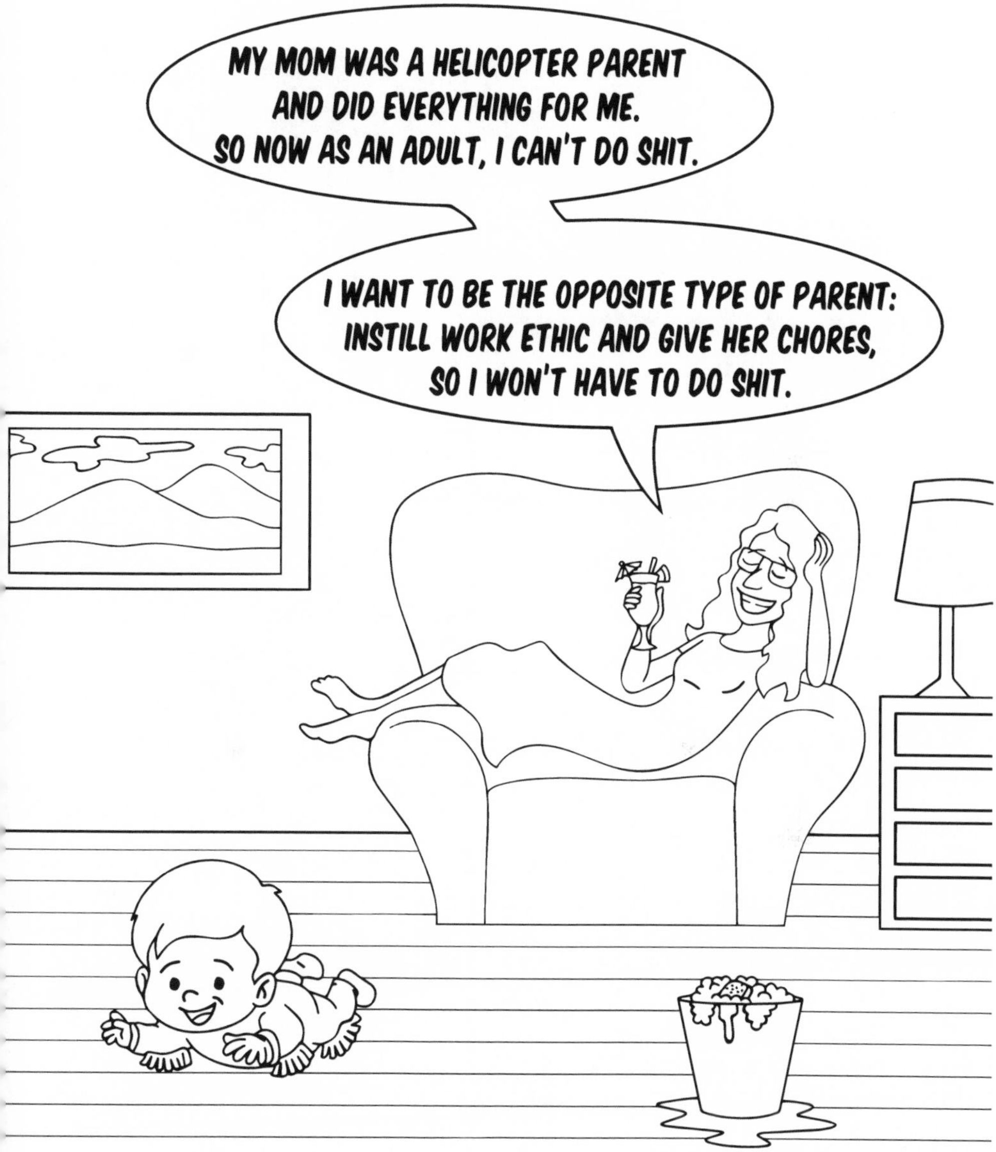
MY MOM WAS A HELICOPTER PARENT AND DID EVERYTHING FOR ME. SO NOW AS AN ADULT, I CAN'T DO SHIT.
I WANT TO BE THE OPPOSITE TYPE OF PARENT: INSTILL WORK ETHIC AND GIVE HER CHORES, SO I WON'T HAVE TO DO SHIT.

SOMEONE IN MY LOCAL MOMMY GROUP POSTED...

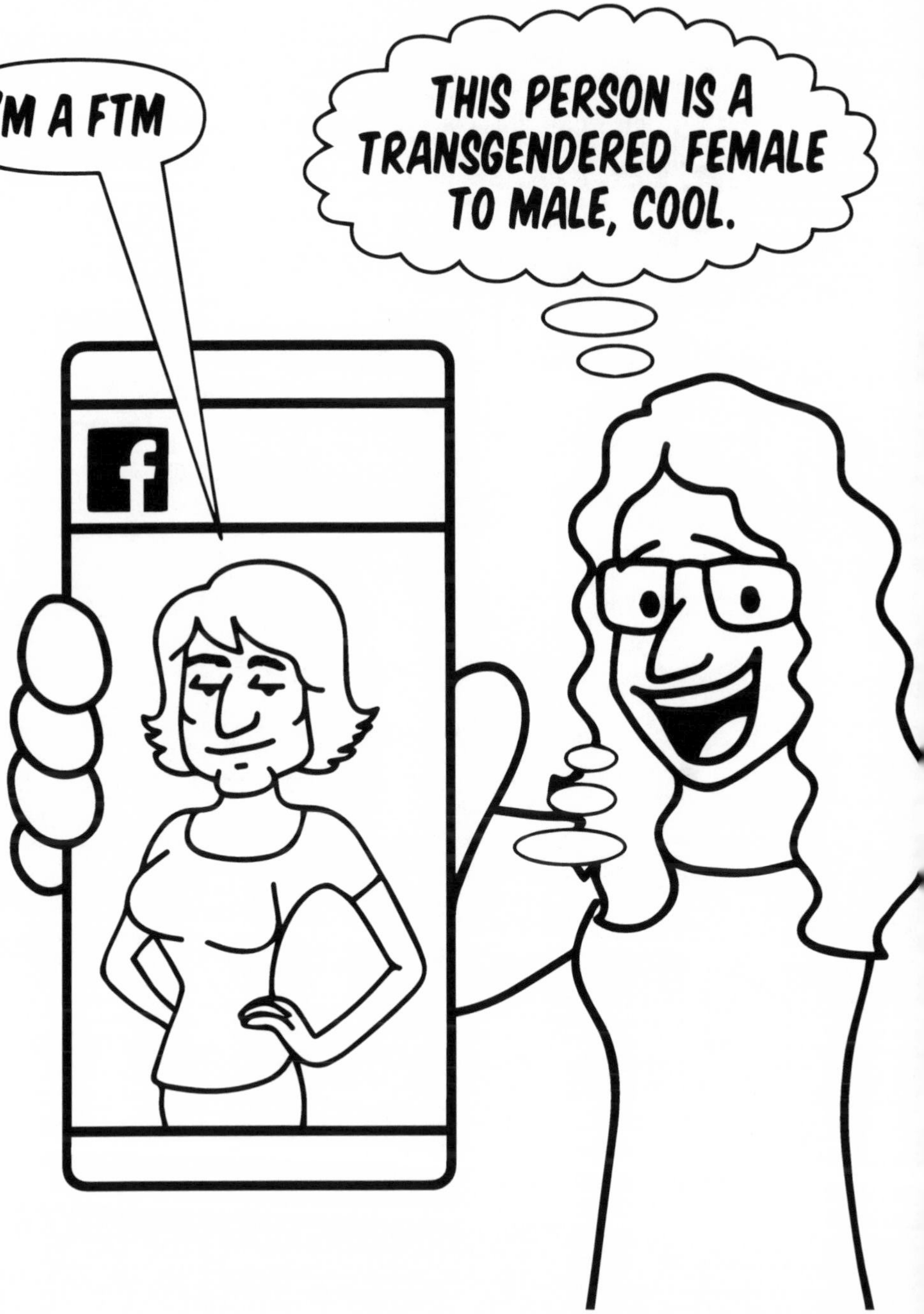
I'M A FTM
THIS PERSON IS A TRANSGENDERED FEMALE TO MALE, COOL.

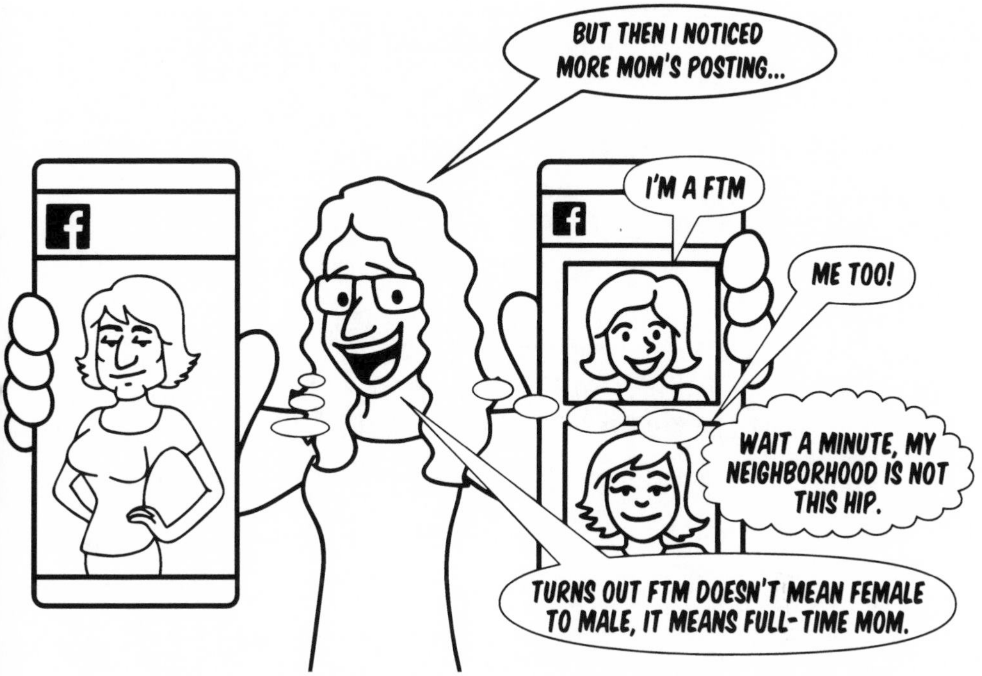
BUT THEN I NOTICED MORE MOM'S POSTING...
I'M A FTM
ME TOO!
WAIT A MINUTE, MY NEIGHBORHOOD IS NOT THIS HIP.
TURNS OUT FTM DOESN'T MEAN FEMALE TO MALE, IT MEANS FULL-TIME MOM.

DISAPPOINTED, I PUT AWAY MY STRAP ON...

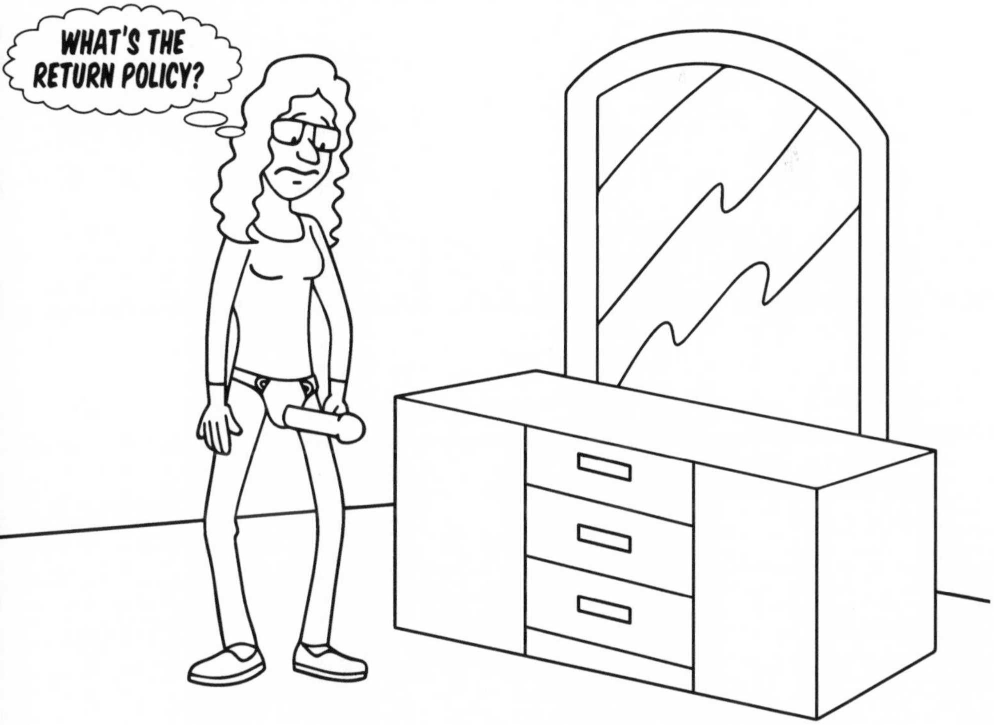
WHAT'S THE RETURN POLICY?

BABY NAMES

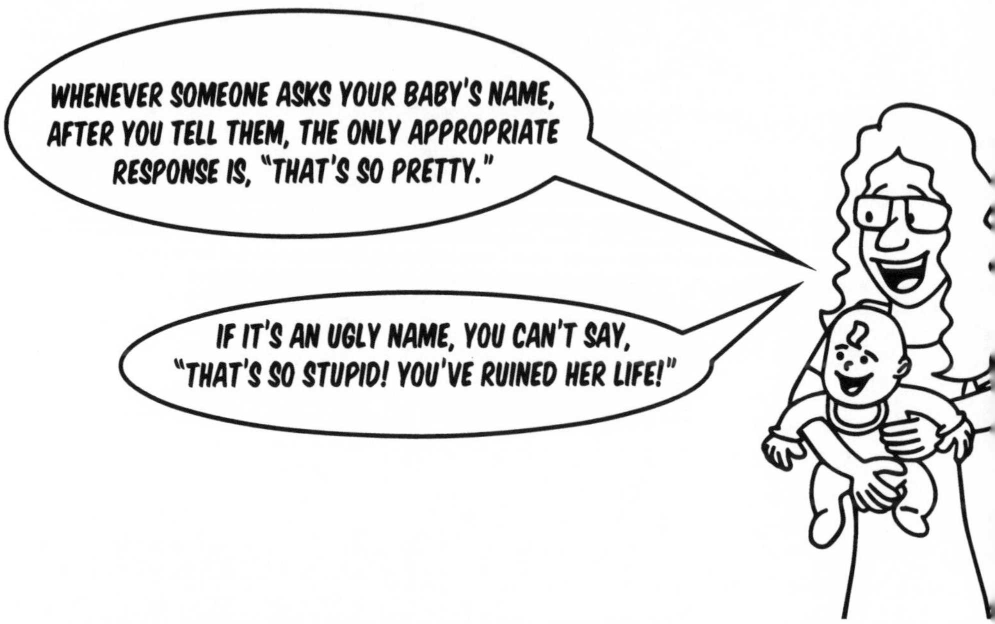
WHENEVER SOMEONE ASKS YOUR BABY'S NAME, AFTER YOU TELL THEM, THE ONLY APPROPRIATE RESPONSE IS, "THAT'S SO PRETTY."
IF IT'S AN UGLY NAME, YOU CAN'T SAY, "THAT'S SO STUPID! YOU'VE RUINED HER LIFE!"

SO TO AMUSE MYSELF, I STARTED MESSING WITH PEOPLE...

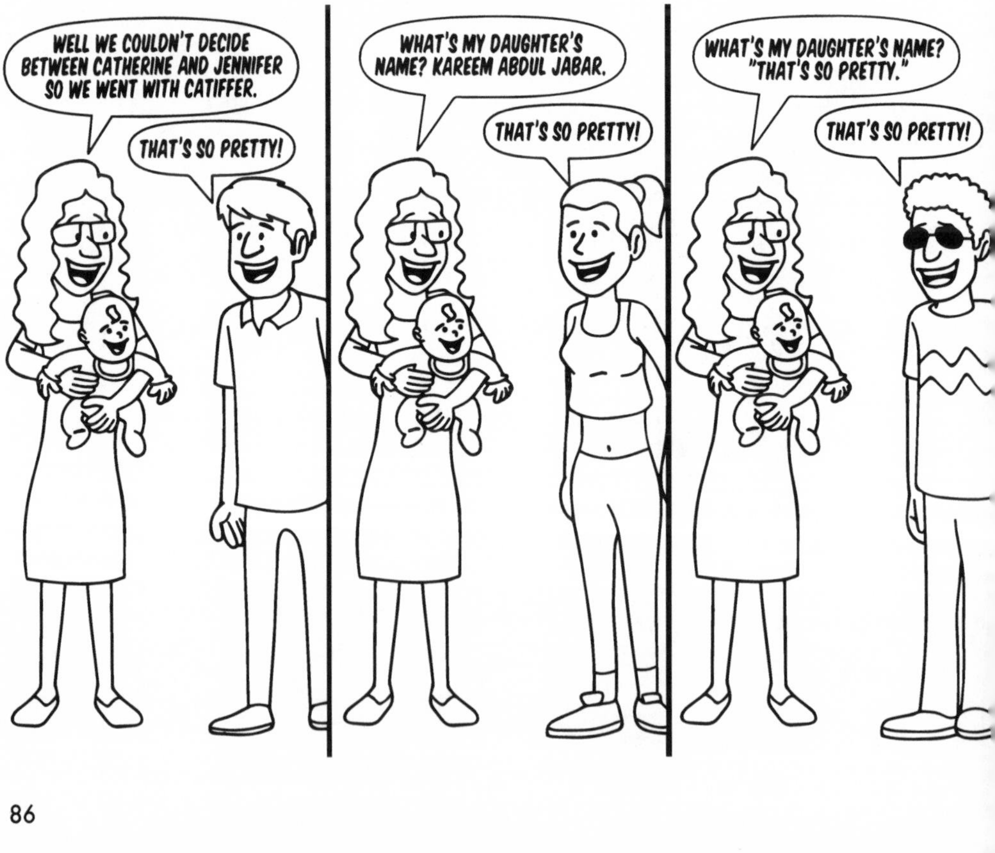
WELL WE COULDN'T DECIDE BETWEEN CATHERINE AND JENNIFER SO WE WENT WITH CATIFFER.
THAT'S SO PRETTY!
WHAT'S MY DAUGHTER'S NAME? KAREEM ABDUL JABAR.
THAT'S SO PRETTY!
WHAT'S MY DAUGHTER'S NAME? "THAT'S SO PRETTY."
THAT'S SO PRETTY!

PEANUT

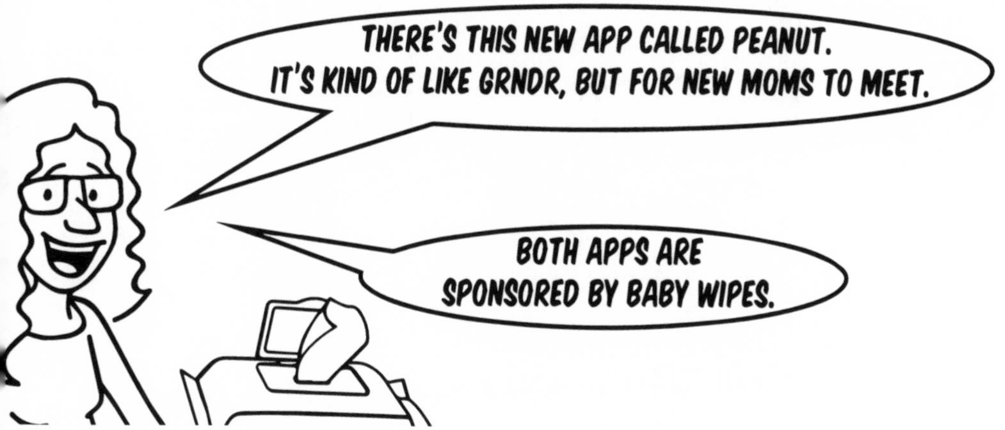
THERE'S THIS NEW APP CALLED PEANUT.
IT'S KIND OF LIKE GRNDR, BUT FOR NEW MOMS TO MEET.
BOTH APPS ARE SPONSORED BY BABY WIPES.

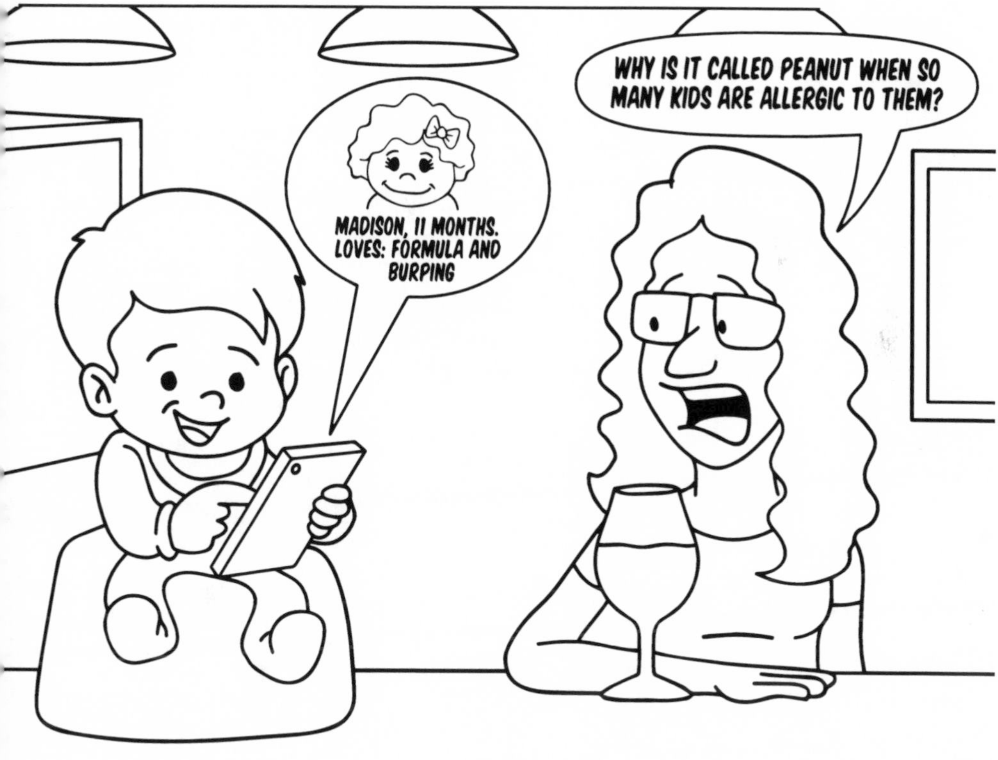
MADISON, 11 MONTHS. LOVES: FORMULA AND BURPING
WHY IS IT CALLED PEANUT WHEN SO MANY KIDS ARE ALLERGIC TO THEM?

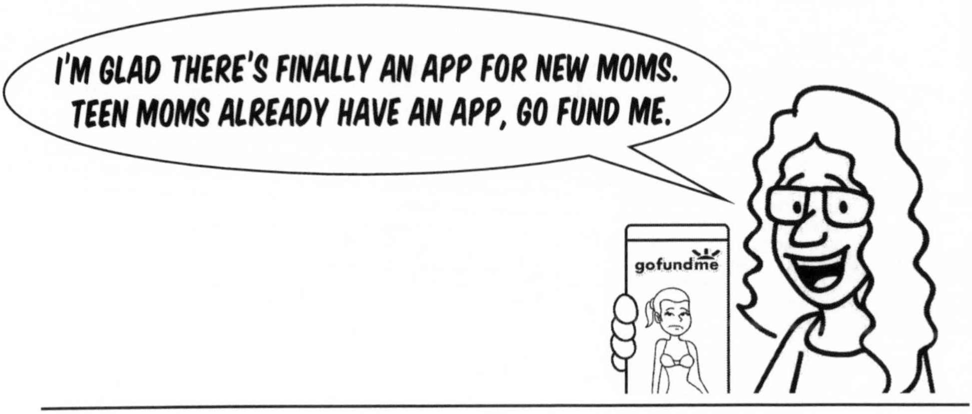
I'M GLAD THERE'S FINALLY AN APP FOR NEW MOMS. TEEN MOMS ALREADY HAVE AN APP, GO FUND ME.
gofundme

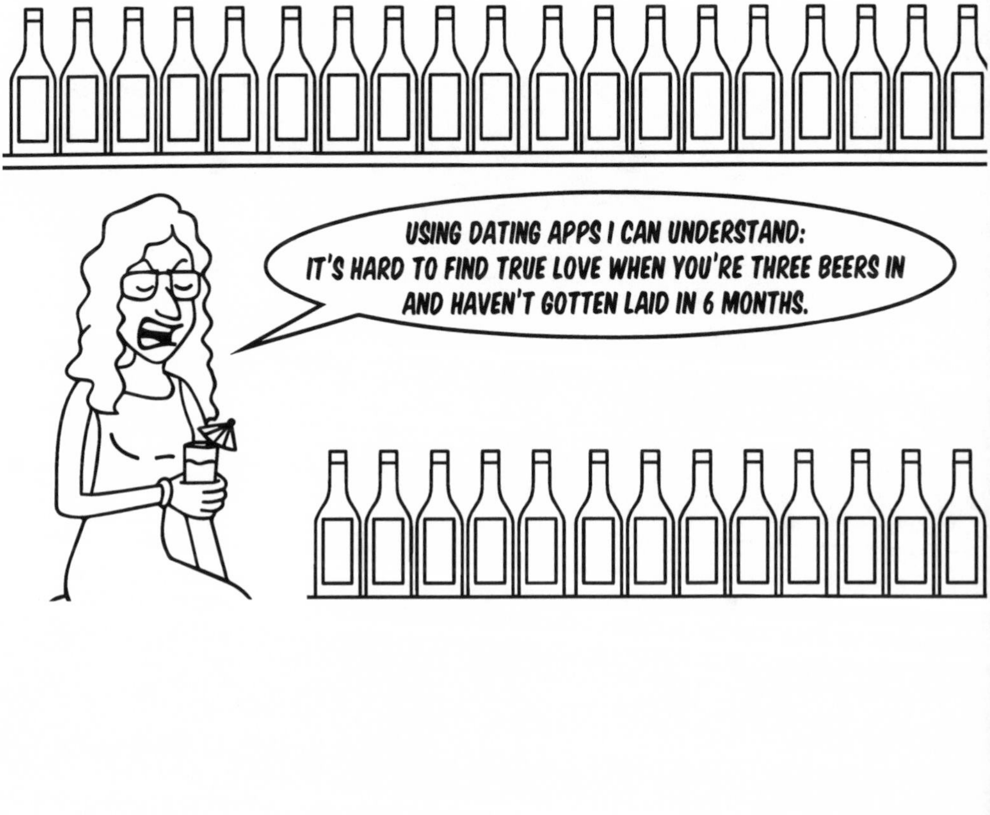
USING DATING APPS I CAN UNDERSTAND: IT'S HARD TO FIND TRUE LOVE WHEN YOU'RE THREE BEERS IN AND HAVEN'T GOTTEN LAID IN 6 MONTHS.

BUT TO FIND A MOM FRIEND, GO TO A PLAYGROUND...

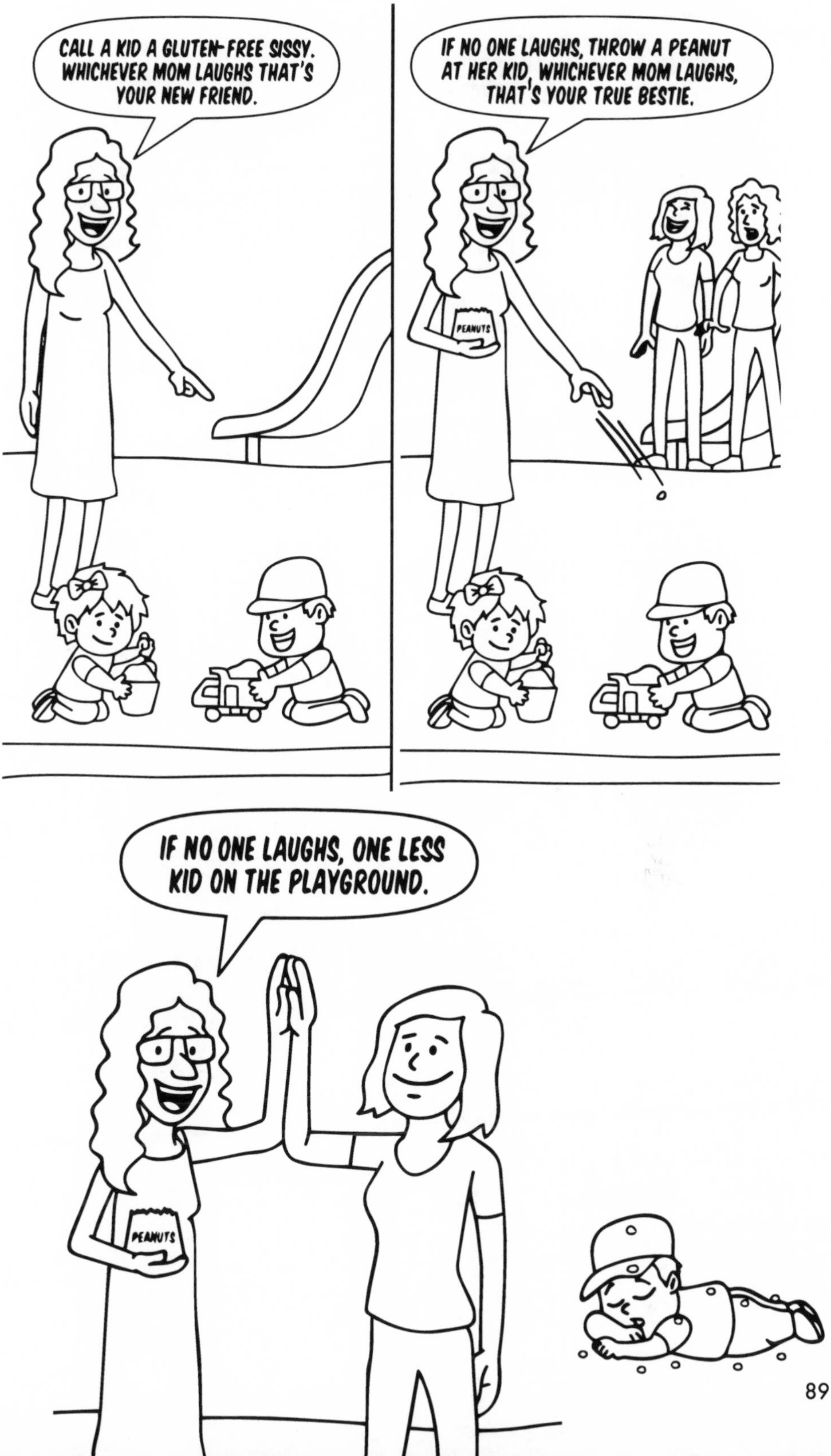
CALL A KID A GLUTEN-FREE SISSY. WHICHEVER MOM LAUGHS THAT'S YOUR NEW FRIEND.
IF NO ONE LAUGHS, THROW A PEANUT AT HER KID, WHICHEVER MOM LAUGHS, THAT'S YOUR TRUE BESTIE.
PEANUTS
IF NO ONE LAUGHS, ONE LESS KID ON THE PLAYGROUND.
PEANUTS

PARENTING STYLES

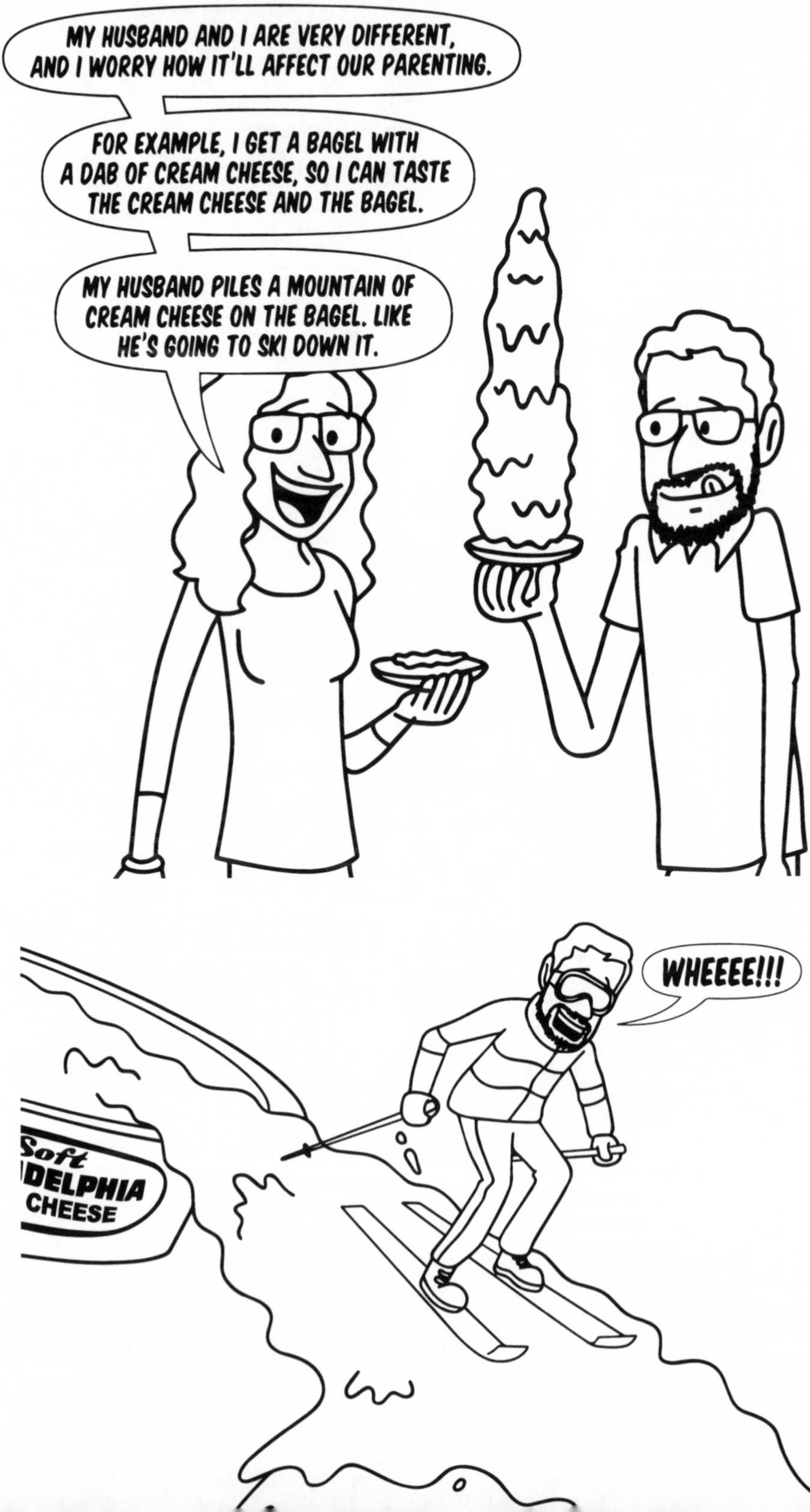
MY HUSBAND AND I ARE VERY DIFFERENT, AND I WORRY HOW IT'LL AFFECT OUR PARENTING.
FOR EXAMPLE, I GET A BAGEL WITH A DAB OF CREAM CHEESE, SO I CAN TASTE THE CREAM CHEESE AND THE BAGEL.
MY HUSBAND PILES A MOUNTAIN OF CREAM CHEESE ON THE BAGEL. LIKE HE'S GOING TO SKI DOWN IT.
WHEEEE!!!
Soft
DELPHIA
CHEESE

IF WE DISAGREE ON BAGEL TECHNIQUE, IMAGINE THE MORE SERIOUS ISSUES. FOR EXAMPLE, WHEN OUR DAUGHTER GRADUATES HIGH SCHOOL, MY ADVICE WILL BE MUCH MORE SENSIBLE THAN MY HUSBAND'S...

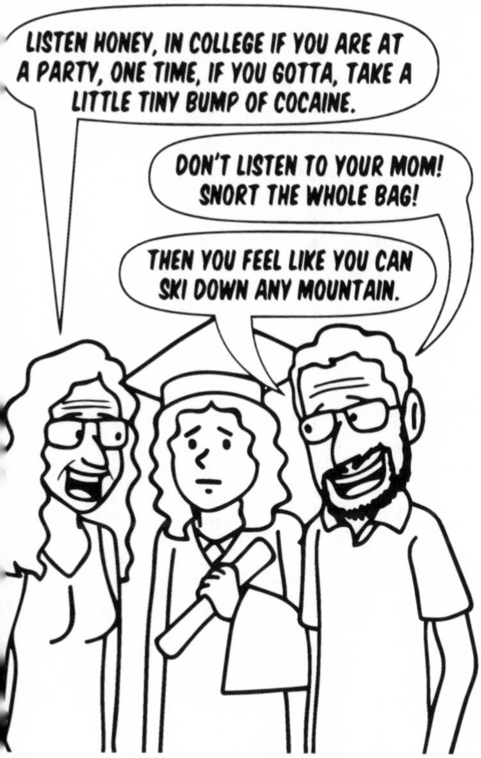
LISTEN HONEY, IN COLLEGE IF YOU ARE AT A PARTY, ONE TIME, IF YOU GOTTA, TAKE A LITTLE TINY BUMP OF COCAINE.
DON'T LISTEN TO YOUR MOM! SNORT THE WHOLE BAG!
THEN YOU FEEL LIKE YOU CAN SKI DOWN ANY MOUNTAIN.

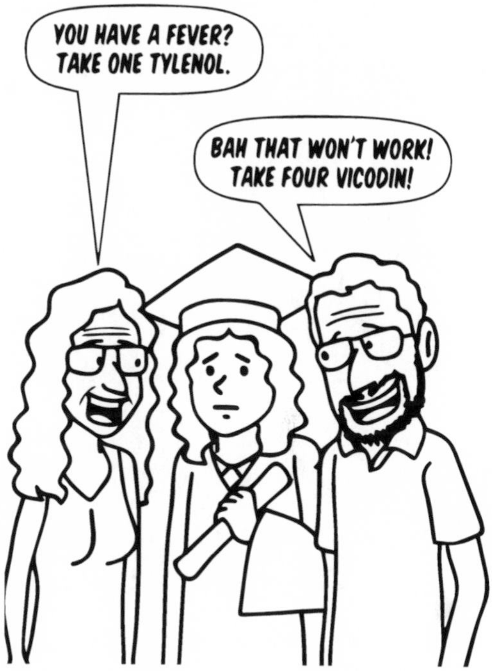
YOU HAVE A FEVER? TAKE ONE TYLENOL.
BAH THAT WON'T WORK! TAKE FOUR VICODIN!

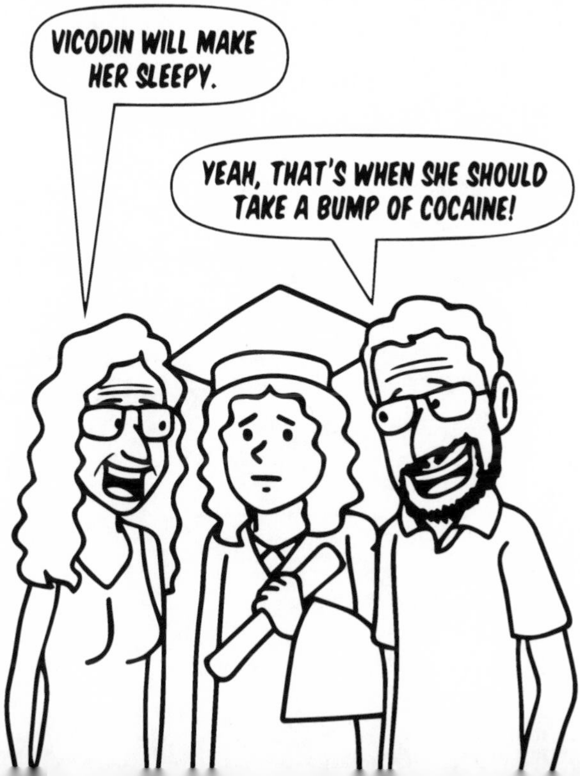
VICODIN WILL MAKE HER SLEEPY.
YEAH, THAT'S WHEN SHE SHOULD TAKE A BUMP OF COCAINE!

SO HARD

PEOPLE SAY PARENTING IS SO HARD. BUT PARENTING IS NOT HARD, IT'S BORING.

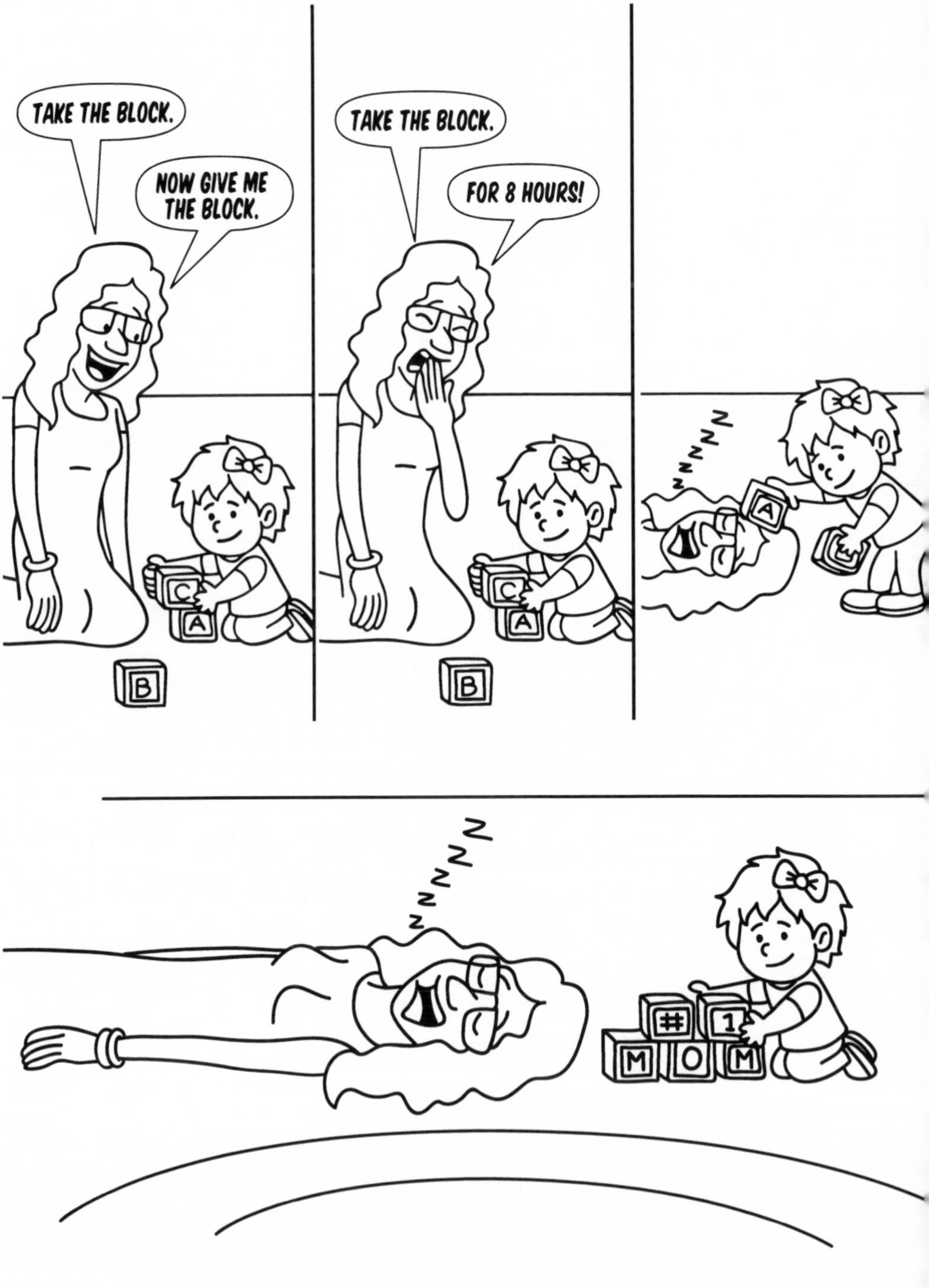

TAKE THE BLOCK.
NOW GIVE ME THE BLOCK.
C
A
B
TAKE THE BLOCK.
FOR 8 HOURS!
C
A
B
ZZZZZ
A
ZZZZZ
#1
MOM

OVERPROTECTIVE

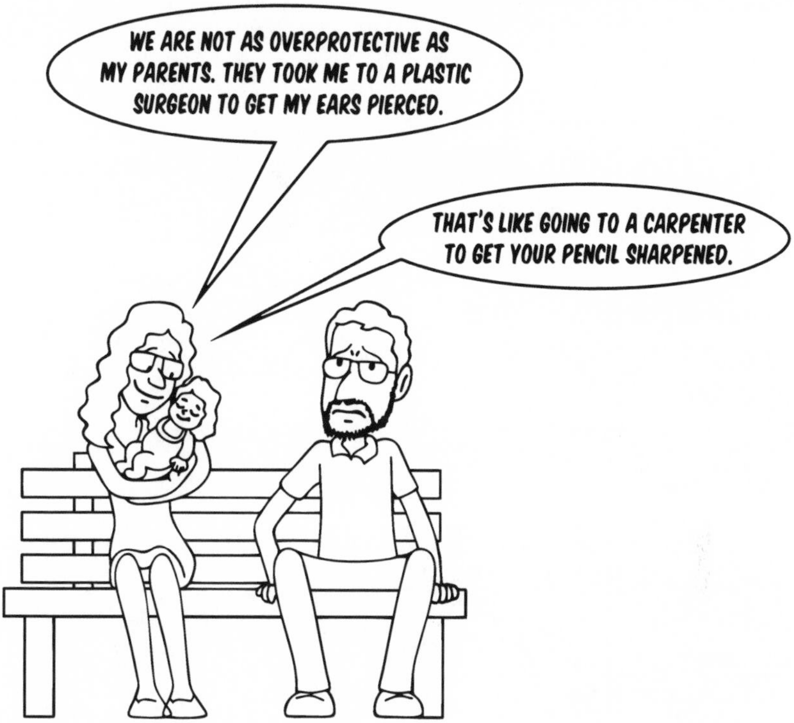
WE ARE NOT AS OVERPROTECTIVE AS MY PARENTS. THEY TOOK ME TO A PLASTIC SURGEON TO GET MY EARS PIERCED.
THAT'S LIKE GOING TO A CARPENTER TO GET YOUR PENCIL SHARPENED.

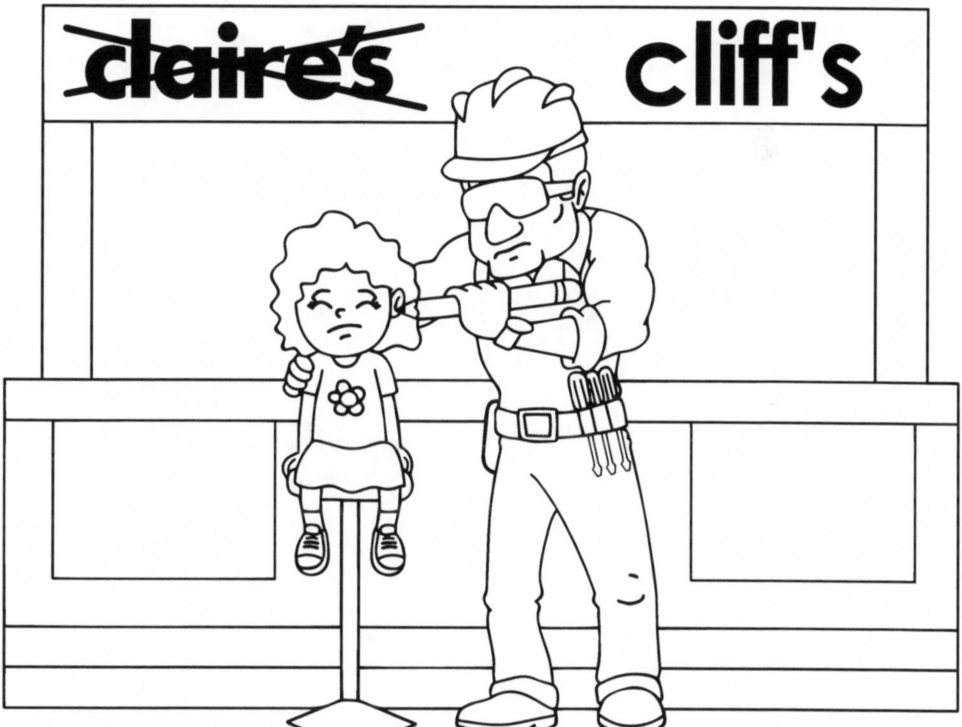
~~claire's~~
cliff's

EDIBLE ARRANGEMENTS

WHEN WE GOT BACK FROM THE HOSPITAL, WE GOT A FRUIT BASKET...

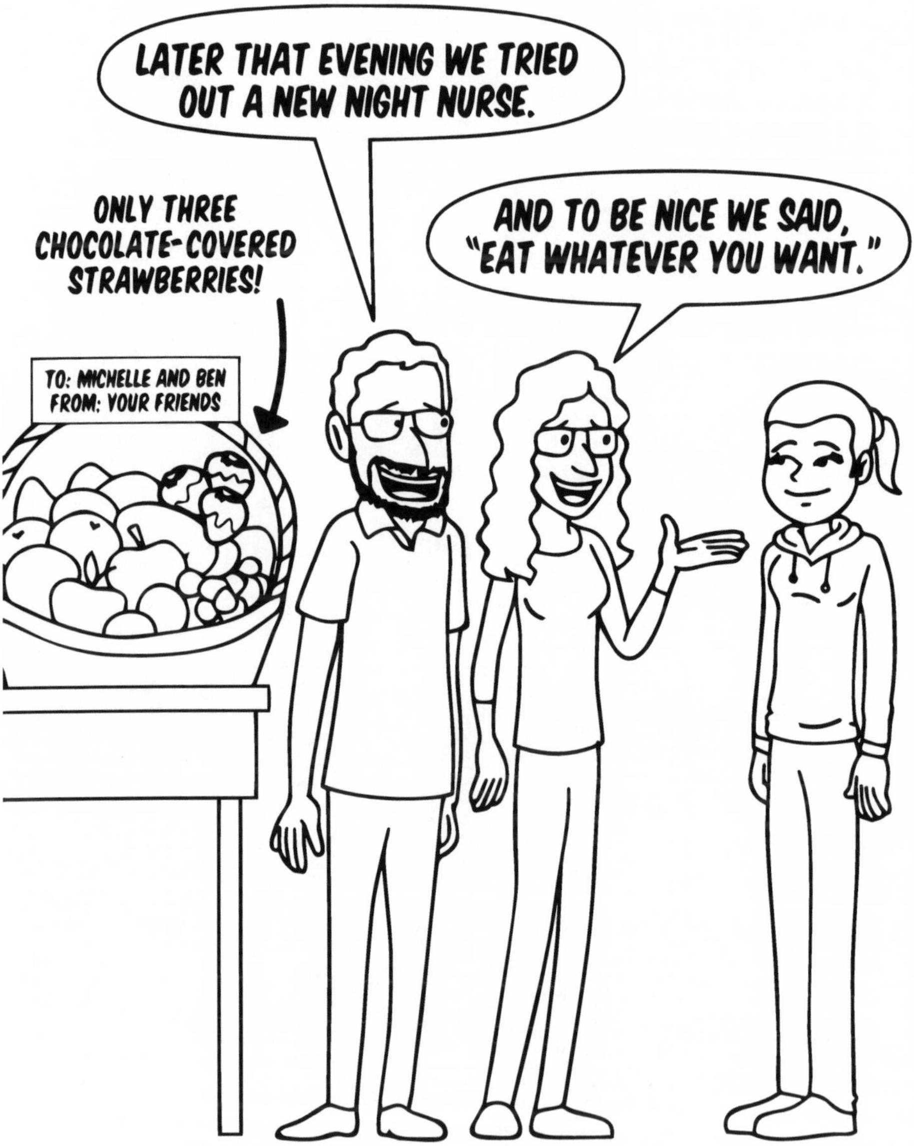
LATER THAT EVENING WE TRIED OUT A NEW NIGHT NURSE.
AND TO BE NICE WE SAID, "EAT WHATEVER YOU WANT."
ONLY THREE CHOCOLATE-COVERED STRAWBERRIES!
TO: MICHELLE AND BEN
FROM: YOUR FRIENDS

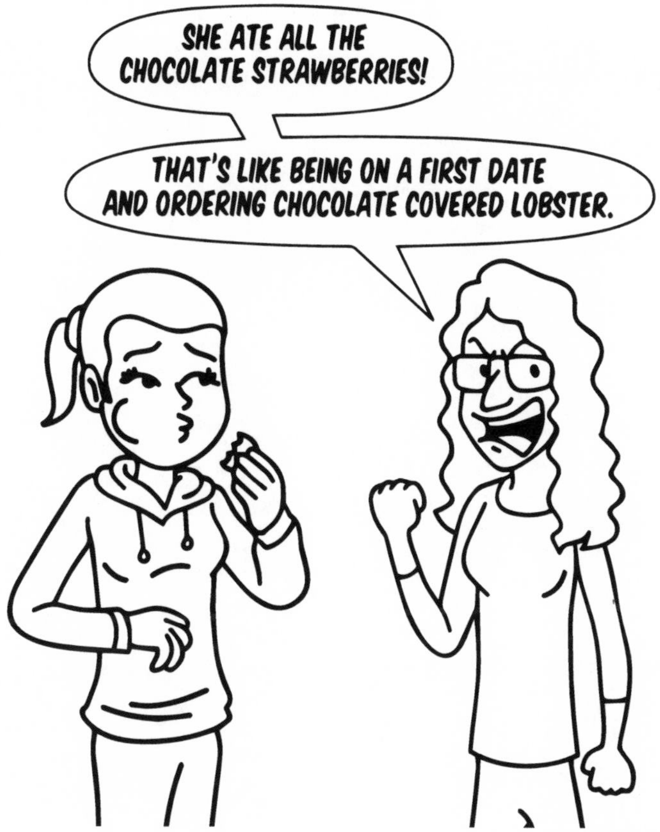
SHE ATE ALL THE CHOCOLATE STRAWBERRIES!
THAT'S LIKE BEING ON A FIRST DATE AND ORDERING CHOCOLATE COVERED LOBSTER.

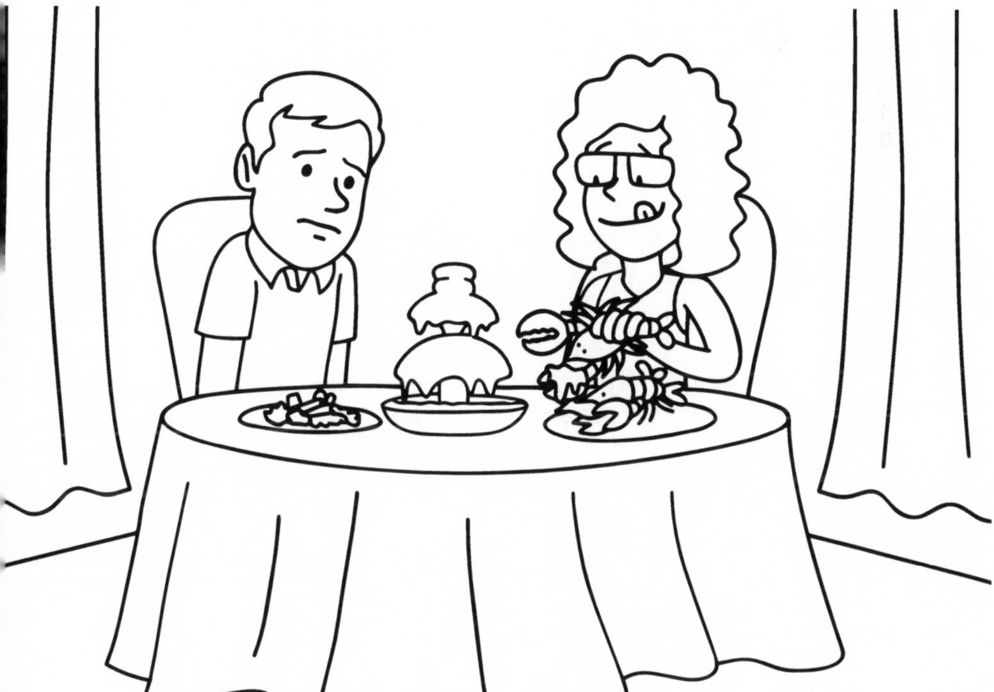

BABY GYM

I RECENTLY LEARNED THAT MY GYM OFFERS FREE DAYCARE, EVERY DAY FOR THREE HOURS.

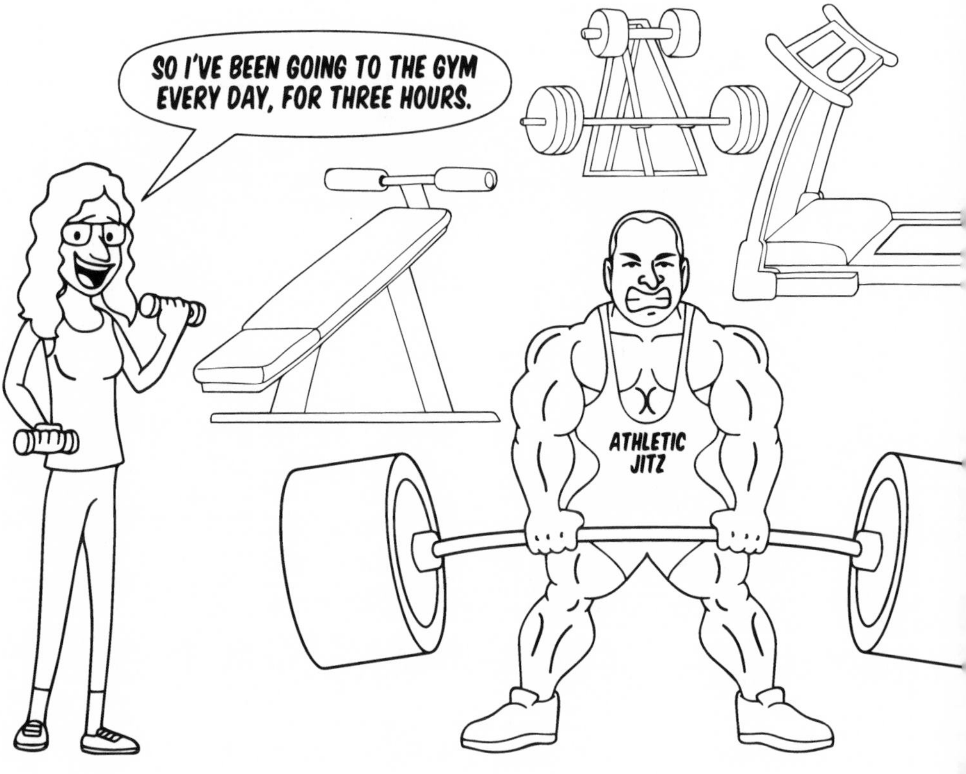
SO I'VE BEEN GOING TO THE GYM EVERY DAY, FOR THREE HOURS.
ATHLETIC JITZ

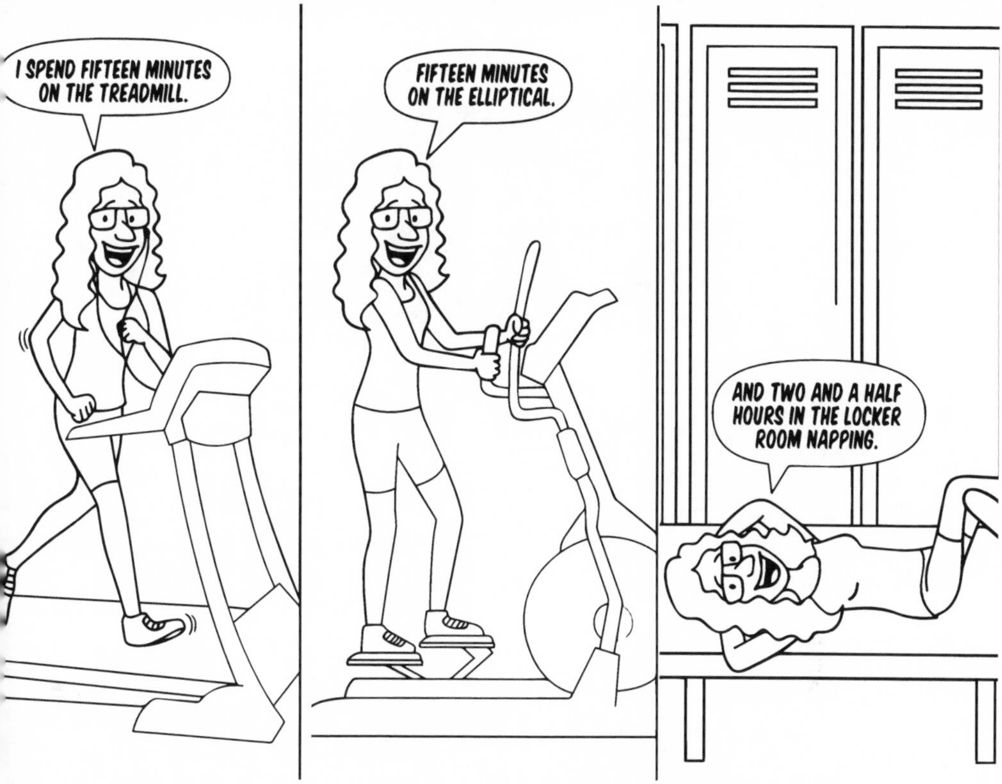
I SPEND FIFTEEN MINUTES ON THE TREADMILL.
FIFTEEN MINUTES ON THE ELLIPTICAL.
AND TWO AND A HALF HOURS IN THE LOCKER ROOM NAPPING.

MY BABY'S AT THE GYM SO OFTEN, SHE CAN BENCH PRESS ANOTHER BABY.

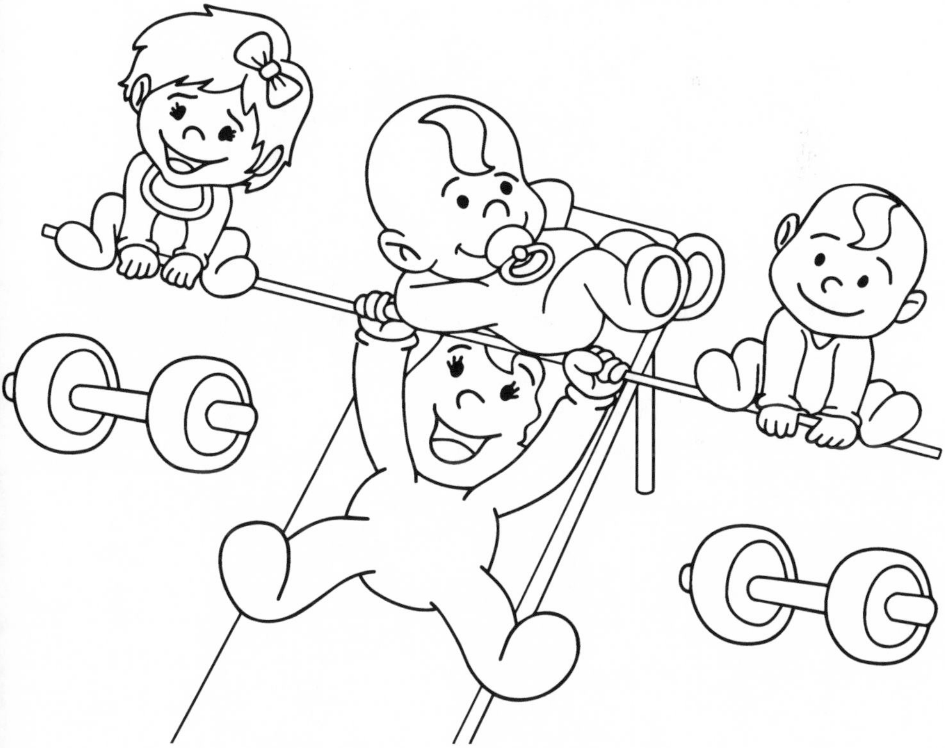

BEN'S BABY JOKES

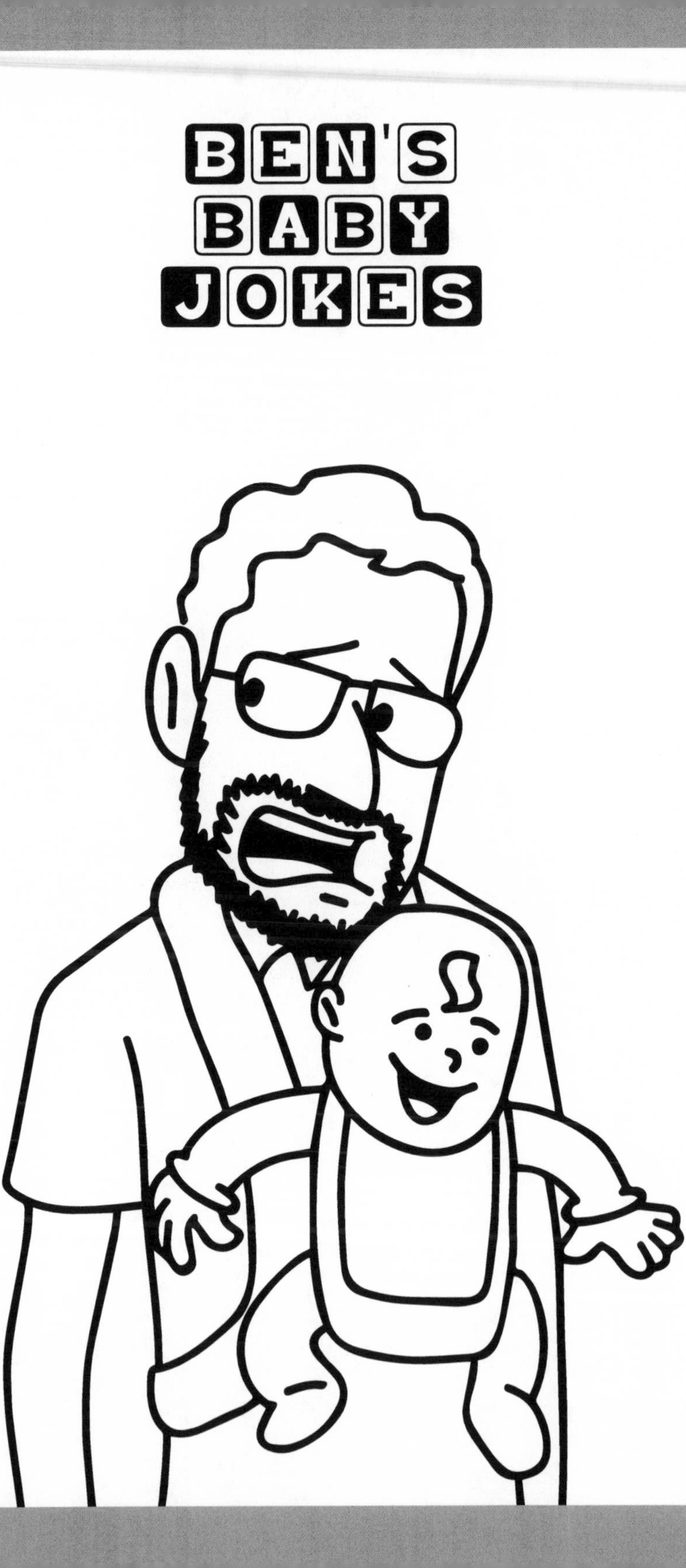

5 DAYS AFTER BIRTH

AFTER MY WIFE GAVE BIRTH, I STAYED HOME FOR FIVE DAYS NOT DOING COMEDY. BUT THEN...

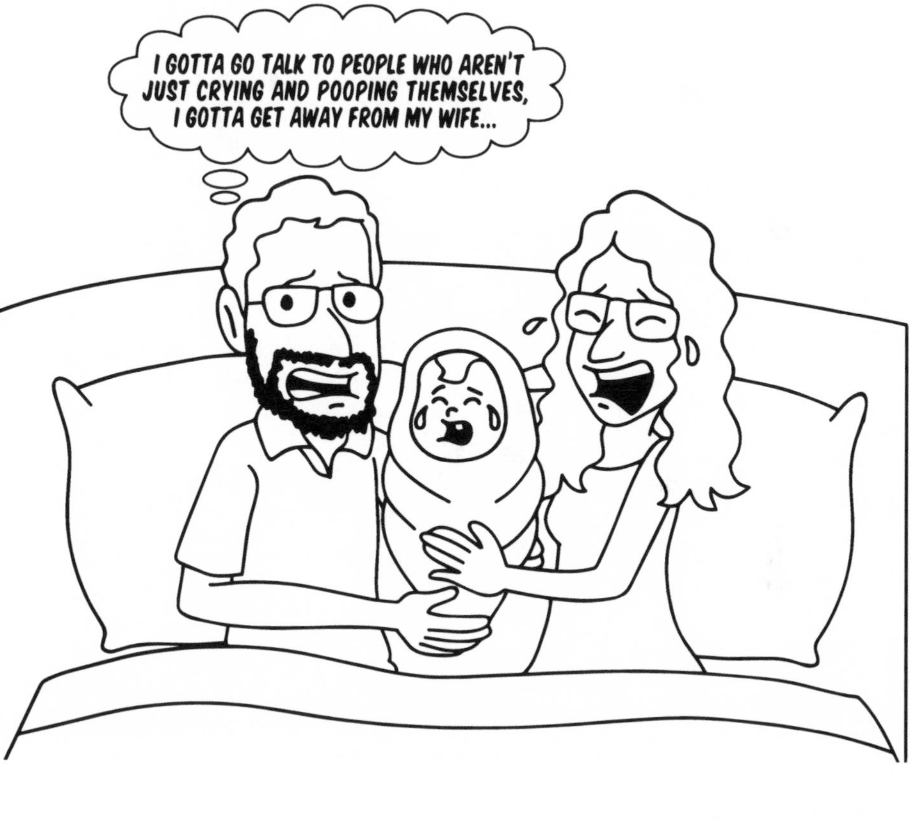
I GOTTA GO TALK TO PEOPLE WHO AREN'T JUST CRYING AND POOPING THEMSELVES, I GOTTA GET AWAY FROM MY WIFE...

ADJUSTMENT

HAVING A BABY IS AN ADJUSTMENT. BACK WHEN I WAS SINGLE AND I'D HEAR SOMEONE'S KID CRY...

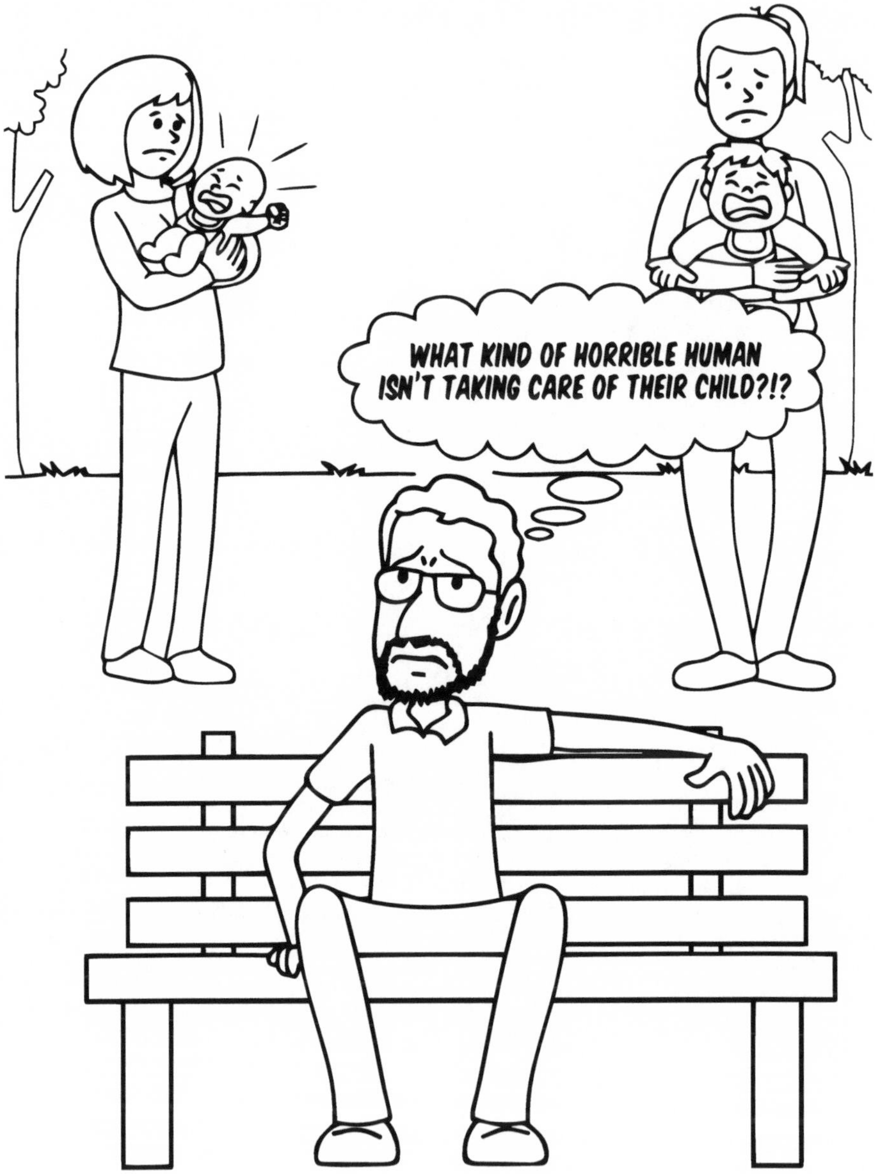

WHAT KIND OF HORRIBLE HUMAN ISN'T TAKING CARE OF THEIR CHILD?!?

NOW THAT I'M A DAD, WHEN I HEAR SOMEONE'S KID CRY...

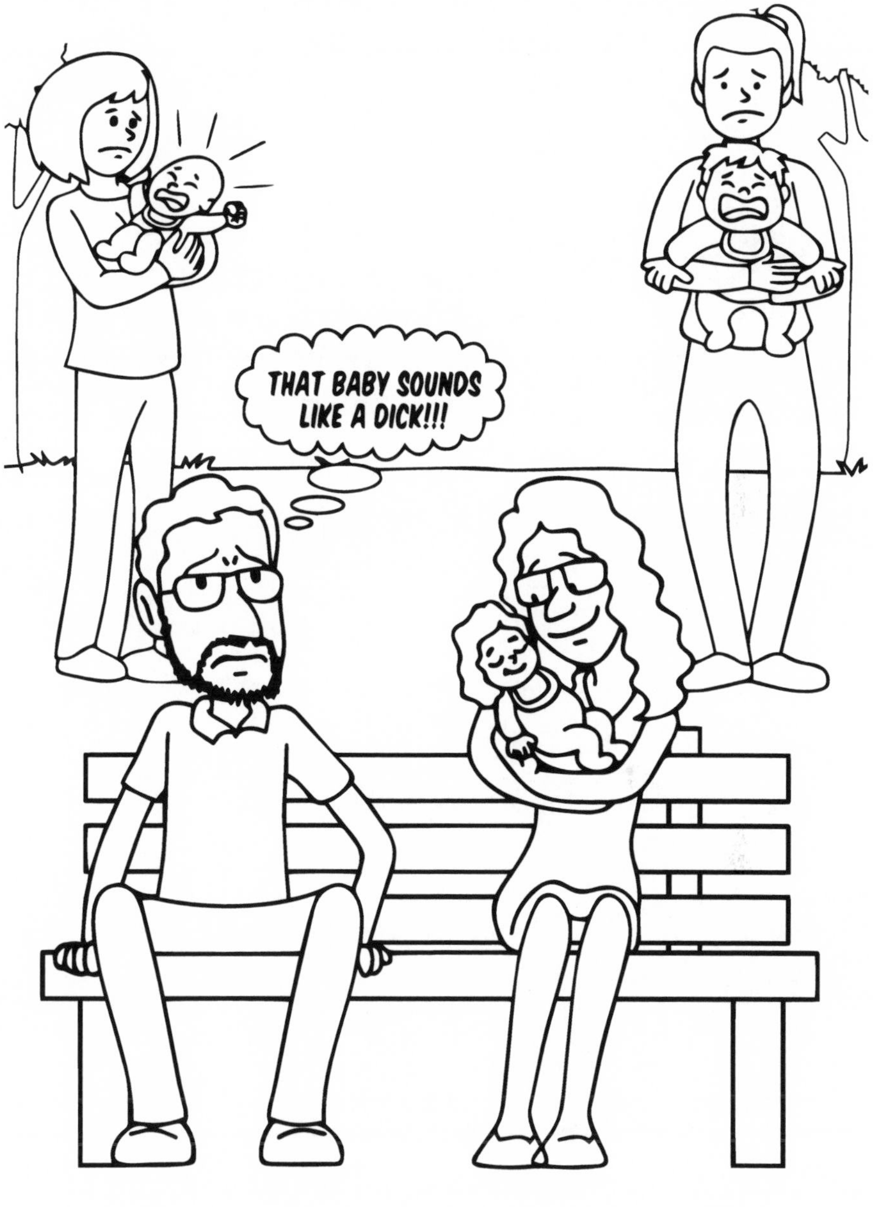
THAT BABY SOUNDS LIKE A DICK!!!

NO PERSPECTIVE

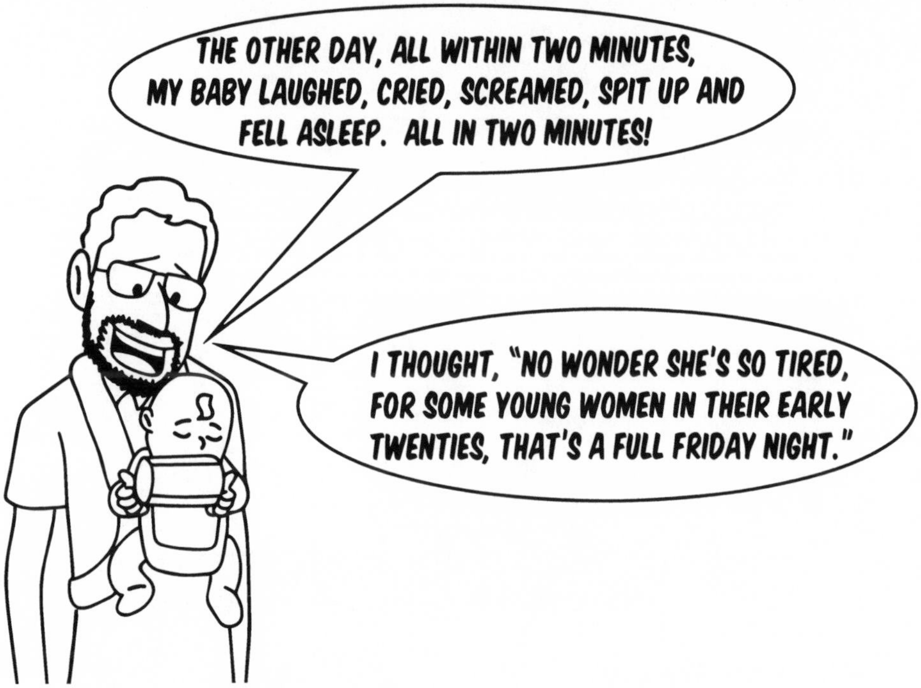
THE OTHER DAY, ALL WITHIN TWO MINUTES, MY BABY LAUGHED, CRIED, SCREAMED, SPIT UP AND FELL ASLEEP. ALL IN TWO MINUTES!
I THOUGHT, "NO WONDER SHE'S SO TIRED, FOR SOME YOUNG WOMEN IN THEIR EARLY TWENTIES, THAT'S A FULL FRIDAY NIGHT."

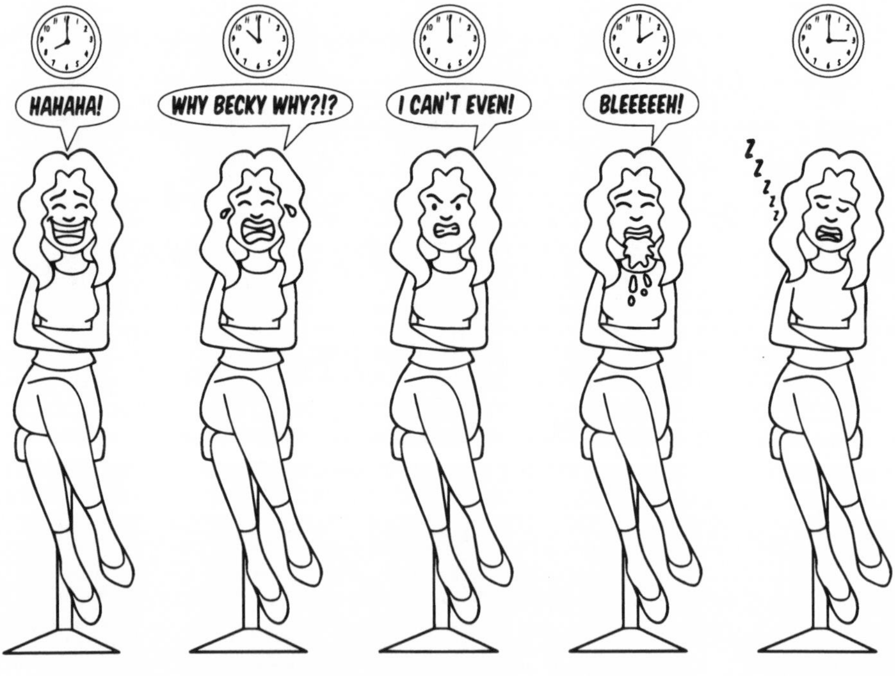
HAHAHA!
WHY BECKY WHY?!?
I CAN'T EVEN!
BLEEEEEH!
ZZZZZ

THE CALM BABY SECRET

MY SECRET TO A CALM BABY IS, WHENEVER SHE GETS UPSET, I JUST THROW HER UP AND DOWN THREE TIMES AND SHE'S ALL BETTER. AND I WISH YOU COULD DO THAT WITH ADULTS, RIGHT?

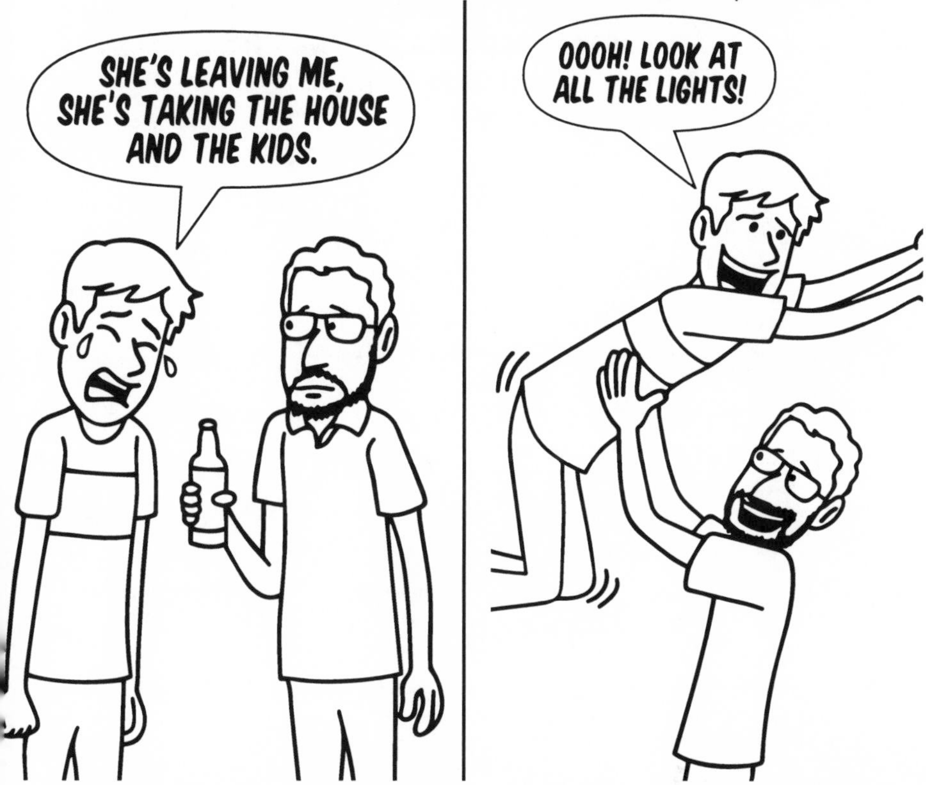
SHE'S LEAVING ME, SHE'S TAKING THE HOUSE AND THE KIDS.
OOOH! LOOK AT ALL THE LIGHTS!

ALTHOUGH IF THIS WAS TRUE, THERAPISTS WOULD GO OUT OF BUSINESS, AND FAT PEOPLE WOULD BE INCONSOLABLE...

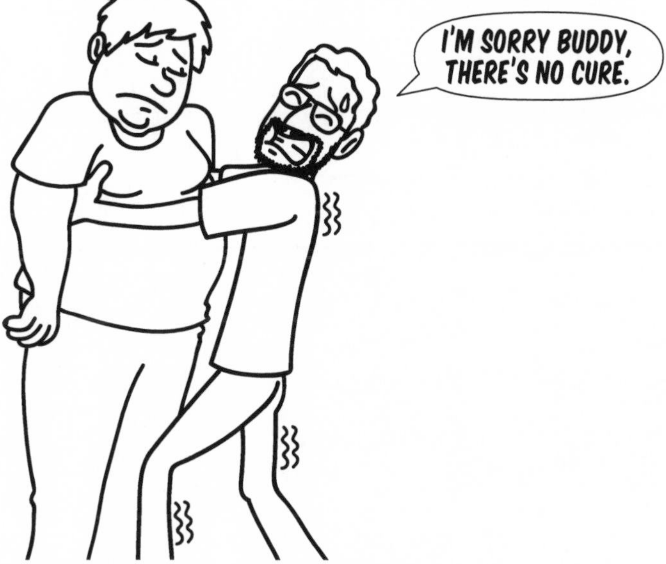
I'M SORRY BUDDY, THERE'S NO CURE.

THE UPSIDE ABOUT NO SLEEP

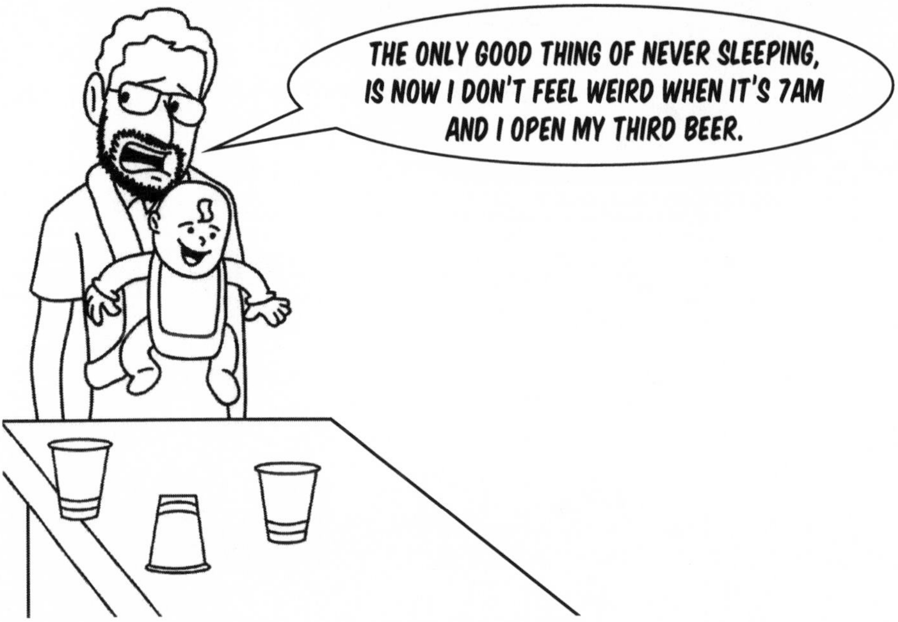
THE ONLY GOOD THING OF NEVER SLEEPING, IS NOW I DON'T FEEL WEIRD WHEN IT'S 7AM AND I OPEN MY THIRD BEER.

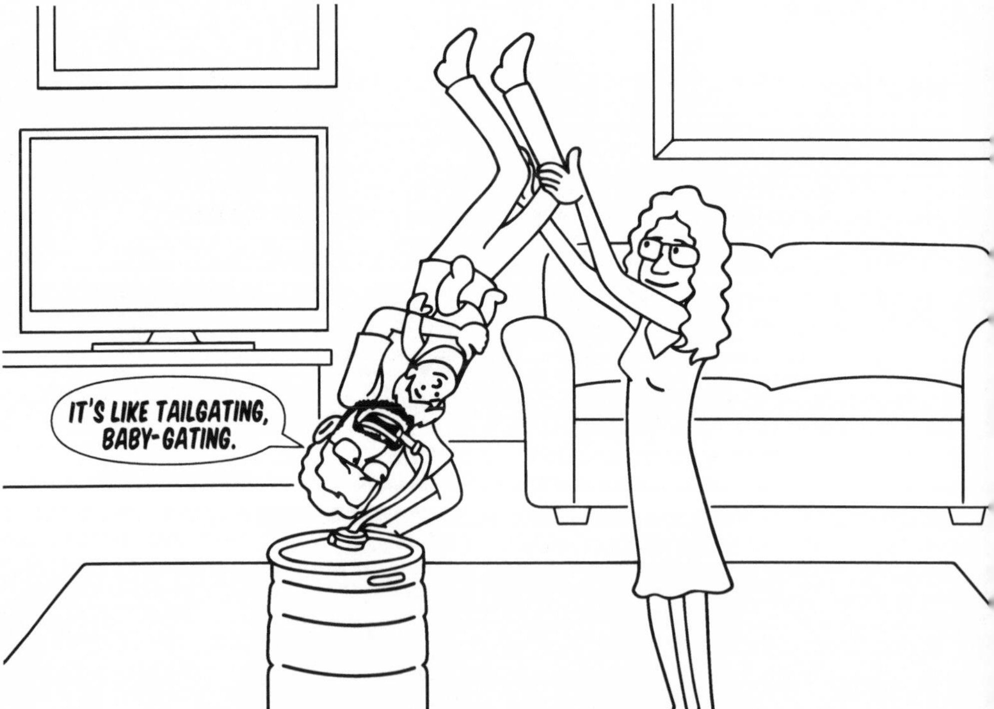
IT'S LIKE TAILGATING, BABY-GATING.

BEN'S LIST

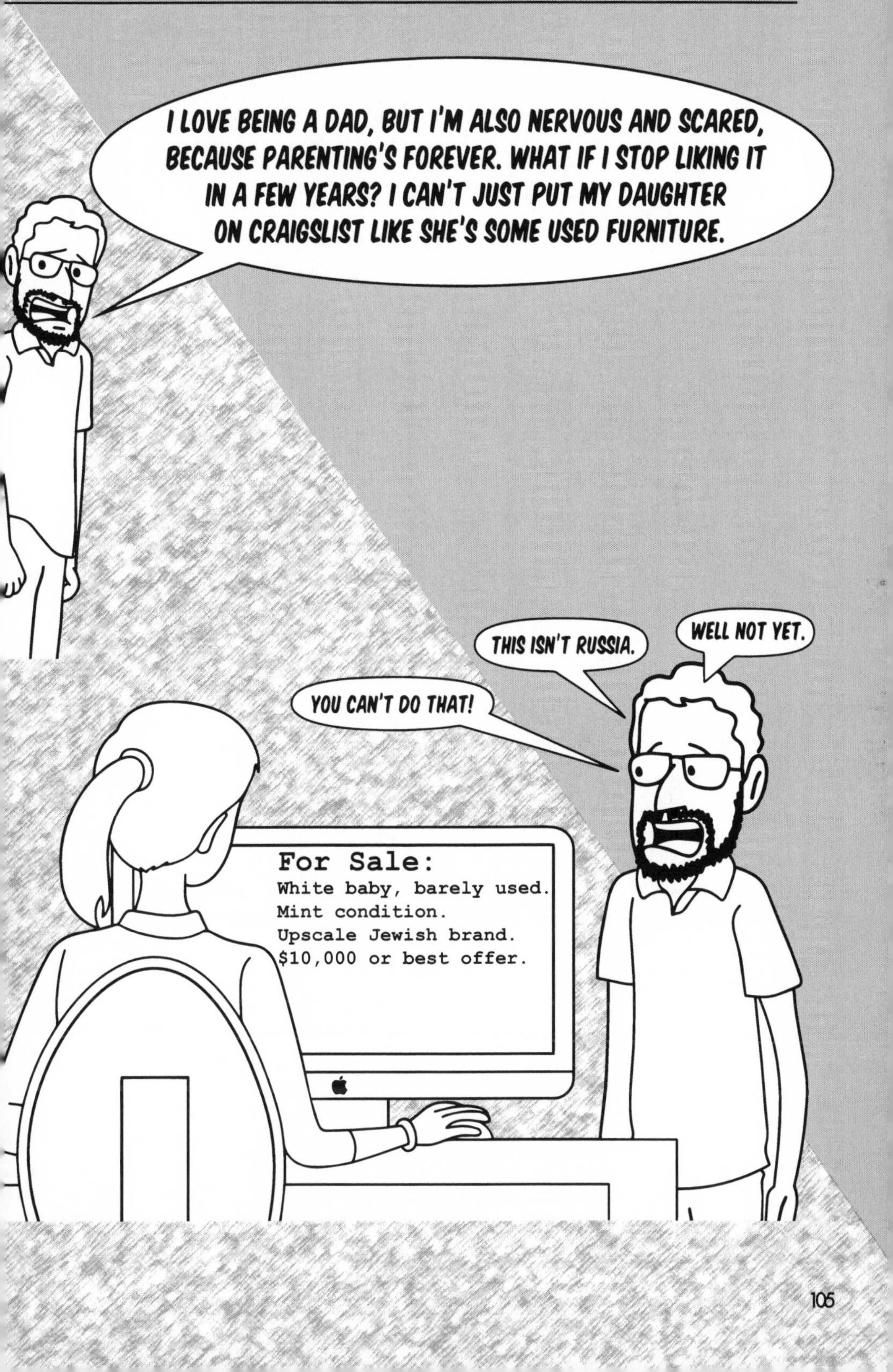
I LOVE BEING A DAD, BUT I'M ALSO NERVOUS AND SCARED, BECAUSE PARENTING'S FOREVER. WHAT IF I STOP LIKING IT IN A FEW YEARS? I CAN'T JUST PUT MY DAUGHTER ON CRAIGSLIST LIKE SHE'S SOME USED FURNITURE.
For Sale:
White baby, barely used.
Mint condition.
Upscale Jewish brand.
$10,000 or best offer.
YOU CAN'T DO THAT!
THIS ISN'T RUSSIA.
WELL NOT YET.

ANCHOR BABY

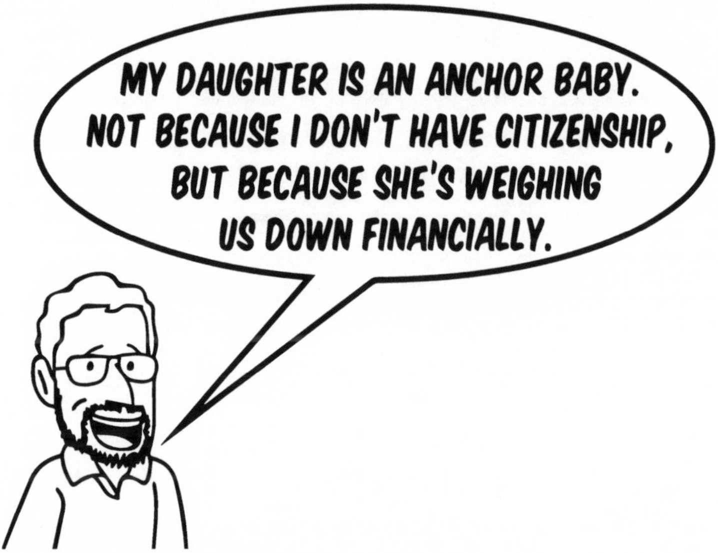
MY DAUGHTER IS AN ANCHOR BABY. NOT BECAUSE I DON'T HAVE CITIZENSHIP, BUT BECAUSE SHE'S WEIGHING US DOWN FINANCIALLY.

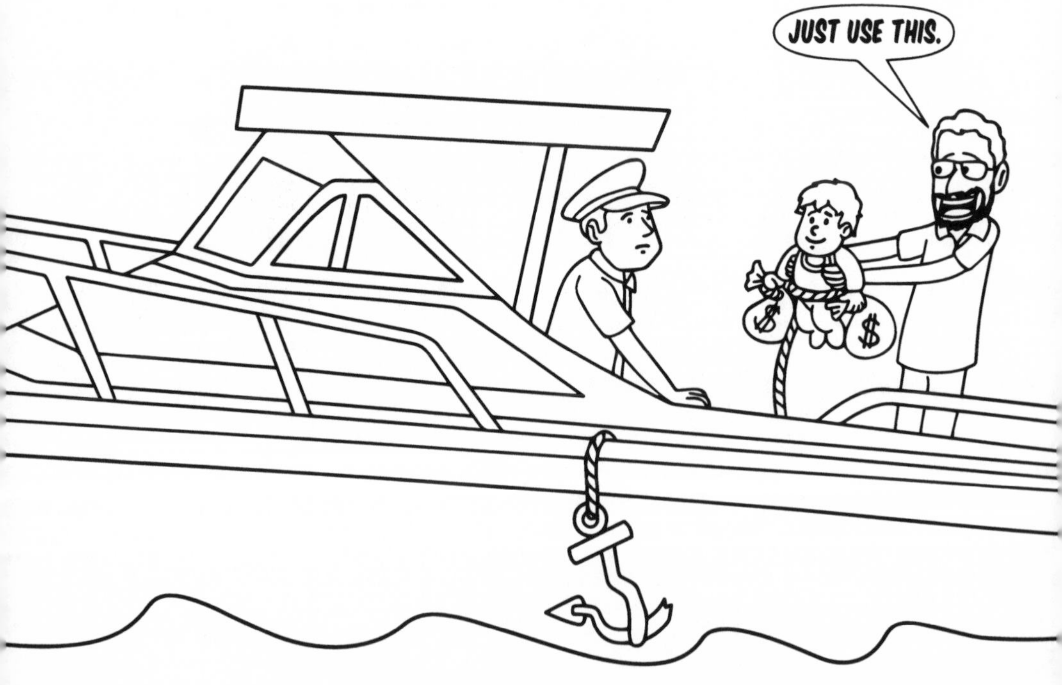
JUST USE THIS.
$
$

CAR WASH

I CAN'T AFFORD TO TAKE MY DAUGHTER TO DISNEY LAND,
SO WHAT I DO INSTEAD, I PUT HER THROUGH THE CAR WASH...

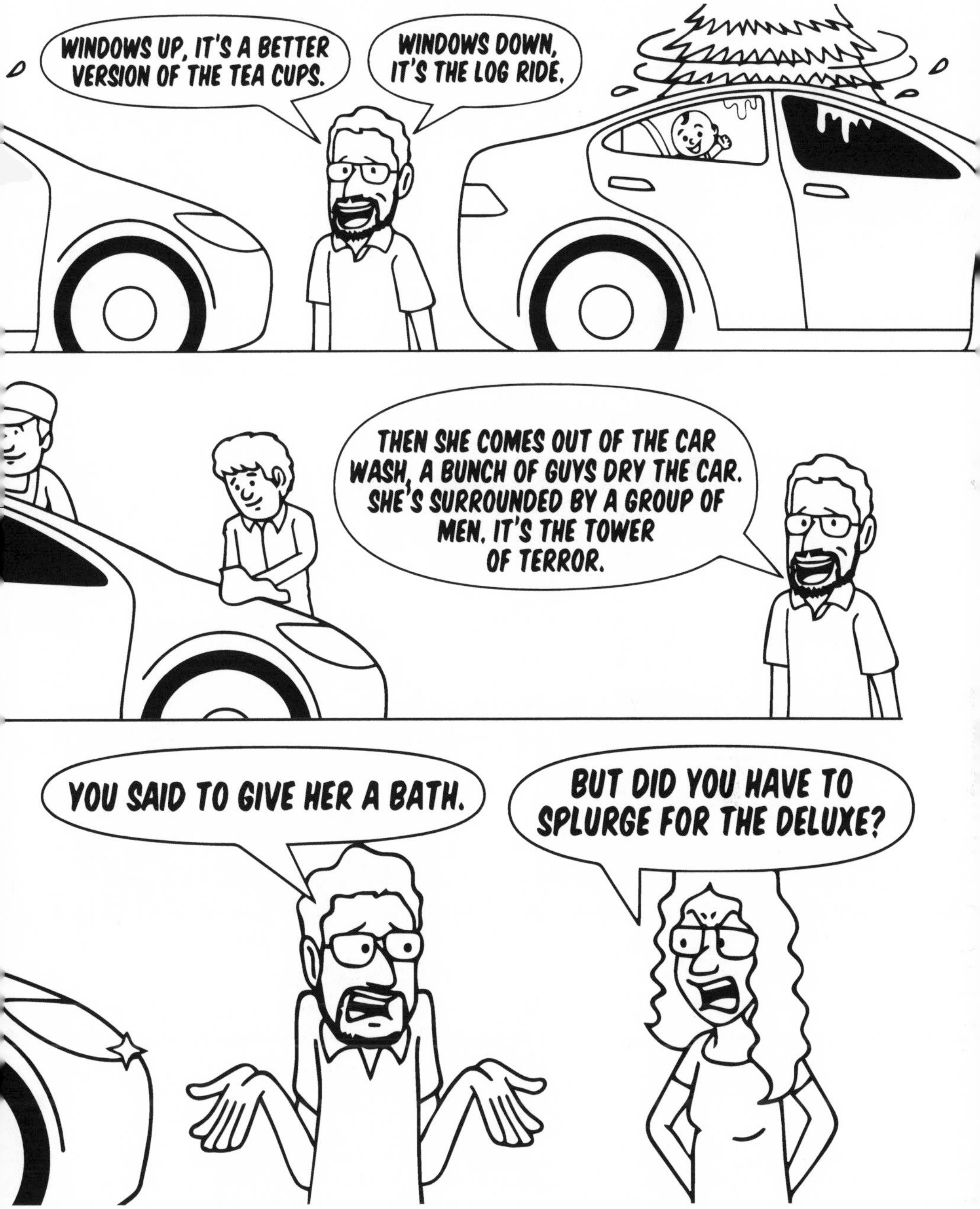

WINDOWS UP, IT'S A BETTER VERSION OF THE TEA CUPS.
WINDOWS DOWN, IT'S THE LOG RIDE.
THEN SHE COMES OUT OF THE CAR WASH, A BUNCH OF GUYS DRY THE CAR. SHE'S SURROUNDED BY A GROUP OF MEN, IT'S THE TOWER OF TERROR.
YOU SAID TO GIVE HER A BATH.
BUT DID YOU HAVE TO SPLURGE FOR THE DELUXE?

SCREEN TIME

MY PHONE ADDICTION IS SO BAD, HERE'S MY DAY...

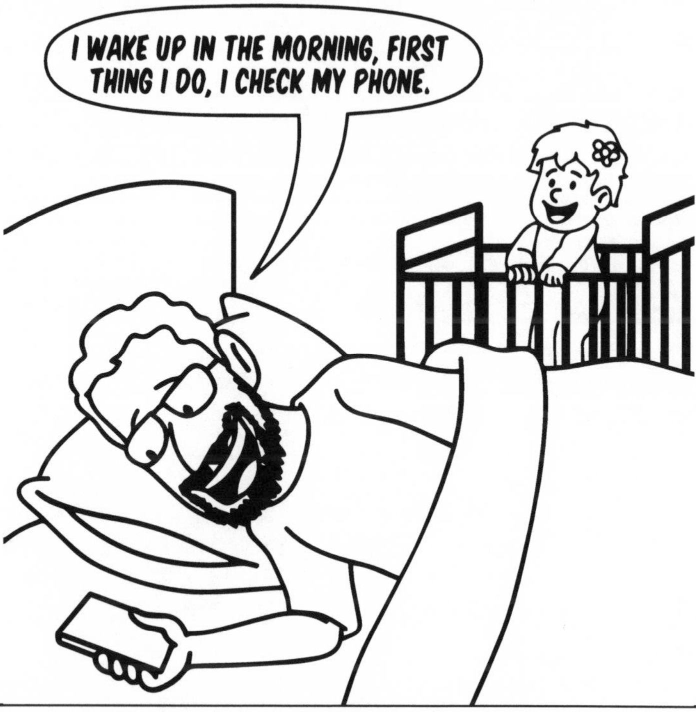
I WAKE UP IN THE MORNING, FIRST THING I DO, I CHECK MY PHONE.

THEN AN HOUR LATER, I CHECK ON MY BABY.

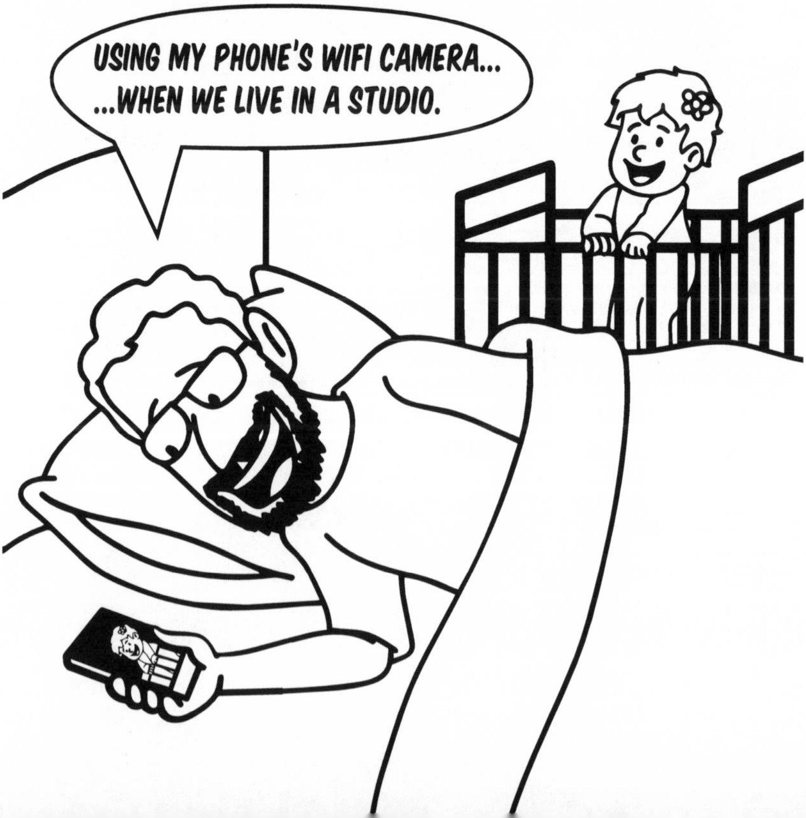
USING MY PHONE'S WIFI CAMERA...
...WHEN WE LIVE IN A STUDIO.

IF I REALLY WANTED TO USE MY PHONE LESS,
I'D MOVE SOME PLACE THAT LIMITS DATA, LIKE...

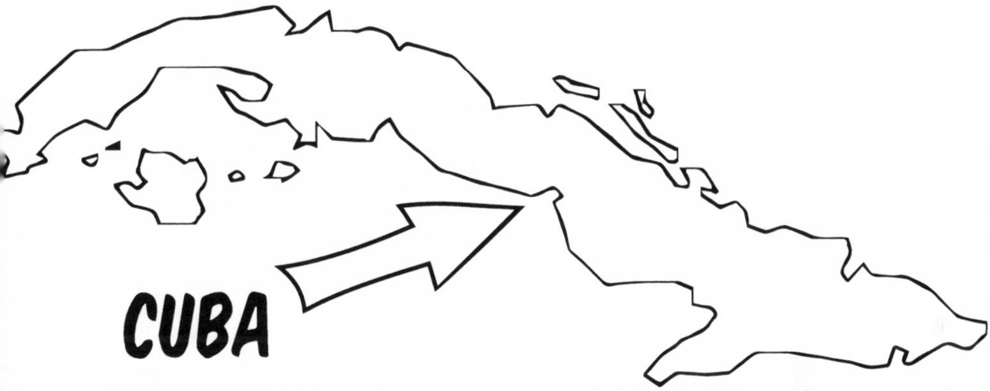
CUBA

OR...

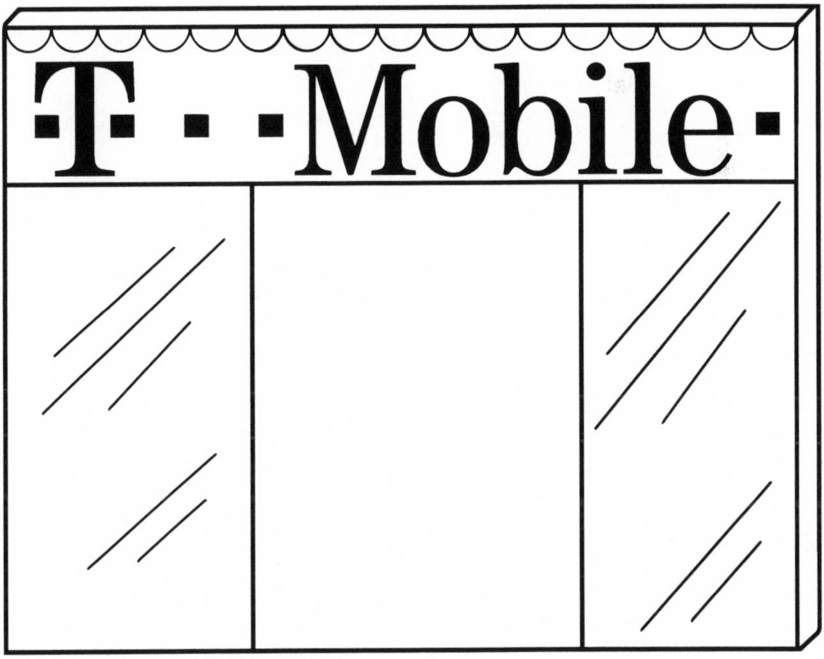
T · · Mobile ·

LAST WEEK, I'M WALKING DOWN THE STREET,
I SEE A GUY IN A PHONE BOOTH...

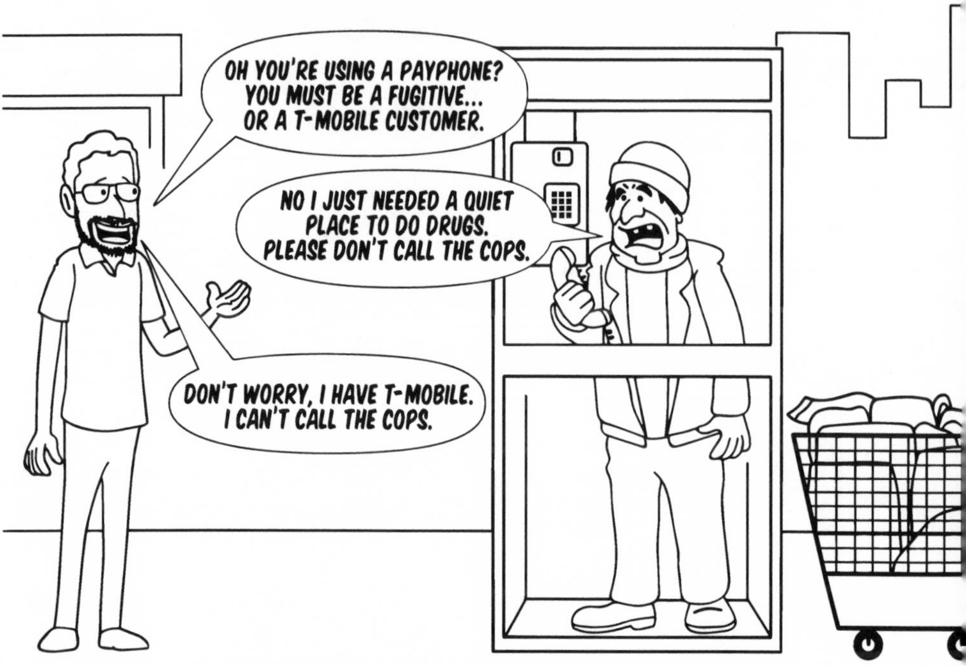
OH YOU'RE USING A PAYPHONE? YOU MUST BE A FUGITIVE... OR A T-MOBILE CUSTOMER.
NO I JUST NEEDED A QUIET PLACE TO DO DRUGS. PLEASE DON'T CALL THE COPS.
DON'T WORRY, I HAVE T-MOBILE. I CAN'T CALL THE COPS.

MY BABY'S ADDICTED TO THE CELLPHONE TOO.
SHE SAY'S LITTLE WORDS LIKE "HI" AND "BYE."
AND SHE THINKS ANY RECTANGULAR OBJECT IS A PHONE.

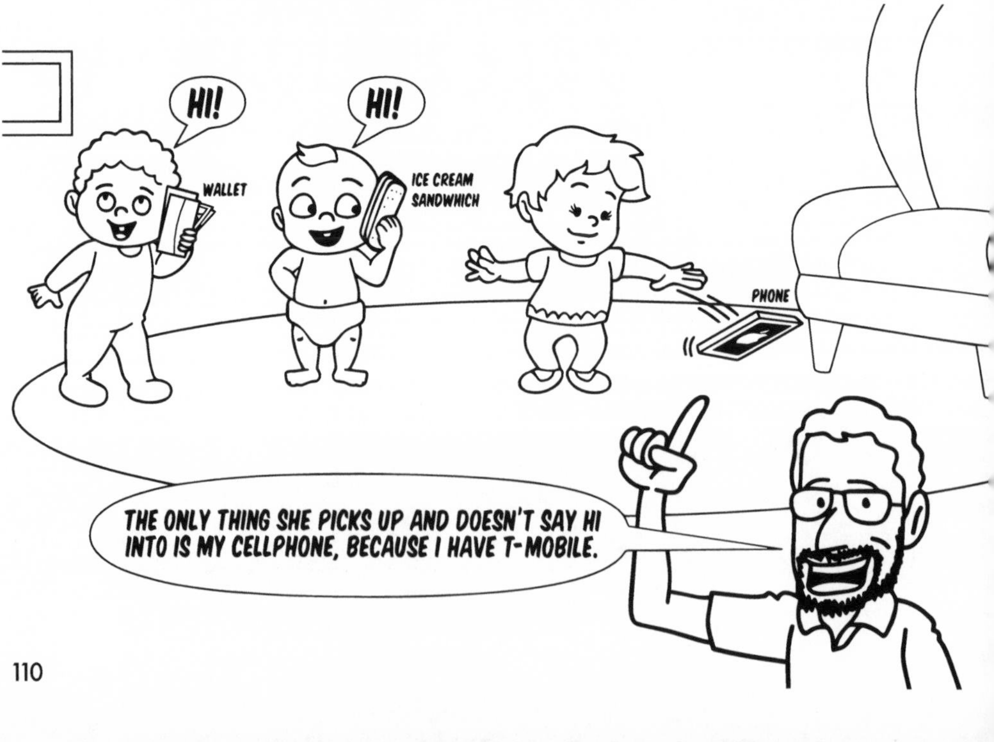
HI!
WALLET
HI!
ICE CREAM SANDWHICH
PHONE
THE ONLY THING SHE PICKS UP AND DOESN'T SAY HI INTO IS MY CELLPHONE, BECAUSE I HAVE T-MOBILE.

I'M CONCERNED THAT I'M SO ADDICTED TO MY CELL PHONE, I'M GONNA LEAVE MY BABY SOMEWHERE SO...

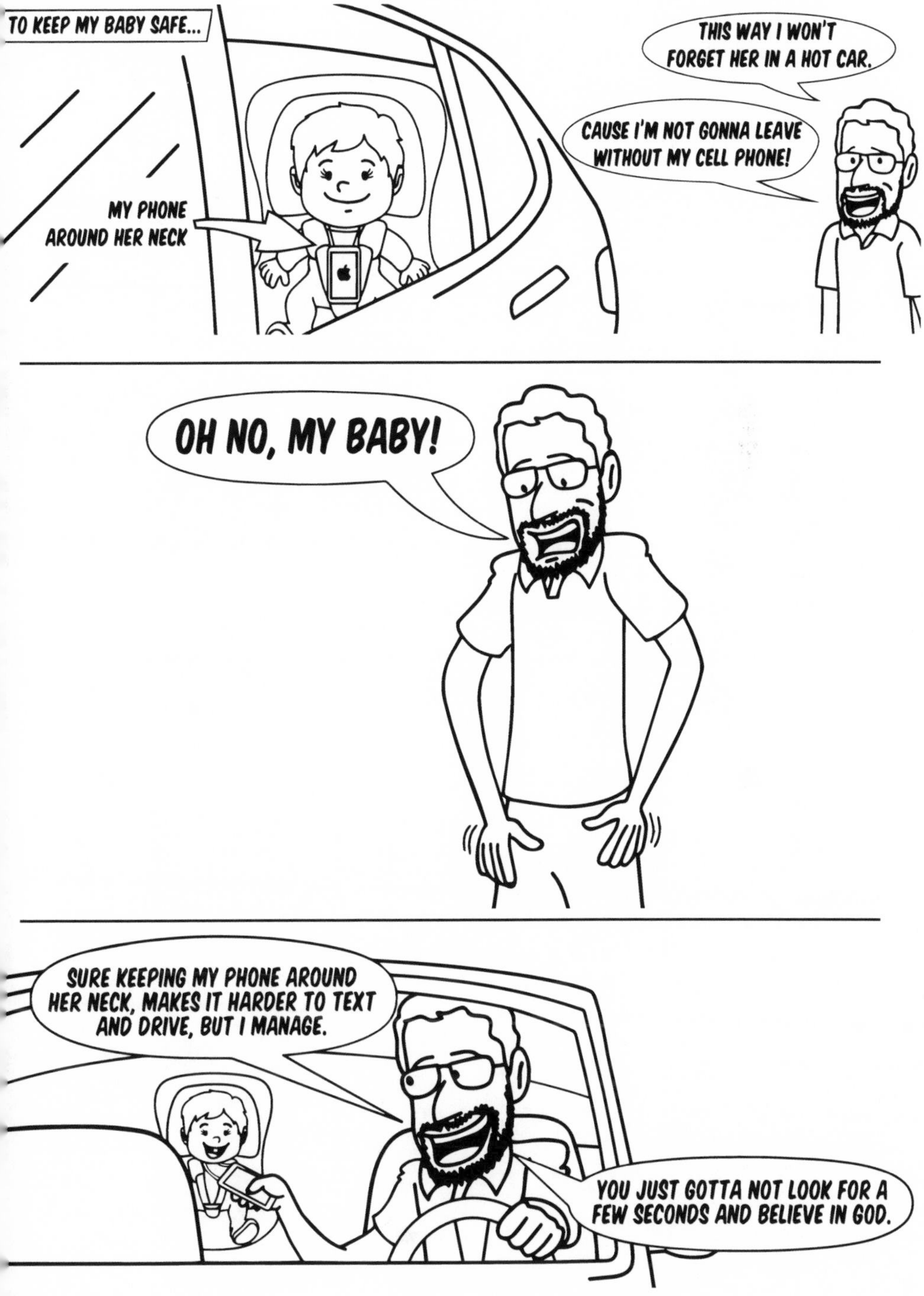
TO KEEP MY BABY SAFE...
THIS WAY I WON'T FORGET HER IN A HOT CAR.
CAUSE I'M NOT GONNA LEAVE WITHOUT MY CELL PHONE!
MY PHONE AROUND HER NECK
OH NO, MY BABY!
SURE KEEPING MY PHONE AROUND HER NECK, MAKES IT HARDER TO TEXT AND DRIVE, BUT I MANAGE.
YOU JUST GOTTA NOT LOOK FOR A FEW SECONDS AND BELIEVE IN GOD.

HAPPINESS

THIS IS TRUE: THEY'VE DONE STUDIES FINDING THE BIRTH OF YOUR FIRST CHILD DECREASES YOUR HAPPINESS MORE THAN UNEMPLOYMENT, DIVORCE OR DEATH OF A SPOUSE.

A GOOD DAY
HAPPY
SAD
BIRTH OF FIRST CHILD
DIVORCE
UNEMPLOYMENT
DEATH OF A SPOUSE

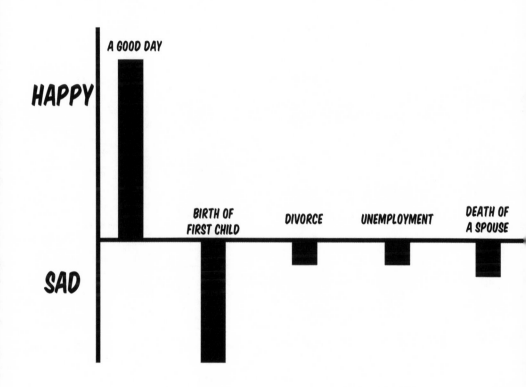

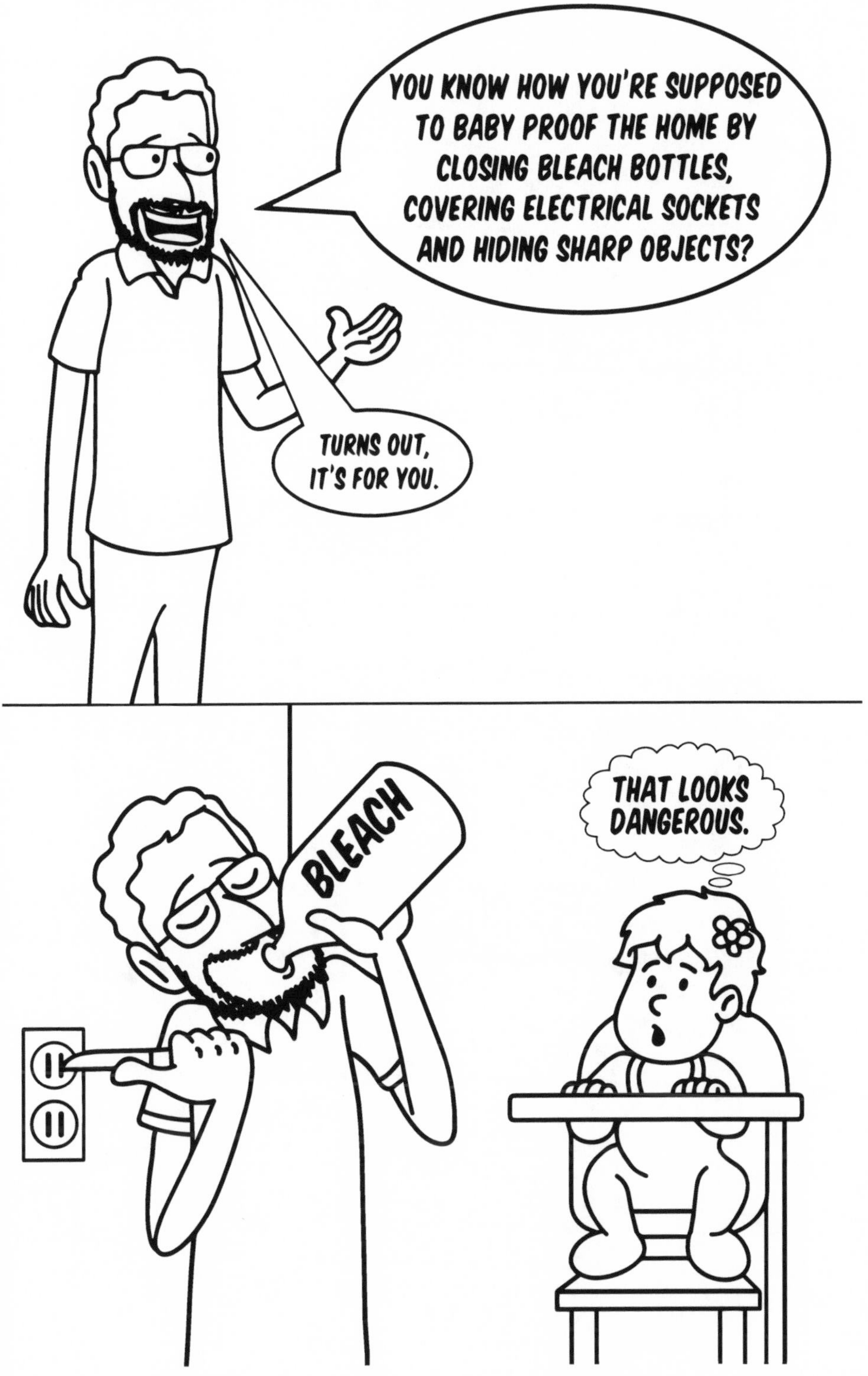
YOU KNOW HOW YOU'RE SUPPOSED TO BABY PROOF THE HOME BY CLOSING BLEACH BOTTLES, COVERING ELECTRICAL SOCKETS AND HIDING SHARP OBJECTS?
TURNS OUT, IT'S FOR YOU.
BLEACH
THAT LOOKS DANGEROUS.

DAD JOKES

I'VE ONLY BEEN A DAD FOR A FEW MONTHS AND I'M ALREADY MAKING TERRIBLE DAD JOKES.

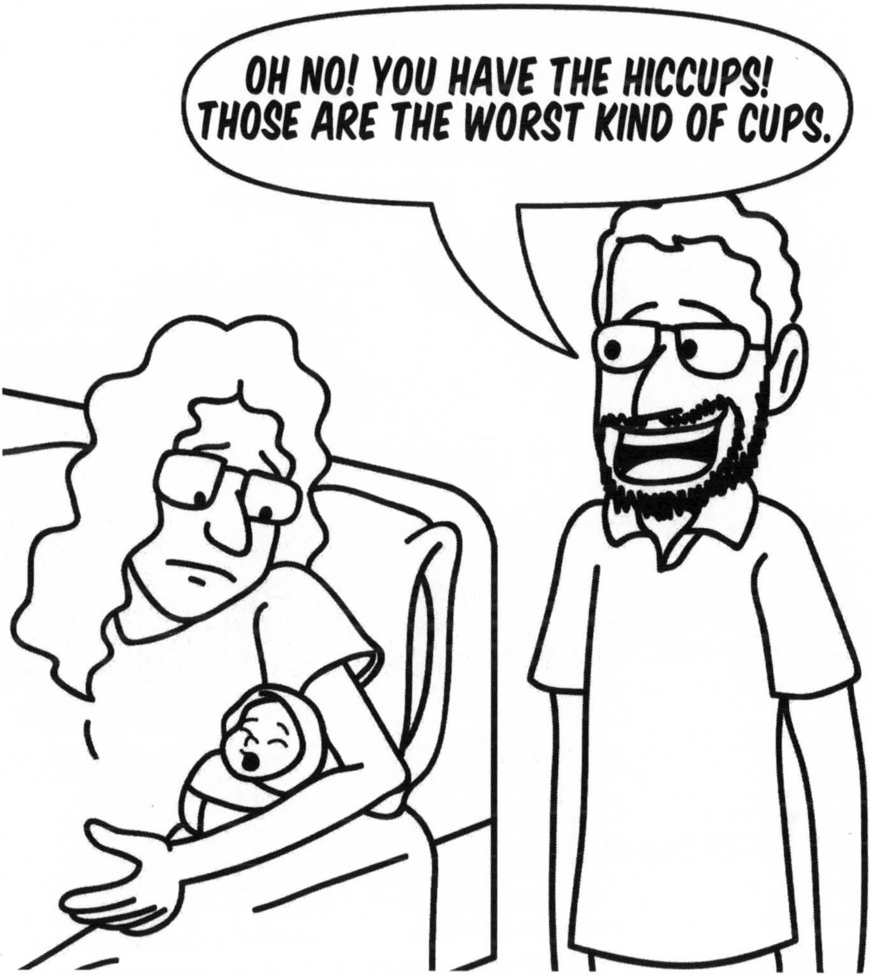
OH NO! YOU HAVE THE HICCUPS! THOSE ARE THE WORST KIND OF CUPS.

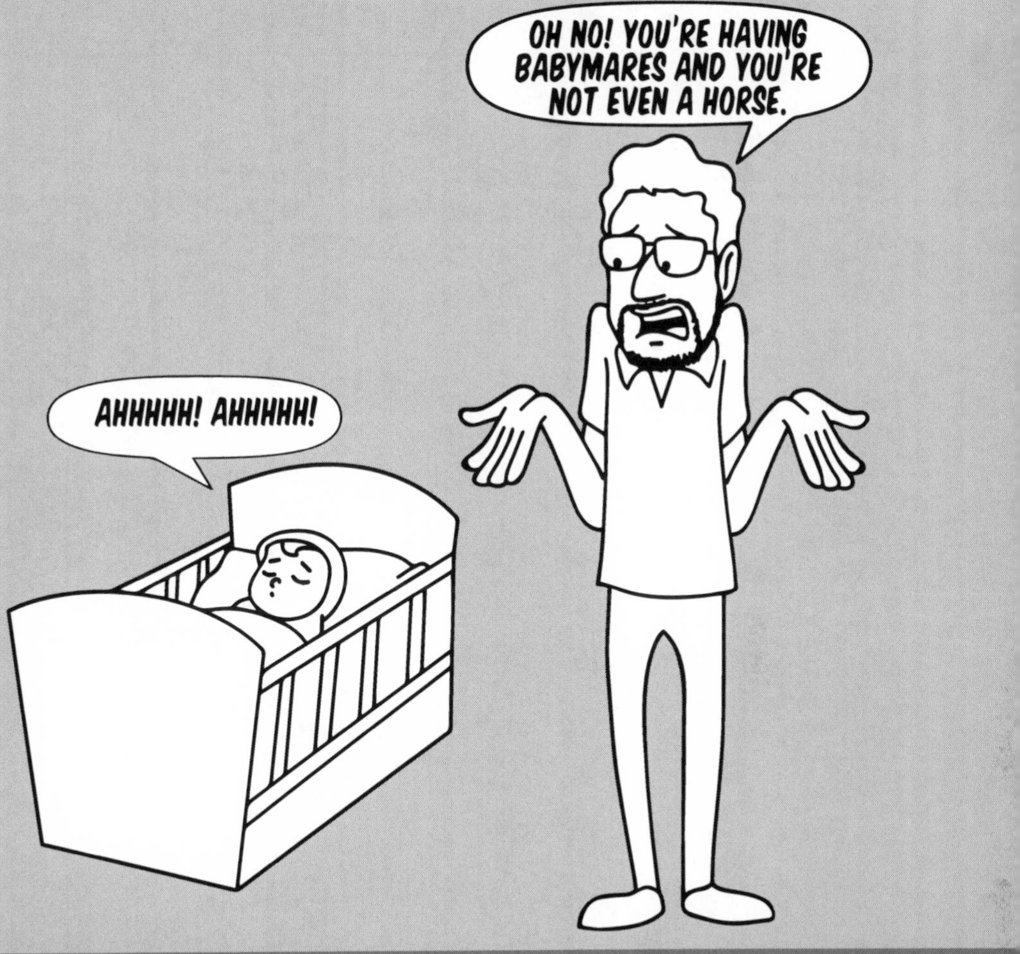
OH NO! YOU'RE HAVING BABYMARES AND YOU'RE NOT EVEN A HORSE.
AHHHHH! AHHHHH!

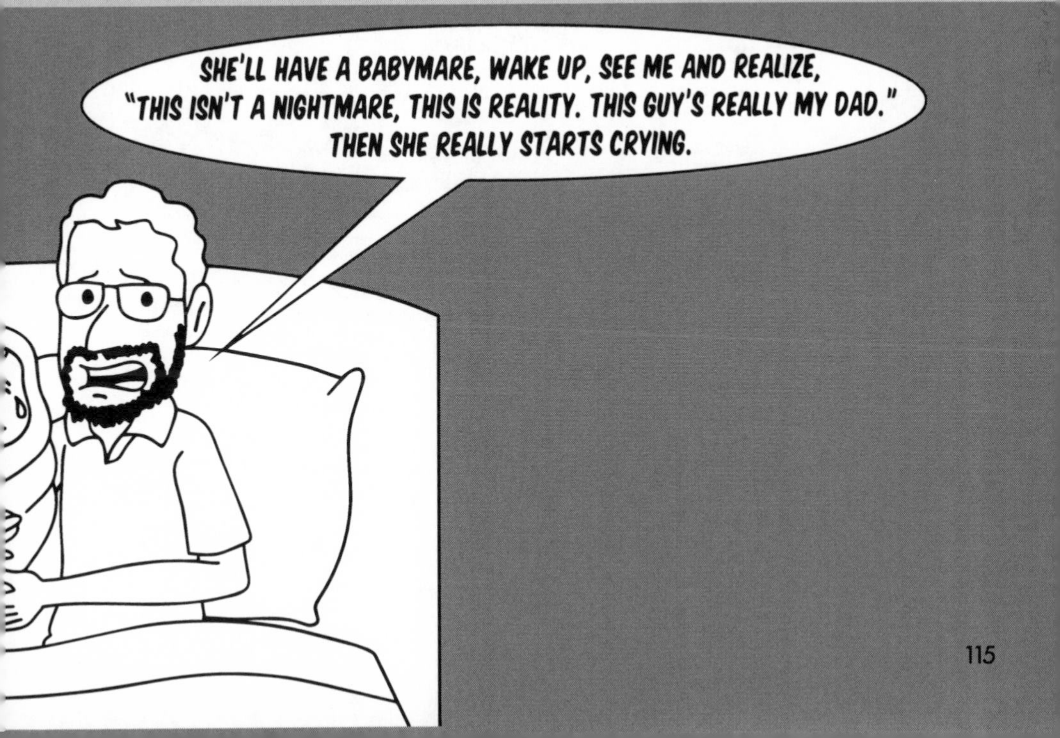
SHE'LL HAVE A BABYMARE, WAKE UP, SEE ME AND REALIZE, "THIS ISN'T A NIGHTMARE, THIS IS REALITY. THIS GUY'S REALLY MY DAD." THEN SHE REALLY STARTS CRYING.

CRYING IN PUBLIC

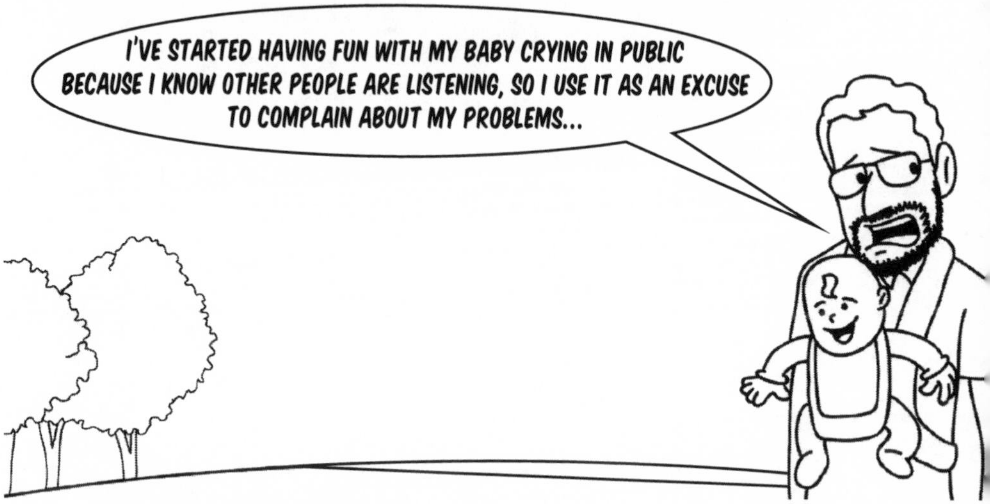
I'VE STARTED HAVING FUN WITH MY BABY CRYING IN PUBLIC BECAUSE I KNOW OTHER PEOPLE ARE LISTENING, SO I USE IT AS AN EXCUSE TO COMPLAIN ABOUT MY PROBLEMS...

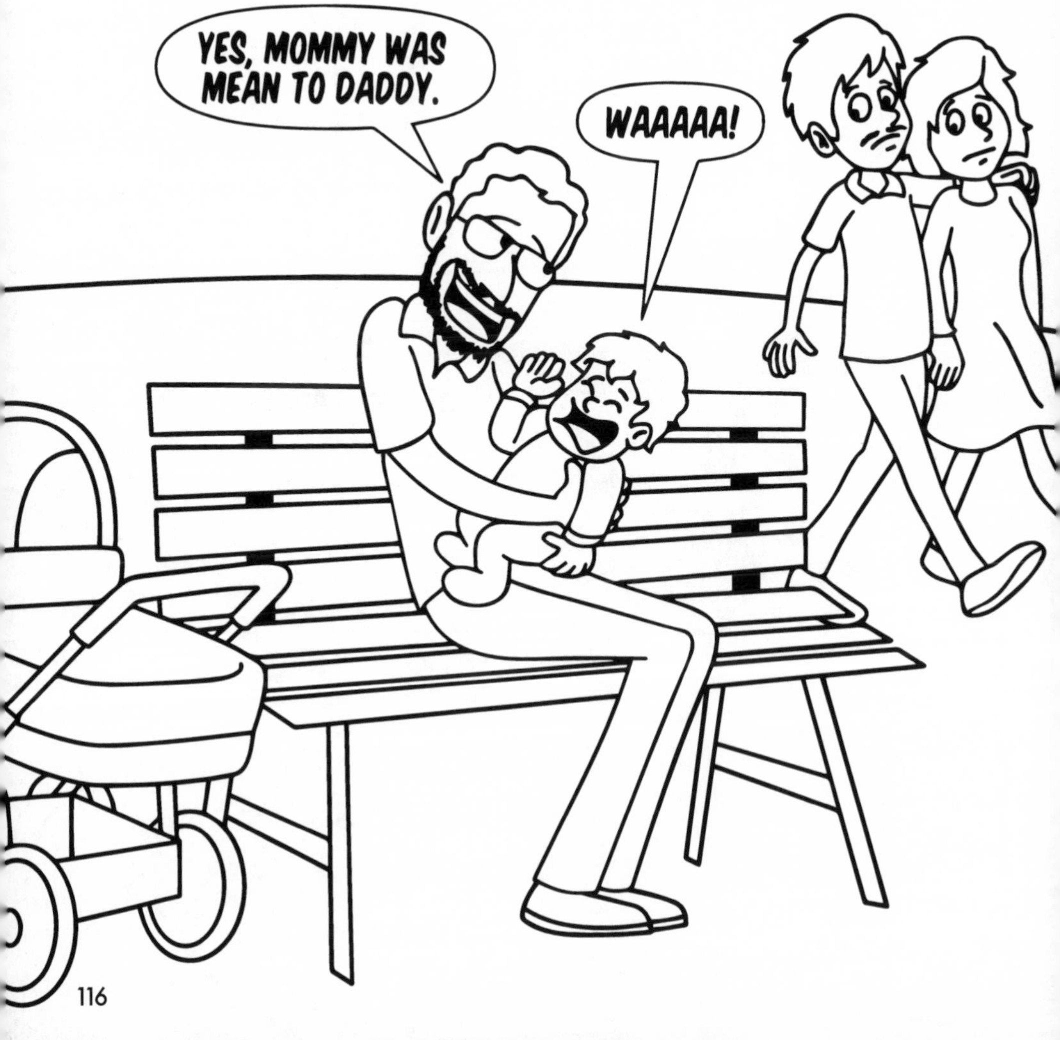
YES, MOMMY WAS MEAN TO DADDY.
WAAAAA!

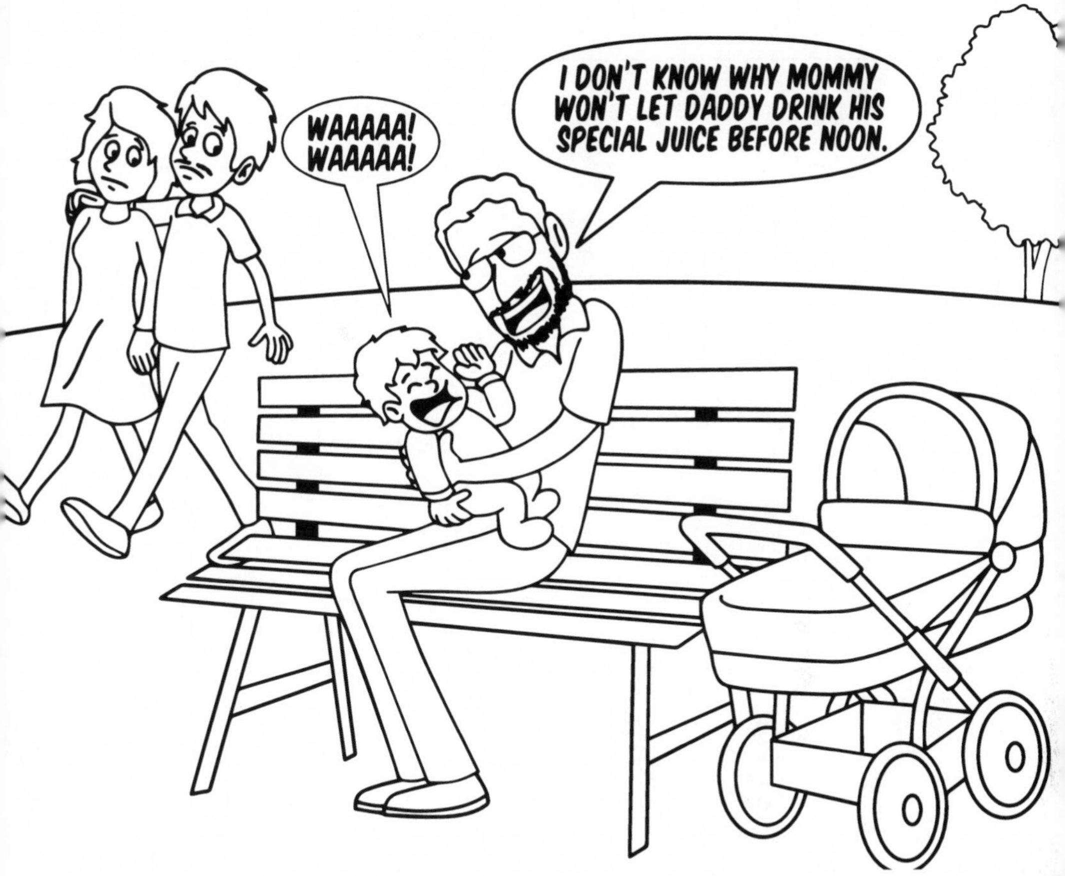
WAAAAA! WAAAAA!
I DON'T KNOW WHY MOMMY WON'T LET DADDY DRINK HIS SPECIAL JUICE BEFORE NOON.

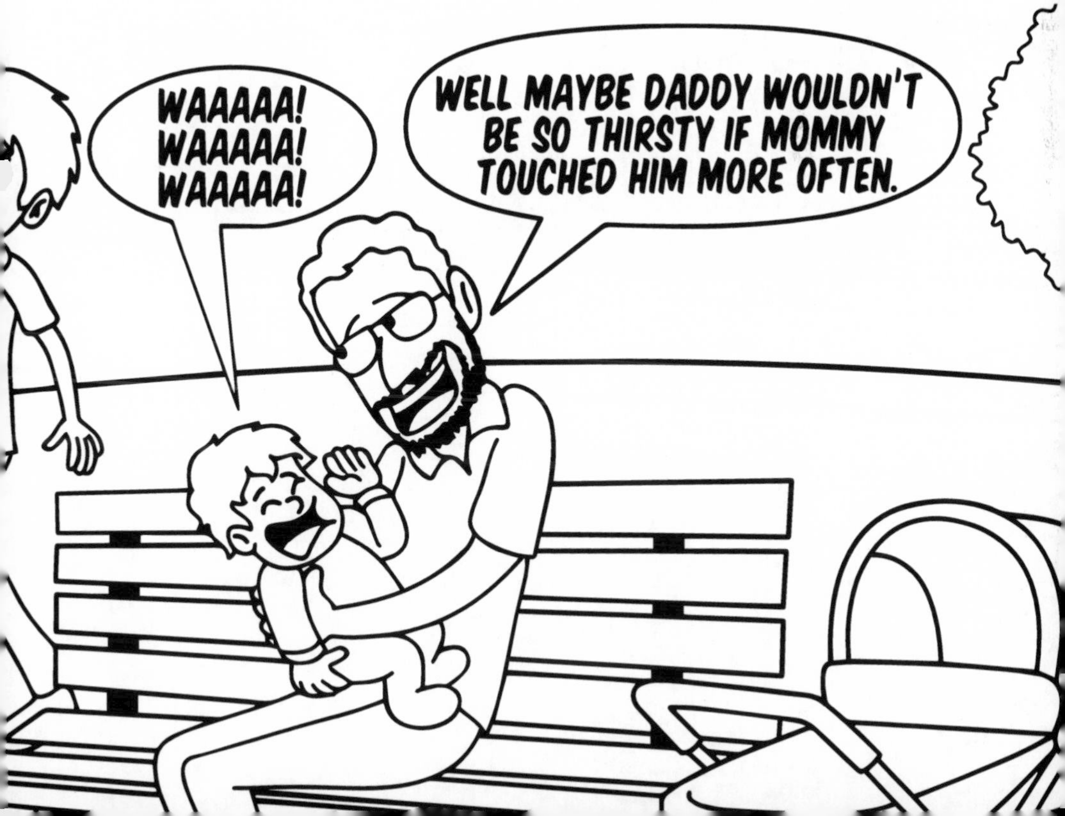
WAAAAA! WAAAAA! WAAAAA!
WELL MAYBE DADDY WOULDN'T BE SO THIRSTY IF MOMMY TOUCHED HIM MORE OFTEN.

JENGA

KEEPING AN INFANT SAFE IS LIKE PLAYING A GAME OF JENGA. IT CAN ALL FALL APART AT ANY MINUTE AND I JUST DON'T WANT IT TO BE MY FAULT.

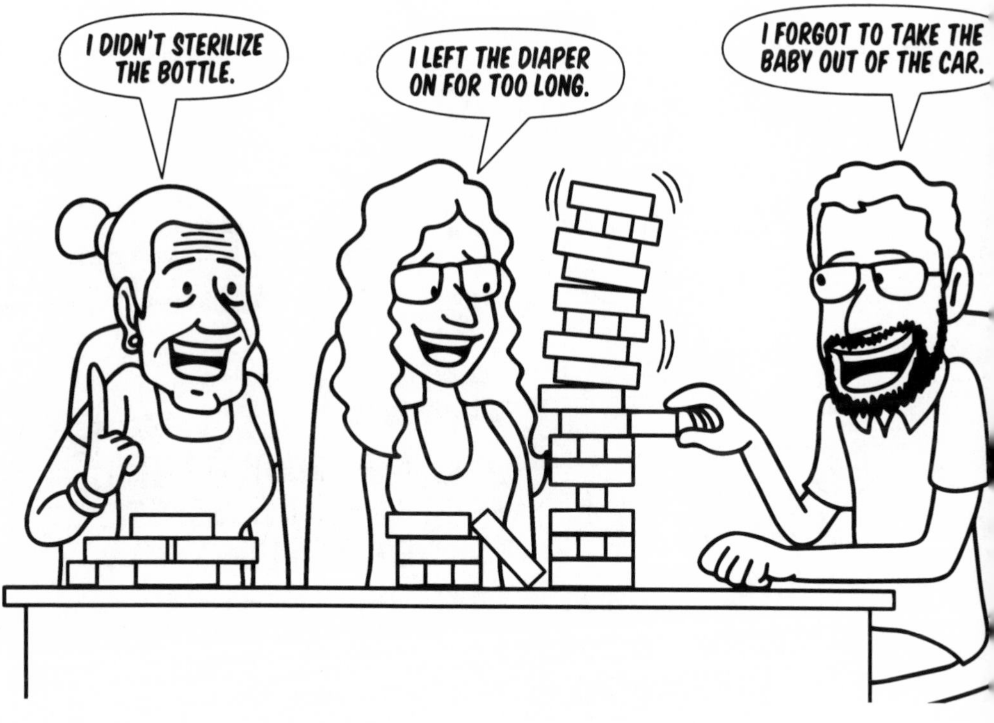
I DIDN'T STERILIZE THE BOTTLE.
I LEFT THE DIAPER ON FOR TOO LONG.
I FORGOT TO TAKE THE BABY OUT OF THE CAR.

CRAZY MOMS

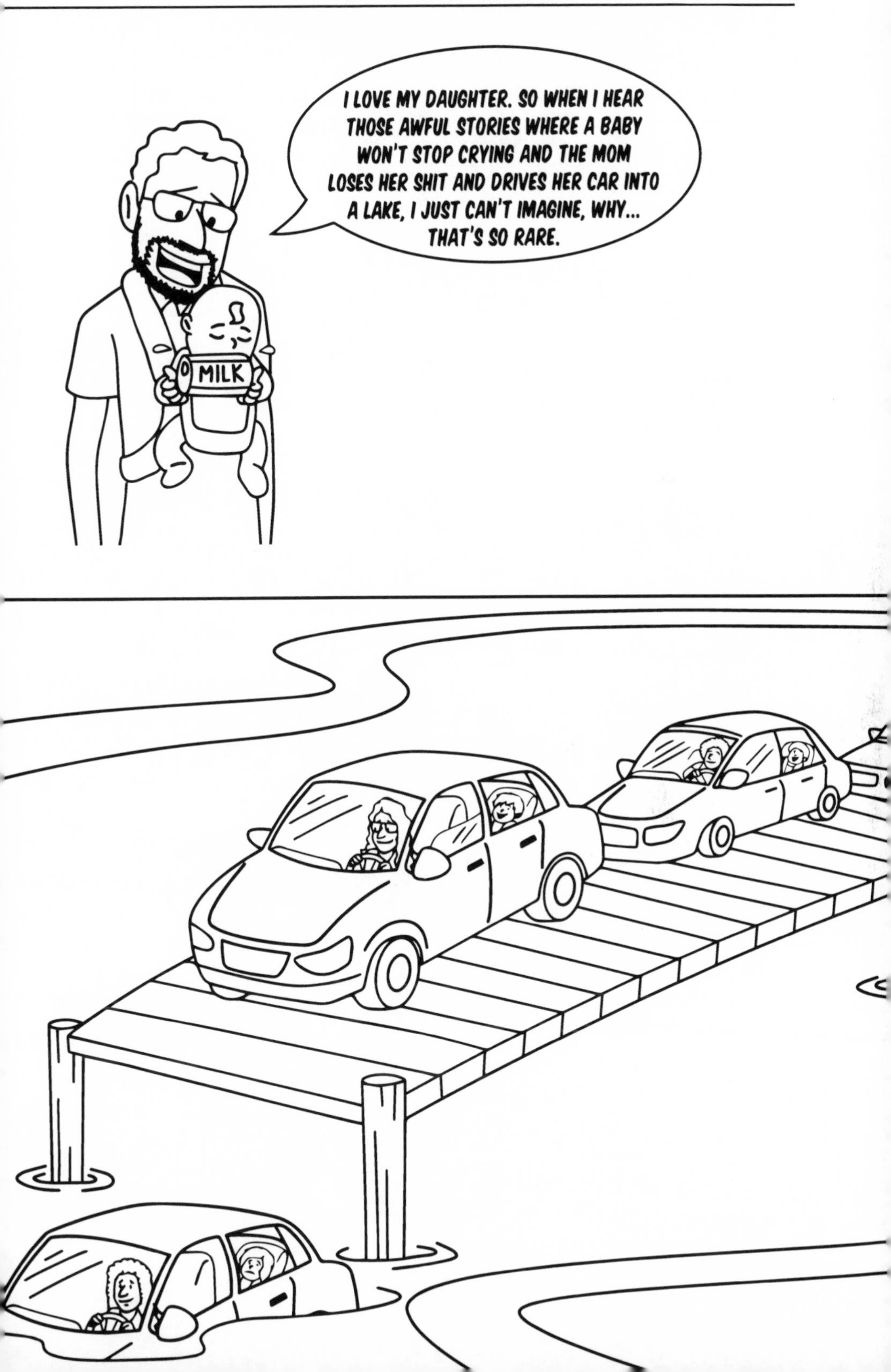
I LOVE MY DAUGHTER. SO WHEN I HEAR THOSE AWFUL STORIES WHERE A BABY WON'T STOP CRYING AND THE MOM LOSES HER SHIT AND DRIVES HER CAR INTO A LAKE, I JUST CAN'T IMAGINE, WHY... THAT'S SO RARE.
MILK

FANTASIZE

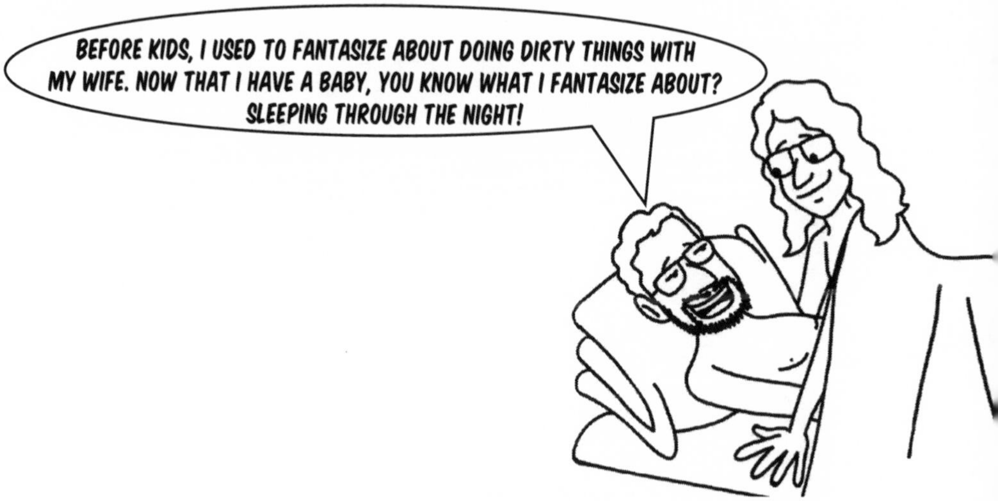

BEFORE KIDS, I USED TO FANTASIZE ABOUT DOING DIRTY THINGS WITH MY WIFE. NOW THAT I HAVE A BABY, YOU KNOW WHAT I FANTASIZE ABOUT? SLEEPING THROUGH THE NIGHT!

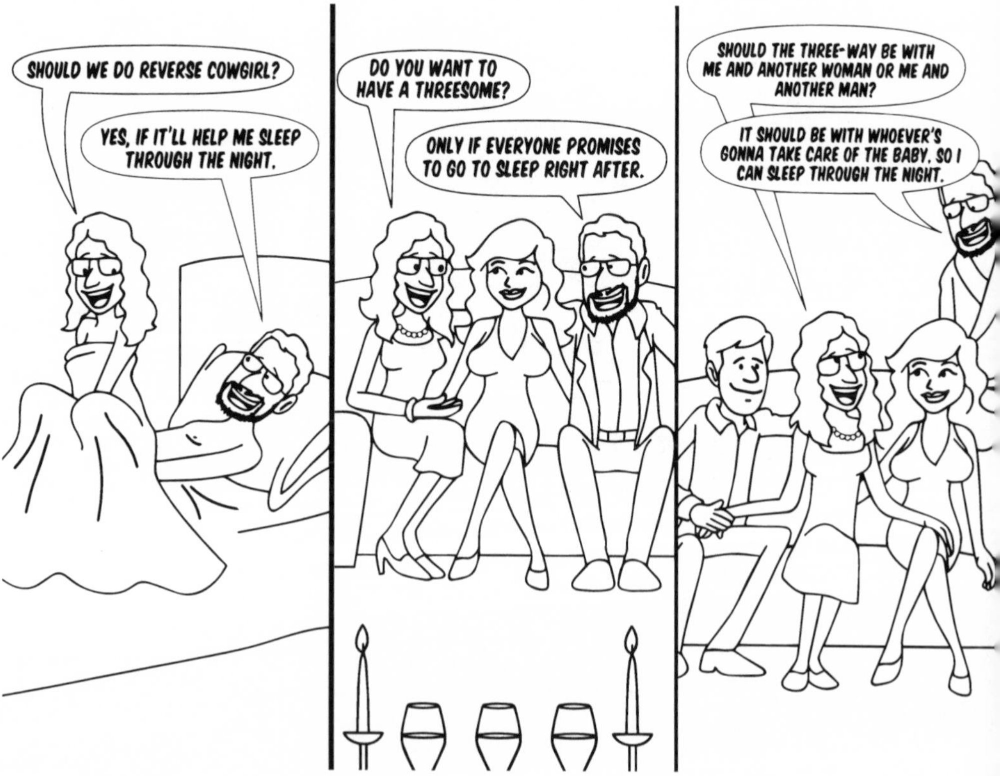

SHOULD WE DO REVERSE COWGIRL?
YES, IF IT'LL HELP ME SLEEP THROUGH THE NIGHT.
DO YOU WANT TO HAVE A THREESOME?
ONLY IF EVERYONE PROMISES TO GO TO SLEEP RIGHT AFTER.
SHOULD THE THREE-WAY BE WITH ME AND ANOTHER WOMAN OR ME AND ANOTHER MAN?
IT SHOULD BE WITH WHOEVER'S GONNA TAKE CARE OF THE BABY, SO I CAN SLEEP THROUGH THE NIGHT.

WIFE LIAR

HAVING A CHILD IS A BEAUTIFUL THING.
BUT IT'S TURNING MY WIFE INTO A LIAR.

BEFORE KIDS, MY WIFE USED TO DO THIS THING WHERE SHE'D WAKE ME FOR SEX...

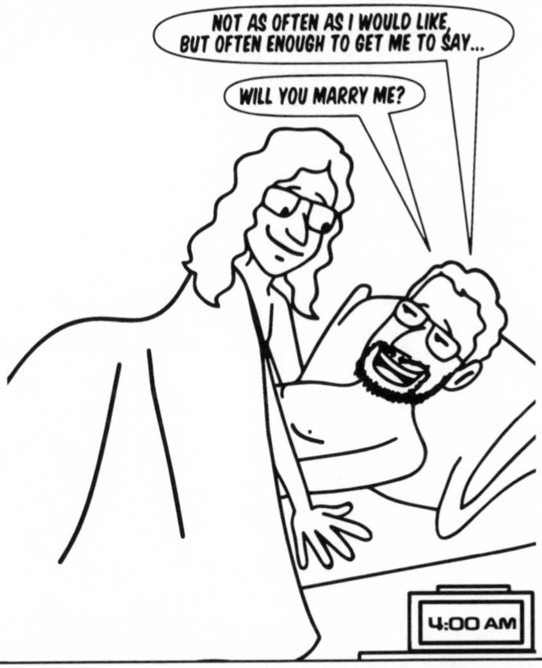
NOT AS OFTEN AS I WOULD LIKE, BUT OFTEN ENOUGH TO GET ME TO SAY...
WILL YOU MARRY ME?
4:00 AM

BUT NOW THAT WE HAVE A CHILD, MY WIFE DOES THIS THING WHERE SHE ACTS LIKE SHE'S WAKING ME FOR SEX...

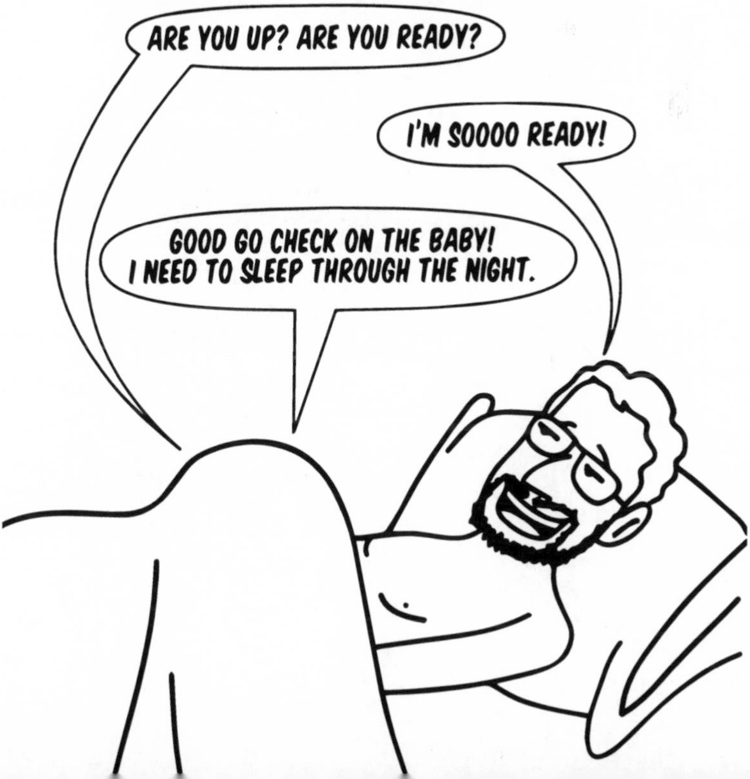
ARE YOU UP? ARE YOU READY?
I'M SOOOO READY!
GOOD GO CHECK ON THE BABY! I NEED TO SLEEP THROUGH THE NIGHT.

MOM YELL

HAVING A BABY MAKES YOU FEEL MORE LOVE, BUT YOU ALSO FEEL ALL SORTS OF EMOTIONS. ONE TIME, MY MOM WAS WATCHING THE BABY WHILE I WAS HOME, AND THE BABY STARTED CRYING...

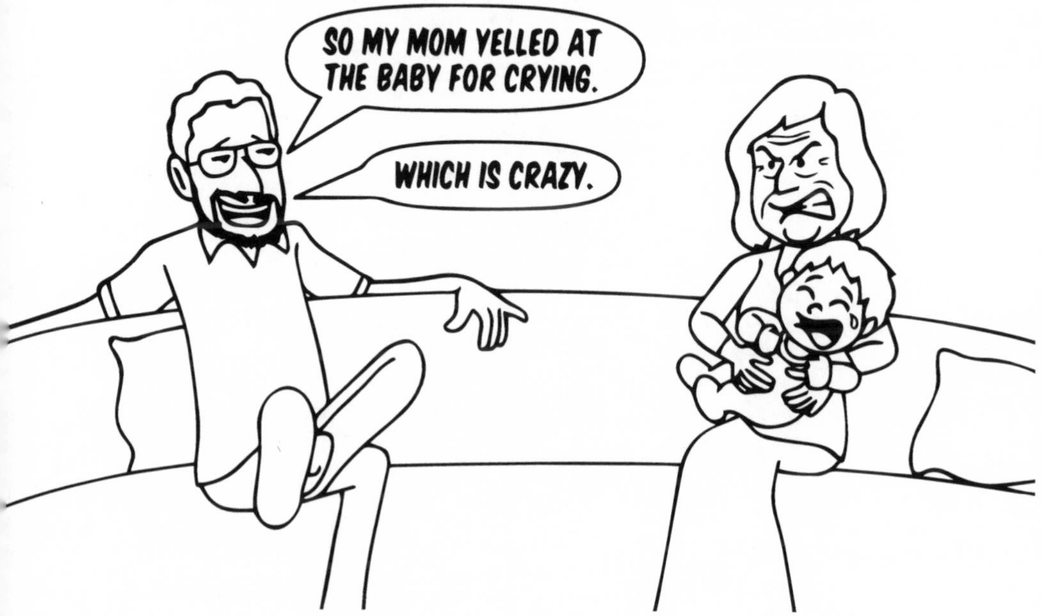
SO MY MOM YELLED AT THE BABY FOR CRYING.
WHICH IS CRAZY.

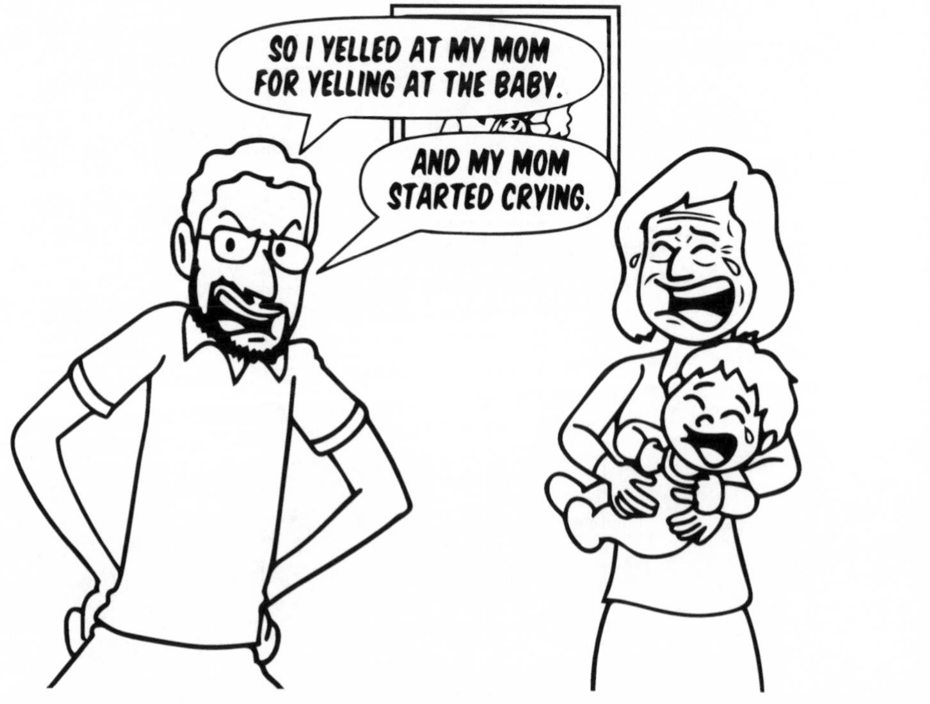
SO I YELLED AT MY MOM FOR YELLING AT THE BABY.
AND MY MOM STARTED CRYING.

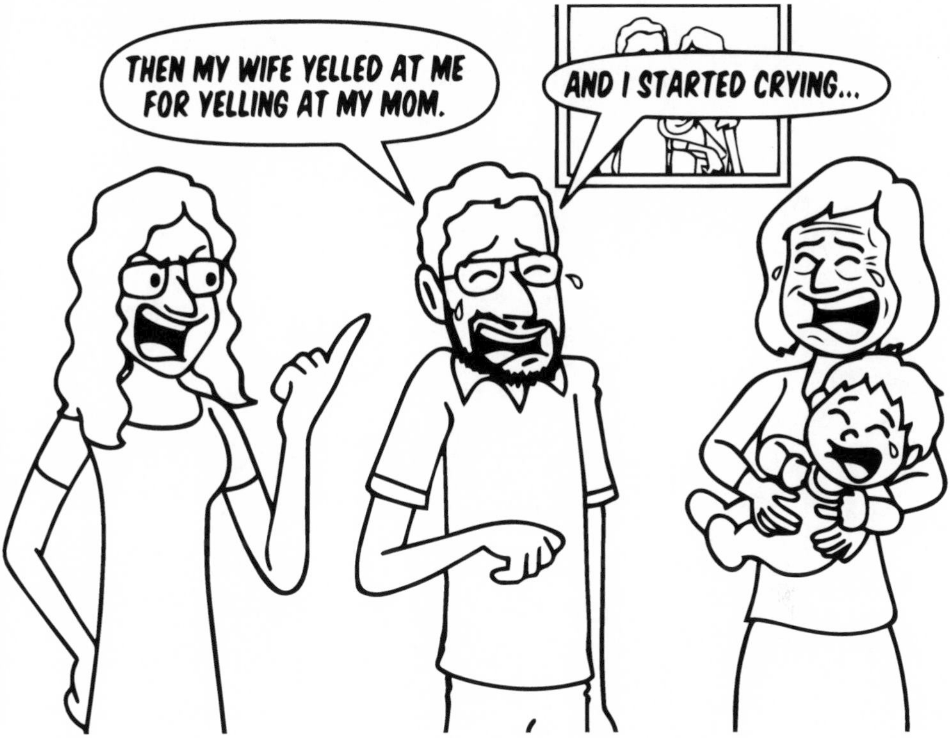
THEN MY WIFE YELLED AT ME FOR YELLING AT MY MOM.
AND I STARTED CRYING...

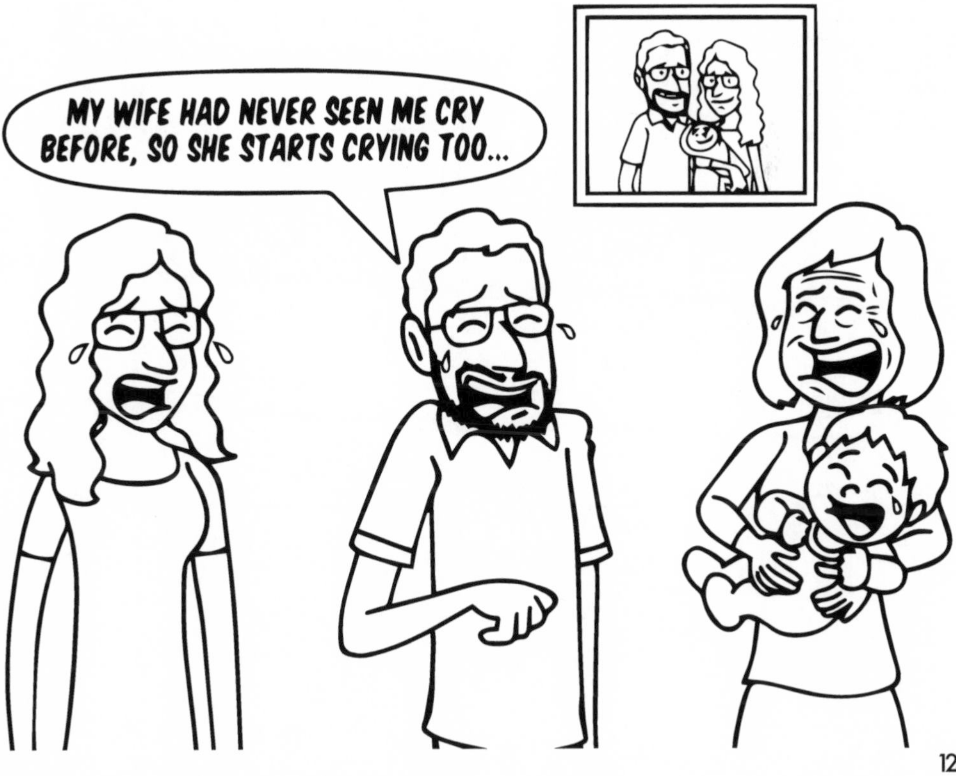
MY WIFE HAD NEVER SEEN ME CRY BEFORE, SO SHE STARTS CRYING TOO...

SO THERE WE ARE, ALL STANDING AROUND SOBBING, LIKE WE JUST WON AN OSCAR...

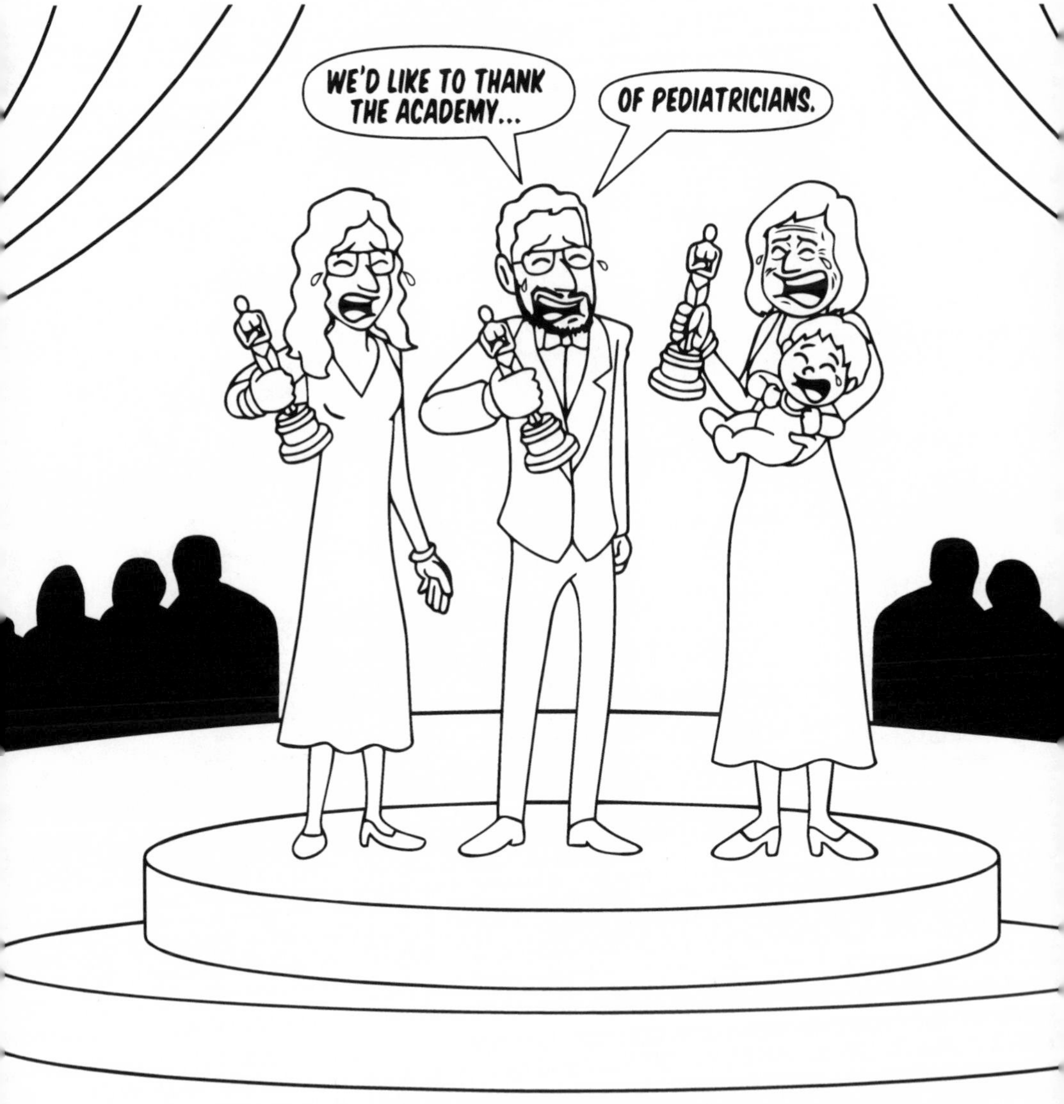
WE'D LIKE TO THANK THE ACADEMY...
OF PEDIATRICIANS.

ON BABYSITTERS

ONE THING I STRUGGLED WITH WAS, HOW DO I FIND A GOOD BABYSITTER THAT I CAN TRUST?

HERE'S MY FOOLPROOF BABYSITTER SCREENING PROCESS...

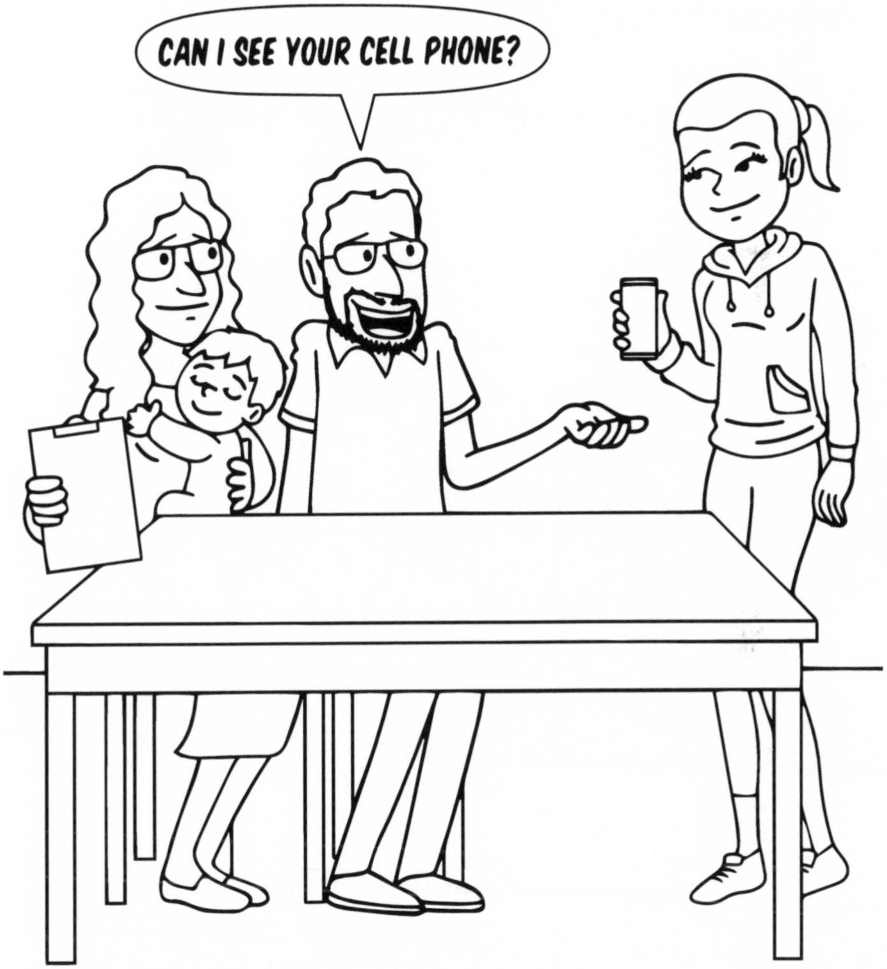
CAN I SEE YOUR CELL PHONE?

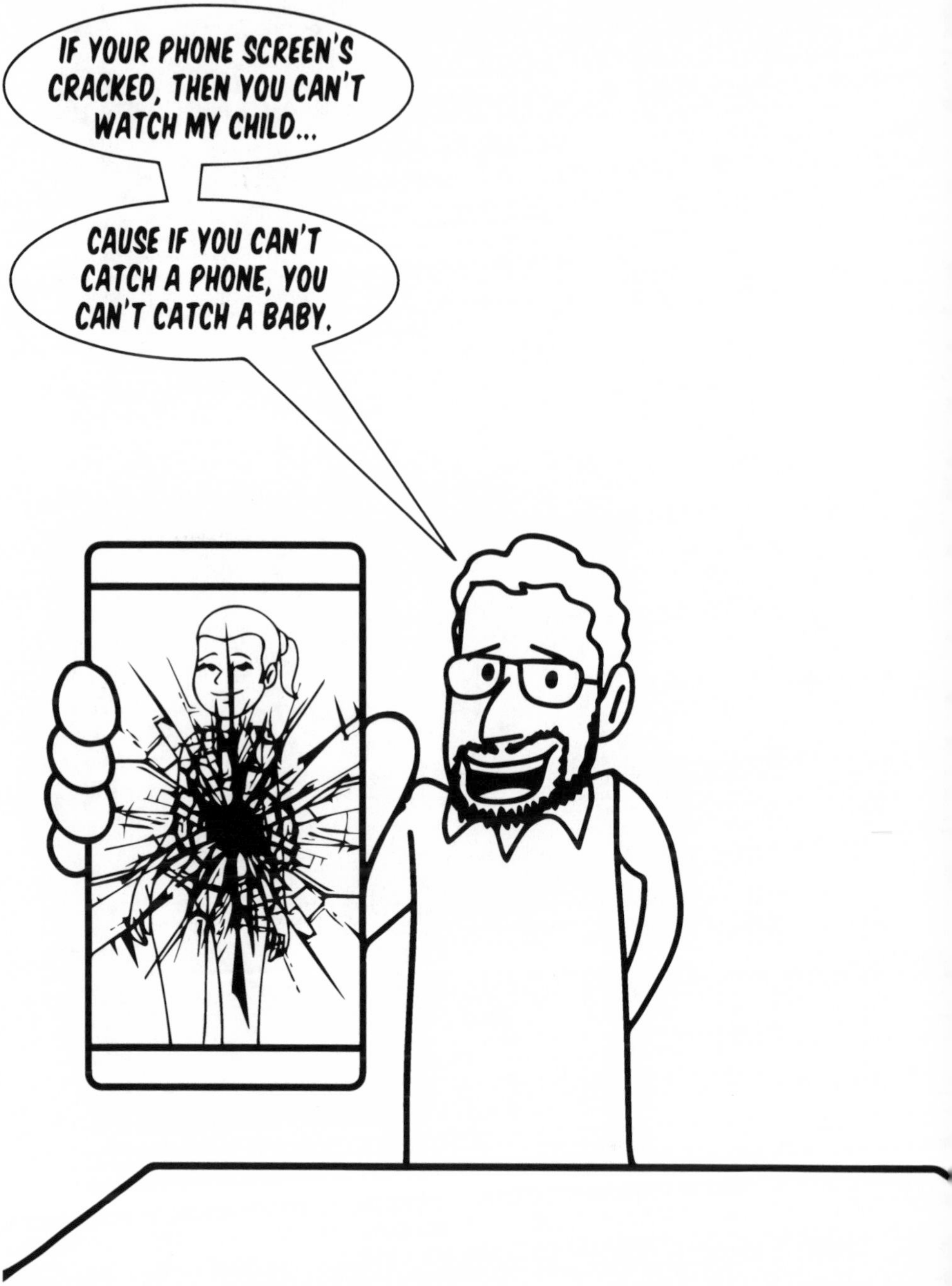
IF YOUR PHONE SCREEN'S CRACKED, THEN YOU CAN'T WATCH MY CHILD...
CAUSE IF YOU CAN'T CATCH A PHONE, YOU CAN'T CATCH A BABY.

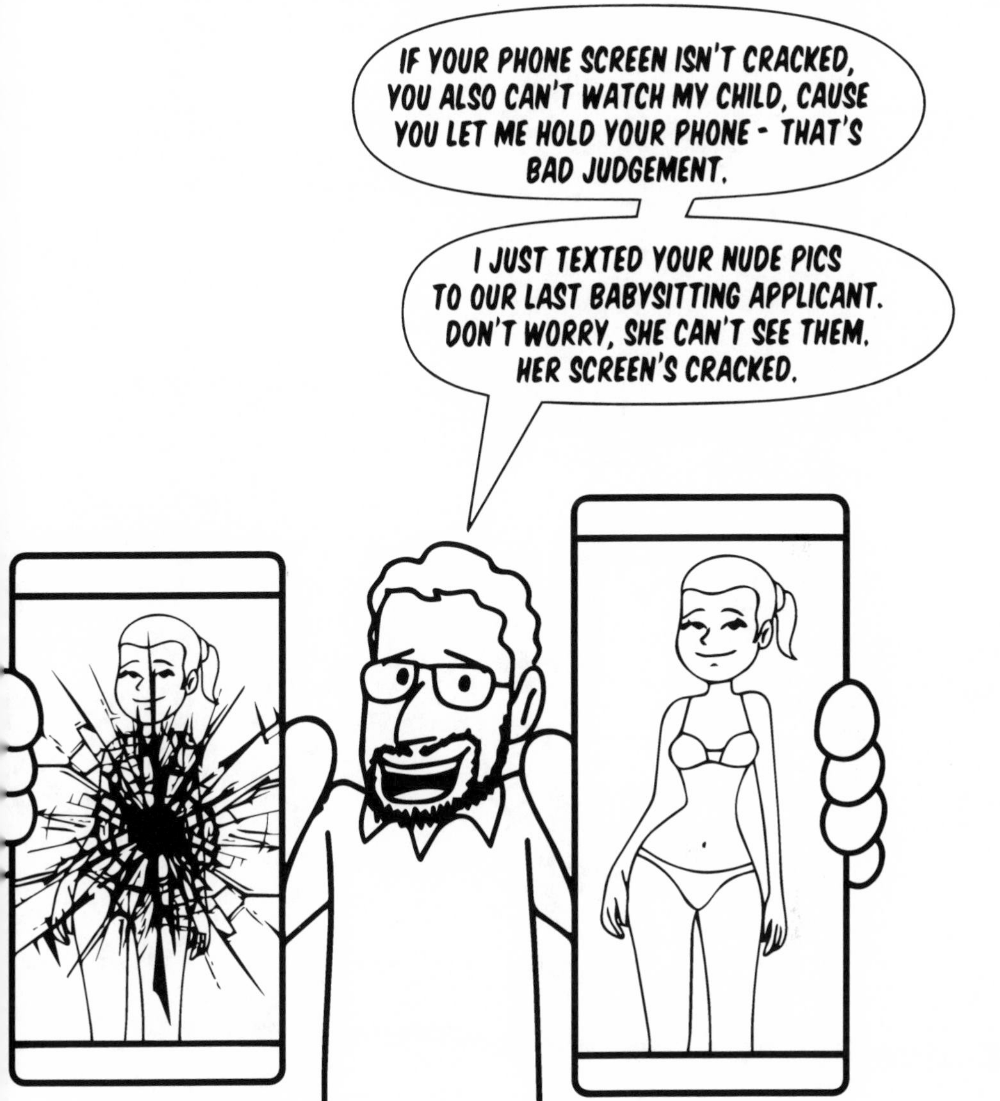
IF YOUR PHONE SCREEN ISN'T CRACKED, YOU ALSO CAN'T WATCH MY CHILD, CAUSE YOU LET ME HOLD YOUR PHONE - THAT'S BAD JUDGEMENT.
I JUST TEXTED YOUR NUDE PICS TO OUR LAST BABYSITTING APPLICANT. DON'T WORRY, SHE CAN'T SEE THEM. HER SCREEN'S CRACKED.

READING TIME

I TOOK MY DAUGHTER TO STORY HOUR AND THE LIBRARIAN READ A BOOK CALLED *TEN FAT TURKEYS*.

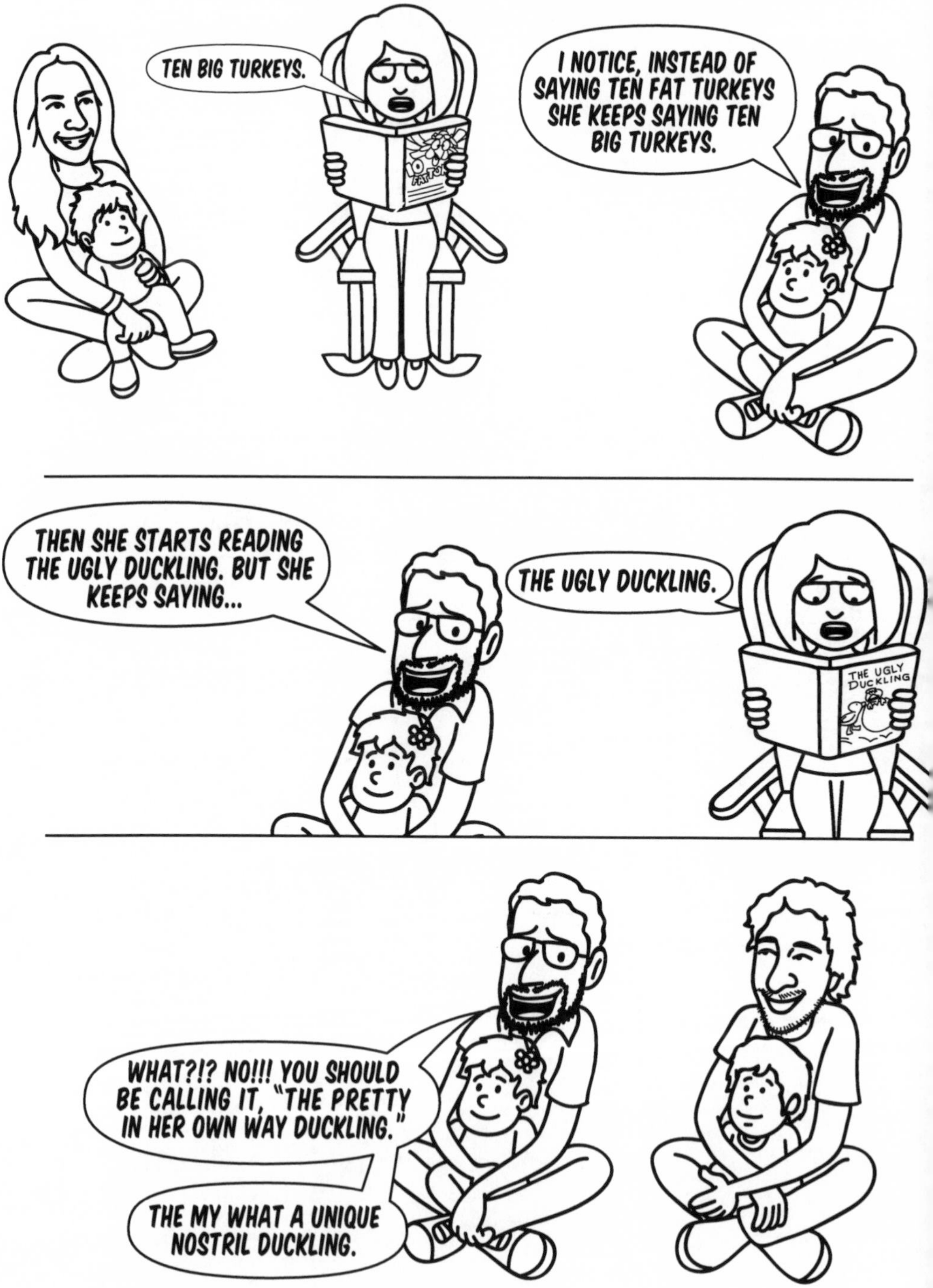
TEN BIG TURKEYS.
I NOTICE, INSTEAD OF SAYING TEN FAT TURKEYS SHE KEEPS SAYING TEN BIG TURKEYS.
THEN SHE STARTS READING THE UGLY DUCKLING. BUT SHE KEEPS SAYING...
THE UGLY DUCKLING.
THE UGLY DUCKLING
WHAT?!? NO!!! YOU SHOULD BE CALLING IT, "THE PRETTY IN HER OWN WAY DUCKLING."
THE MY WHAT A UNIQUE NOSTRIL DUCKLING.

IF WE'RE GONNA CHANGE CHILDREN'S BOOK TITLES,
WE CAN'T ONLY PROTECT OBESE POULTRY.
NO, WE GOTTA FIX ALL CHILDREN'S STORY TITLES.

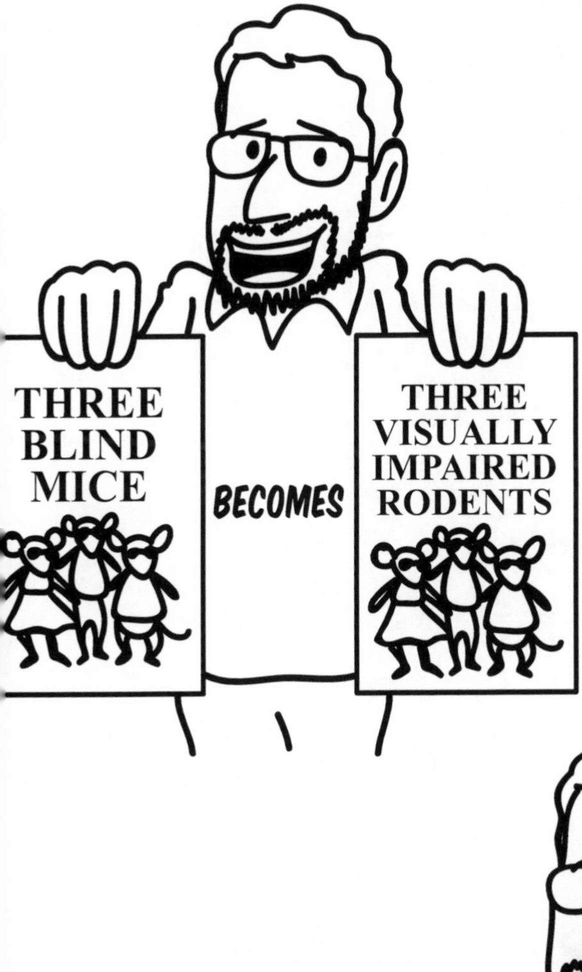
THREE BLIND MICE
BECOMES
THREE VISUALLY IMPAIRED RODENTS

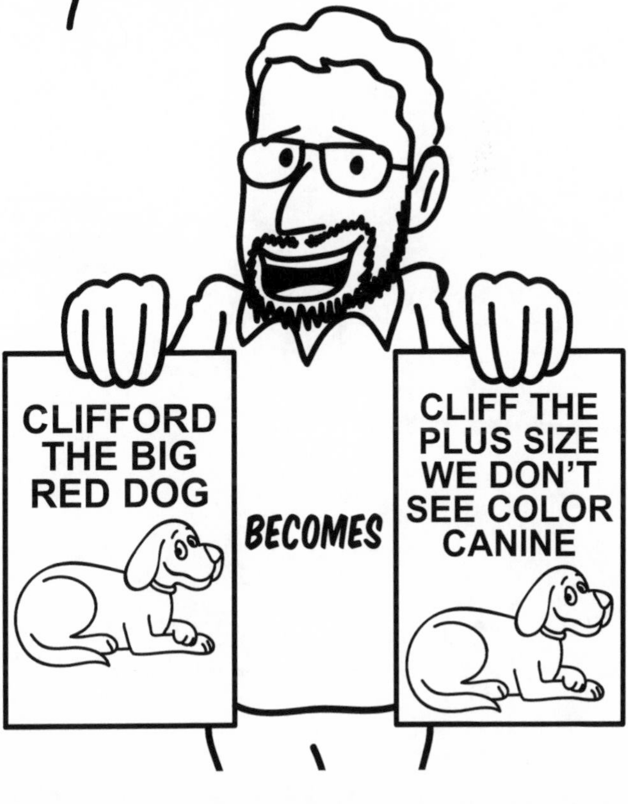
CLIFFORD THE BIG RED DOG
BECOMES
CLIFF THE PLUS SIZE WE DON'T SEE COLOR CANINE

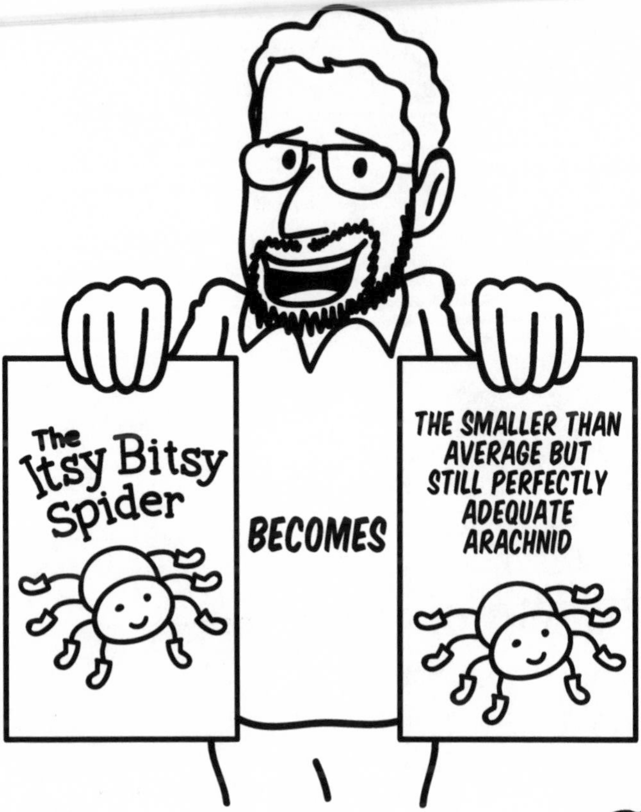
The Itsy Bitsy Spider
BECOMES
THE SMALLER THAN AVERAGE BUT STILL PERFECTLY ADEQUATE ARACHNID

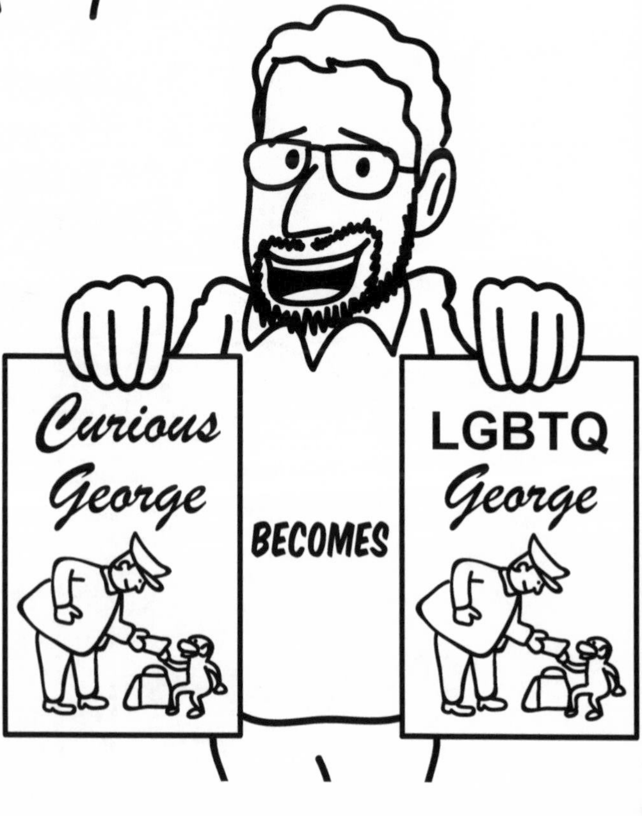
Curious George
BECOMES
LGBTQ George

THE ONLY ACTUALLY USEFUL TIP
IN THIS WHOLE BOOK

IT TAKES BABIES LONGER TO DIGEST FORMULA THAN BREAST MILK.
MEANING THEY'RE NOT HUNGRY AND WILL SLEEP LONGER.
SO EVEN IF YOU'RE BREAST FEEDING, AT NIGHT,
GIVE THE BABY SOME FORMULA.

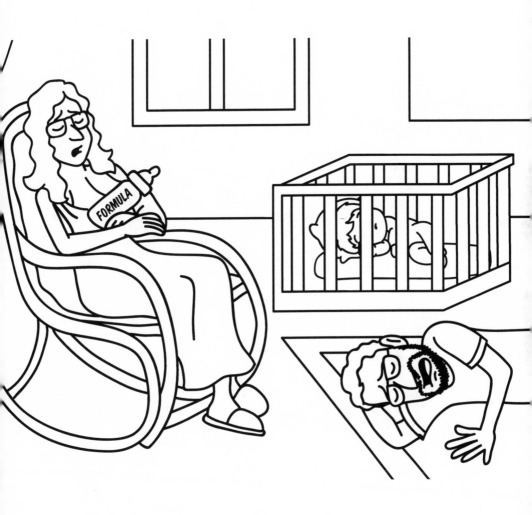

DEAR READER

BEING WITH OUR BABY TOO MUCH MAKES US TALK TO EVERYONE LIKE THEY'RE A BABY.

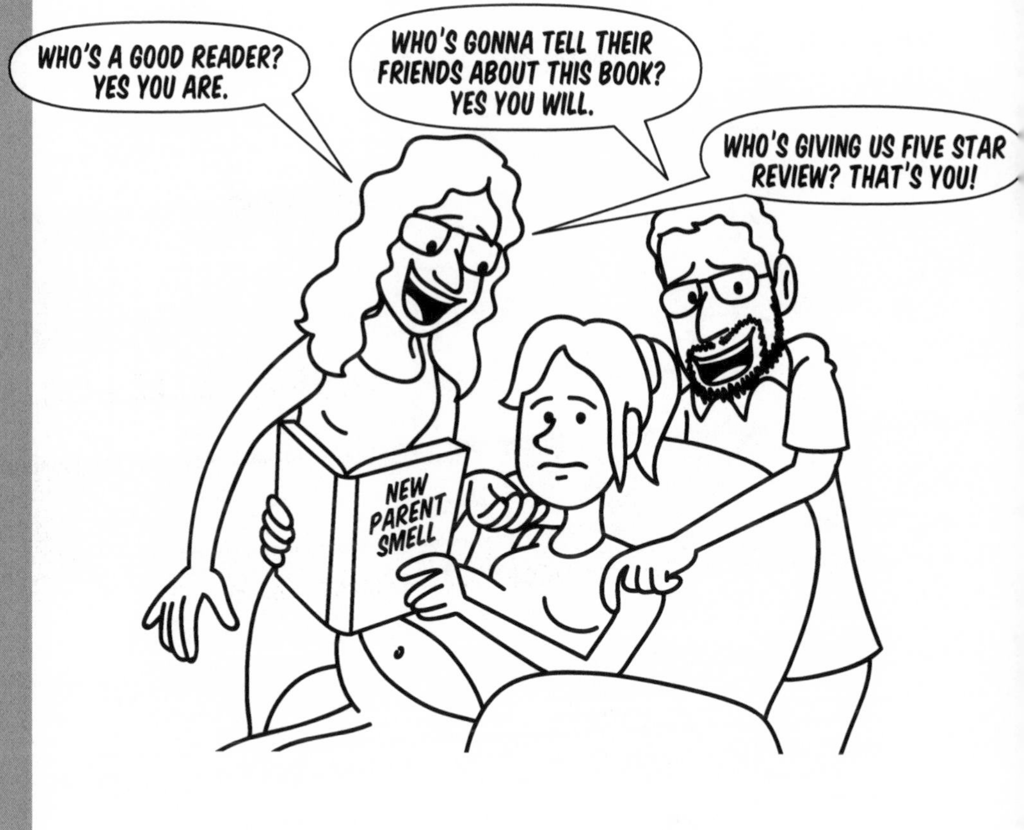
WHO'S A GOOD READER? YES YOU ARE.
WHO'S GONNA TELL THEIR FRIENDS ABOUT THIS BOOK? YES YOU WILL.
WHO'S GIVING US FIVE STAR REVIEW? THAT'S YOU!
NEW PARENT SMELL

Please leave a review at NewParentSmell.com/review

New Parent Smell: Funny Thoughts On Pregnancy, Newborns & Tots is an illustrated humor book that helps ease the stress of parents-to-be. New Parent Smell is the book to read after you've read one of those *What To Expect When You're Expecting* type books, got hit with anxiety and could use some laughs.

Comedians Ben and Michelle Rosenfeld* take you through their hilarious entry into parenthood with pithy jokes and over 200 illustrations. Unlike other humorous new parent books, New Parent Smell is written by two professional stand-up comedians who tested all this material on live audiences, so you'll actually laugh when reading it. They also tested these jokes on their baby, so your baby will laugh too.

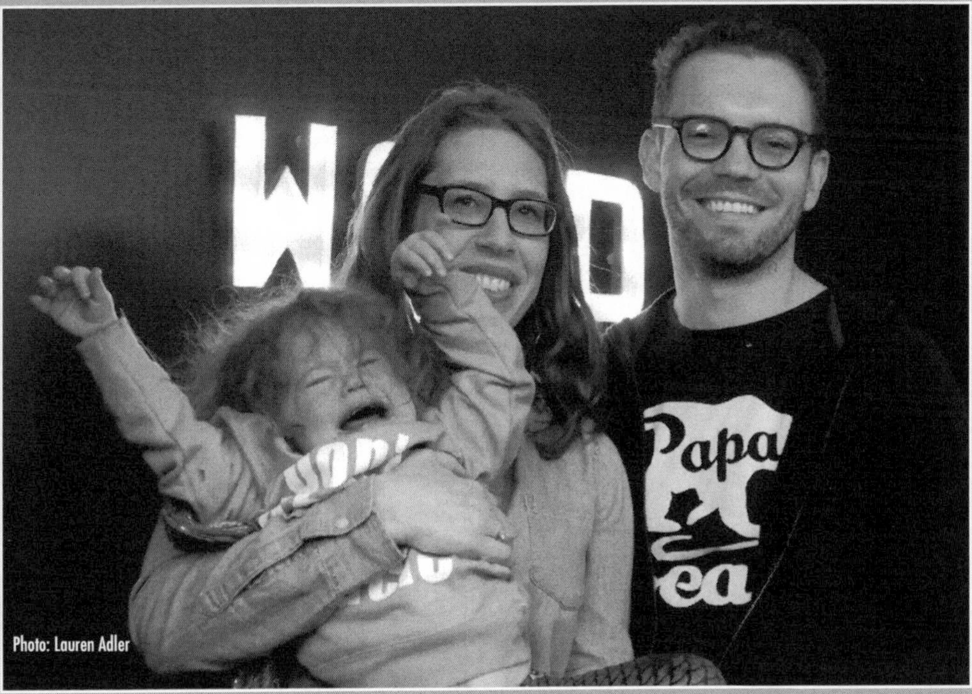
Papa
ea
Photo: Lauren Adler

*Michelle's maiden/stage name is Michelle Slonim, but for this book Ben insisted she use her new government-issued last name so that people would believe they are real-life husband and wife. Michelle responded, "Ugh, fine, as long as you watch the baby today."

Made in the USA
Monee, IL
29 December 2021

87491641R00081